COLONIAL DILEMMA

Critical Perspectives on Contemporary Puerto Rico

Edited by Edwin Meléndez
and Edgardo Meléndez

South End Press   Boston, MA

Edited, designed, and produced by the South End Press collective
Manufactured in the USA

Library of Congress Cataloging-in-Publication Data

Colonial dilemma: critical perspectives on contemporary Puerto Rico/ edited by Edwin Meléndez and Edgardo Meléndez.
p. cm.
Includes bibliographical references and index.
ISBN 0-89608-442-6: $40.00 (alk. paper). —ISBN 0-89608-441-8: $16.00 (pbk.: alk. paper)
1. Puerto Rico—Politics and government—1952- 2. Puerto Rico—Economic conditions—1952- 3. Social movements—Puerto Rico—History—20th century. 4. Nationalism—Puerto Rico—History—20th century. I. Meléndez, Edwin. II. Meléndez, Edgardo.
F1976.C6   1993
320.97295—dc20
92-23475
CIP

South End Press 116 Saint Botolph Street, Boston, MA 02115
98 97 96 95 94 93   1 2 3 4 5 6

Dedicamos este volumen a nuestro padre
Edwin Meléndez Grellasca, luchador
incansable por la justicia y nuestro ejemplo
en la defensa de los más necesitados.

We dedicate this book to our father,
Edwin Meléndez Grellasca, our example in
the struggle for social justice.

CONTENTS

Acknowledgements

We would like to thank Ann Withorn, John Demeter, and other members of the *Radical America* collective for their enthusiasm in producing the special issue on Puerto Rico that served as the basis for this collection. We are also indebted to our editors Karin Aguilar-San Juan, Carlos Suárez-Boulangger, and the other members of the South End Press collective for their keen and diligent attention to our project. Without their encouragement and support, this book would have never been realized.

Introduction

Edwin Meléndez and Edgardo Meléndez

Puerto Rico has been a U.S. neo-colony since 1898, when the island was taken as war booty of the Spanish-American War. For 94 years Puerto Rico has occupied a peculiar status within the U.S. political system. The United States has never had an established colonial policy and nearly all acquired territories eventually have been incorporated into statehood. The island remains an "unincorporated territory," belonging to, but not being a part of, the United States. Yet Puerto Ricans, as people, have been American citizens since 1917.

Colonialism and citizenship define Puerto Rican history in the twentieth century. The island's economy is an appendage of the U.S. economy, and Puerto Rican politics revolve around whether the island should be independent, a state of the Union, or continue as a Commonwealth. Meanwhile, mass migration has led to the formation of a community in the United States which represents two-fifths of the Puerto Rican people.

Puerto Rico is entering a period of rapid political change and transition. The U.S. government is restructuring the colonial administration to meet new international and domestic concerns. In particular, the United States now faces a dissatisfied population demanding change. There is constant tension between the U.S. government's effort to maintain the colonial status quo and the Puerto Rican people's desire to end colonial domination, or at least reform it.

Puerto Rico's colonial structure has not changed in a fundamental way since 1900, when the U.S. government appointed the first colonial administration. In 1952 the then-dominant Popular Democratic Party (PPD, from the Spanish *Partido Popular Democrático*) and the United States created the current Commonwealth status. The Commonwealth granted Puerto Ricans some autonomy over local affairs and enjoyed popular support for as long as the PPD's economic development program, Operation Bootstrap, was successful. During the 1970s, economic crisis encouraged the statehood movement and support for the Commonwealth waned. Sectors of the U.S. government began to question the effectiveness of the colonial arrangement.

The status question

Puerto Rico's status became national news once more when U.S. President George Bush and made public his support for Puerto Rico's statehood in his 1989 State of the Union address. Later that year, the Senate Energy and Natural Resources Committee (ENR) worked out three bills (S710, S711, and S712) detailing the mechanisms for holding a status plebiscite in Puerto Rico. Bill S712, the most fully elaborated of the three, was supported by the three major Puerto Rican parties and submitted to Senate hearings the following June.

Among other things, S112 raised two issues that have created controversy in the United States: a self-executing clause that would force Congress to recognize and immediately implement the winning option; and a simple majority clause to rule the contest. Had these two clauses remained in the final version of any plebiscite bill, they would have compelled Congress to accept any option that won by a simple majority, including statehood. This version of S712 also included the definitions of each status option—Commonwealth, statehood, and independence—given by the three Puerto Rican political parties.

After holding hearings on S112 in the summer of 1989 in Washington and San Juan, the Committee extensively modified the definition of each political status presented by the Puerto Rican parties and resubmitted the bill. The new version of S712 was molded mostly by the concerns of the Bush Administration regarding each status alternative.

The plebiscite process moved along an uncertain path from the time the bill was first submitted. The Senate Finance Committee held hearings twice on S712 and raised several concerns regarding the economic aspects of the plebiscite bill, particularly those dealing with the economic transition to statehood. The House leadership deferred consideration of S712, which was considered unacceptable to Congress (mainly due to the self-executing clause). The House Insular Affairs Subcommittee held hearings on the island's status in March 1990 in Washington and Puerto Rico. In October 1990 the House approved a new bill on Puerto Rico's status (HR4765). The House bill contains no commitment by Congress to accept the Puerto Ricans' choice and no definitions of the status alternatives. The difference between the Senate and the House versions reflects the tension between those who are willing to accept the outcome of the plebiscite, even if it implies accepting Puerto Rico as the 51st State of the Union in the immediate future, and those who are not.

However, differences between the House and Senate did not doom the bill. The plebiscite bill was killed by the same ENR Committee that gave life to it. The initial plebiscite bill (S712) was possible largely due to the bipartisan support given by ENR committee Chairman Bennett Johnston (D-LA) and Republican ranking member James McClure (R-ID). But the new Republican ranking member in the Committee, Senator Malcolm Wallop (R-WY), was a vocal critic of S712. When a new plebiscite bill was debated in February 1991 in the ENR committee, Wallop was able to gather enough votes to kill the bill. The reason for this harsh reaction? Critics—both Republicans and Democrats—argue that the United States is not yet ready to grant statehood to Puerto Rico.

By spring 1991, the plebiscite was dead. Bush seemed to be alone in the Republic Party in his support of Puerto Rican statehood, as the Republican right—spearheaded by Senator Jesse Helms, Pat Buchanan, George Will, and others—steadfastly opposes the idea. On the Democratic side, ENR Committee chairman Johnson, after two years of working hard for the plebiscite, finally gave up on the idea.

Farewell to the plebiscite

The Republicans, and others in Washington, concluded that Congress could not be bought off by a status plebiscite, particularly if Puerto Ricans had not already expressed their positions. Trying to keep the status debate alive in Puerto Rico, Governor Rafael Hernández Colón seized the opportunity to propose a referendum to amend the Puerto Rican Constitution. Among the amendments he put forth were: that a future status plebiscite should present all three status alternatives (Commonwealth, statehood, and independence); the permanence of U.S. citizenship; and the protection of Puerto Rican identity under any status.

After initial consultations between the three major parties (Popular Democratic, New Progressive, and Independence), talks broke off, and the Governor decided to push for the referendum without the backing of the pro-statehood NPP. The PPD Governor faced opposition also from his own ranks. A group of PPD legislators, headed by gubernatorial hopeful Victoria (Melo) Muñoz, opposed the proposition. The Governor submitted the bill anyway and failed to gain the two-thirds majority required to pass. In a second attempt, the PPD was able to garner a simple majority, but the NPP voted against it.

The so-called "Law for Democratic Rights" called for a December 1991 referendum where Puerto Ricans voted for or against including the following issues in the Constitution: the inalienable right of Puerto Ricans to decide their own political status, freely and democratically; the right to choose a status of full political dignity without colonial or territorial subordination to the U.S. Congress; the right to choose from among the three status alternatives (Commonwealth, statehood, or independence) based on the sovereignty of the people of Puerto Rico; the stipulation that the winning alternative in a status consultation shall garner more than half the votes cast; the condition that under any alternative, Puerto Rico's culture, language, and identity are preserved, including its international sports representation; the condition that under any status alternative, Puerto Ricans' U.S. citizenship be safeguarded under the U.S. Constitution.

Clearly, many conflicts and awkward alliances surfaced during the referendum process. For example, the pro-statehood NPP was against U.S. citizenship, and had other reasons to oppose the referendum, the biggest of which was the fact that by including three status alternatives, the referendum would be stacked against statehood. The Independence party favored citizenship. While the PPD and the PIP presented a common "yes" front in the referendum, the NPP equated a "yes" vote to a call for separation from the United States.

"No" won by over 100,000 votes, a margin of 53 percent to 45 percent. The results surprised everyone, from political analysts and pundits to the media and the parties themselves. The PPD and the PIP were sure that the "yes" vote would win; they thought that the only concern was over the size of margin. The NPP expected defeat, arguing that the contest was unfair. A poll taken by the pro-statehood *El Nuevo Dia*, had reported a small but significant lead for the "yes" vote just three days before the referendum.

As in the 1968 plebiscite, the 1991 referendum results realigned Puerto Rican politics. Hernández Colón announced that he would not run for reelection in 1992, and the PPD gubernatorial candidate, Victoria Muñoz, has stated that she will not deal with the status issue if elected. The PIP's objective of creating a "patriotic front" against statehood was crushed. Although the PIP's leadership remains unchanged and unabashed by the referendum's results, the party will probably continue to mobilize insignificant electoral backing. The NPP seems to be the main winner of the referendum scuffle, gaining a political momentum that is likely to result in a victory in the next general election. The statehood movement has also benefitted, with supporters in Puerto Rico and Washington arguing that the referendum results point to a majority sentiment for this alternative on the island.

The most significant result of the referendum is the conflict among the three major political parties. The stalemate will continue for years to come, given the lack of interest in resolving the status queston manifested by the PPD gubernatorial candidates; the PNP proposal to hold a yes-or-no referendum on statehood; and Washington's indifference to the issue. For Puerto

Rican activists, however, the question of how to move beyond colonialism, remains unanswered.

The political crisis of colonialism

No one can predict whether the current crisis of the colonial system will be overcome by a dramatic change in political status, as statehood or independence will imply, or through gradual reforms within the Commonwealth. Our objectives in this anthology are, first, to define the current political and economic situation and, second, to explore the emerging social movements that could redefine the political process in future years.

The first section of this volume examines the current political debate on Puerto Rico and its historical, social, and economic undercurrents. In Chapter 1, Juan Manuel Carrión tackles the national question. He argues that the Puerto Rican independence movement experienced several phases during the twentieth century and that its latest one, the "new struggle for independence," is coming to an end. This phase was characterized by a new radicalism during the seventies, when nationalism and socialism were joined in a single movement. Many organizations, particularly the Puerto Rican Socialist Party (PSP), gained significant support in the labor, student, and community movements. Even the Puerto Rican pro-Independence Party (PIP) complemented its electoral strategy with direct-action campaigns and actively reached out for the support of the popular sectors. Today the situation is dramatically different. The PSP is just a small fraction of what it was in the early 1970s and a weakened and more conservative PIP remains the only significant organization on the left. Despite wide mass support for the PIP legislative candidates, electoral support for the party remains at 5 percent to 7 percent of the electorate.

Carrión argues that although the independence movement has faced several divisive problems, Puerto Rican nationalism is still alive and vibrant. He proposes that even though pro-independence forces have been relatively weak politically during the last three decades, cultural nationalism is very strong. Carrión warns those seeking the annexation of Puerto Rico that the Puerto Rican nation will not be assimilated and will thus remain a burdensome problem for the United States.

The articles by Pedro Cabán, Edgardo Meléndez, and Humberto García analyze the plebiscite debate from different perspectives. Cabán argues that the plebiscite process is the United States' attempt to solve the continuing crisis of colonialism in Puerto Rico. He argues that the current colonial structures are not adequate for the new needs of global capitalism. The Commonwealth has failed economically and politically and its legitimacy is questioned internationally and domestically. Economic and social stability in Puerto Rico largely depend on federal transfer payments to the island and federal subsidies to U.S. multi-nationals. Section 936 of the IRS code exempts U.S. corporations from paying taxes in Puerto Rico. Cabán believes that Section 936 may very well have been the pivotal concern of the plebiscite process, as sectors of U.S. capital and branches of the U.S. government struggled for dominance. Nevertheless, disputes between the Executive and Congress, between U.S. corporate and other special interests, and between the three Puerto Rican political parties have doomed the plebiscite. Although the United States is looking for a solution to the problem of Puerto Rico, Cabán explains why the plebiscite process was not one.

In Chapter 2 Edgardo Meléndez traces the history of the statehood movement and discusses the statehood proposal in the plebiscite hearings. The modern statehood movement in Puerto Rico developed a populist appeal in low-income communities. The New Progressive Party (PNP, *Partido Nuevo Progresista*) program of economic and social reform and equality received electoral support in 1968, 1976, and 1980. Since their electoral victories in 1968, pro-statehood administrations have used Federal money to lure popular support. But there is no strong support in Washington for a 51st state. Like Cabán, Meléndez concludes that the plebiscite falls short of being the mechanism to solve the colonial status of Puerto Rico.

Another prominent issue in the plebiscite process was the U.S. military presence on the island. Puerto Rico is a valuable strategic and military asset for the United States. Ever since its occupation in 1898, the United States has used Puerto Rico as a strategic site in its military expansion in the Caribbean. Humberto García Muñiz discusses the structure and uses of U.S. military installations in Puerto Rico. The author pinpoints how these installations have been influenced by changing U.S. military and political interests in the Caribbean, and discusses the increase in U.S. military presence on the island since the 1950s, as the United States struggled for world hegemony. The U.S. military presence on the island was reinforced and relegitimated by the post-Cold War mentality.

U.S. military installations in Puerto Rico not only play a role in U. S. military strategy worldwide, but also play a security role in the Caribbean (the island was used as a launching pad for the U.S. invasions of the Dominican Republic and Grenada) and in Puerto Rico itself (facitilitating persecution of "independentistas"). García also discusses the consequences of the U.S. military presence for Puerto Rico. The island could be used as base for submarines carrying nuclear weapons, which together with nuclear-related intelligence installations in Puerto Rico make it a possible target in case of nuclear war. The militarization of Puerto Rican society has intensified in the last two decades, and military spending plays an important role in stimulating an otherwise stagnant economy. García discusses the down side of this process: how the militarization of Vieques has led to displacement, unemployment, and the disintegration of the community. The author finally discusses how the United States plans to keep its military installations despite any change that may occur in the political status of Puerto Rico.

Puerto Rico's economy and its new role in the Caribbean

The second section of the volume examines recent economic developments in Puerto Rico and the Caribbean and their relation to current political events. The most salient characteristic of the Puerto Rican economy is its dependence on the U. S. economy. This relationship is perhaps most evident during the post-war industrialization. Operation Bootstrap, the Commonwealth government's industrial program, began in 1947 and relied on U.S. capital and markets. U.S. corporations borrowed money from the Commonwealth (which in turn sold bonds in the U.S. municipal funds markets) and invested in labor-intensive manufacturing. These factories brought raw materials from abroad, processed or assembled the products in Puerto Rico, and then sold their products in continental markets. Operations tended to be labor-intensive, paid significantly lower wages than those earned by U.S. workers, and enjoyed almost full tax exemptions.

Operation Bootstrap promoted economic growth until about the late 1960s. Many domestic and international factors contributed to the deterioration of the Commonwealth's model of industrial development. Puerto Rico became a less attractive place for low-wage manufacturing when many other countries were allowed to compete for a share of the U.S. market following the "Kennedy rounds" and new trade agreements. Many of the internal conditions that allowed for a long economic expansion changed as well.

The trough of the mid-1970s business cycle represented a turning point for the Puerto Rican economy. In contrast to the experience of previous business cycles, in which U.S. economic activity remained relatively strong in Puerto Rico, this time GNP declined sharply, the unemployment rate almost doubled, and income levels stagnated. Many factories closed their operations in Puerto Rico and moved to other low-wage countries. Partially as a response to these economic conditions, the Commonwealth government, with the support of U.S. corporations operating in Puerto Rico, petitioned Congress for revisions to the U.S. tax code. Tax benefits, which had been the cornerstone of industrial policy in the 1950s and 1960s became even more central to the Commonwealth's economic program after 1976.

The Tax Reform Act of 1976 removed corporations with operations in U.S. possessions from Section 931 of the Internal Revenue Code and placed them into Section 936. Section 936 leaves intact tax exemption of earnings from investments in Puerto Rico but eliminates tax exemptions for income derived outside the possession. Section 936 accelerates the repatriation of profits and dividends remitted by a possession corporation to its U S. parent from taxation.

The most obvious effect of Section 936 has been to boost profitability for U.S. corporations operating in Puerto Rico. The average profit rate of manufacturing operations in the United States was 10.3 percent, but it was 54.1 percent for Section 936 corporations. Average profits were four times higher in pharmaceutical industries and eight times higher in electrical and electronic equipment.

Section 936 regulations have overwhelmingly benefitted pharmaceutical and electrical and electronic equipment manufacturing operations. In 1983, Section 936 tax benefits amounted to $1.64 billion. Pharmaceutical corporations accounted for $760 million or 46.3 percent of total tax benefits and electrical and electronic equipment for $382 million or 23.3 percent of total tax benefits. Apparel and other labor-intensive industries have benefitted much less from Section 936 even though they provide a large share of employment.

However, the net effect of Section 936 on the Puerto Rican economy is the subject of a heated debate, particularly because of its implications for the status debate. While Section 936 may have induced the expansion of a few high-tech sectors, total manufacturing employment remained about 140,000 between 1977 and 1986. During the same period, unemployment remained above 20 percent. The Puerto Rican economy performed better in the late 1980s but the expansion of employment and the decline in the unemployment rate can hardly be attributed to the new tax regime. In any case, employment growth has not reached the annual growth rate of previous decades, nor has the unemployment rate dropped near the 10.7 percent annual rate of 1970.

It is apparent from the above discussion that current political events in Puerto Rico cannot be understood without an appropriate examination of the economic crisis that hit the island during the late 1970s and 1980s. Edwin Meléndez argues that the pro-annexation administrations won electoral support because many poor people perceived their economic program as a positive alternative to the PPD's model of economic development. However, the pro-statehood economic program failed to stabilize the economy, and popular support for statehood was momentarily interrupted. The PPD's 1984 electoral victory gave them a second chance to implement an effective economic program constituting an alternative to conservatism. Despite favorable economic conditions, the PPD has wasted an opportunity to regain political momentum. The island's economy continues to show structural weaknesses and long-term economic prosperity seems elusive.

Chapters 6 and 7 deal with important aspects of industrial development in Puerto Rico. Palmira Ríos examines the relation of export-oriented industrialization to the expansion of female labor. She finds that, between 1950 and 1980, women's labor force participation increased from 21.2 percent to 29.1 percent, while men's participation declined from 70.6 percent to 54.4 percent. Although this change in the structure of employment affected all economic sectors, women represented about half of the labor force in manufacturing throughout the period. However, by 1980, women were concentrated in five manufacturing sectors, accounting for 71.5 percent of women workers. These female-dominated industries, contrary to expectations, are not declining manufacturing sectors but an integral part of export-oriented industrialization. As Ríos argues, Puerto Rican women "were key actors in [an export-oriented] development strategy." In fact, she concludes, "low-paid women workers are the key to the survival of these highly competitive industries in the new global economy."

Chapter 7 discusses the evolution of the Puerto Rican economy during the last two decades and the implications of those transformations for the Caribbean. James Dietz and Emilio Pantojas-García discuss how Puerto Rico has become a financial center that serves as a regional base for U.S. corporations in the Caribbean. At the center of Puerto Rico's new role in the Caribbean are Section 936 of the U.S. Internal Revenue Code and the Caribbean Basin Economic Recovery Act (CBERA). Taking advantage of these programs, the Puerto Rican government launched the Caribbean Development Program (CDP). The CDP, according to Dietz and Pantojas, is "the key to the accelerating attempt to transform the Caribbean Basin into a huge tax- and duty-free export-processing zone and financial center that allows the legal, tax-free repatriation of profits of productive operations to the United States." For the Puerto Rican government, they conclude, becoming an intermediary is the only strategy that may stabilize industrial employment in Puerto Rico. Whether U.S. corporations will locate the "top end" of the production process in Puerto Rico remains to be seen.

Emerging social movements

Throughout the last two centuries of colonial history, Puerto Ricans have persevered in the struggle for independence and social justice, first under the Spanish, then under the U.S. regime. There are many faces to the Puerto Rican struggle. Chapters 8 through 11 deal with emerging social movements in popular sectors such as local neighborhoods, women, and labor. New popular movements in Puerto Rico, those which emerged during the period of *populismo,* or the Popular Democratic Party's hegemony over local politics, reached a peak by the mid-1970s but continued to grow throughout the 1980s. During the early post-war years, industrialization and economic prosperity marginalized popular movements. At best, workers' demands were limited to better working conditions and strikes were few, while feminism remained an intellectual endeavor and community struggles were coopted or practically nonexistent. This situation began to change in the late 1960s. The pro-independence, student, women, community, and labor movements developed new strategies and mobilized popular support.

The early 1970s were years of great political activism. Union membership grew and workers' strikes were common, community squatter movements occupied vacant lands, and students rallied against the Vietnam War. The pro-independence organizations were active in all of these struggles and helped to fuel a new nationalistic sentiment. Many of these struggles, like the squatters' and students' movements, were very successful. However, popular struggles subsided by the end of the 1970s, partially as a response to high unemployment and to the government's response of repression and accommodation.

The economic and political crisis in Puerto Rico has affected all institutions, including popular and radical political movements. The ascendance of conservative solutions to the economic and political crisis results in part from the inability of progressive organizations to respond to new circumstances. That inability to adjust quickly to changes in the economic and political environment is particularly evident in the pro-independence, student, community, and labor movements. Now however, these traditional popular movements are not only beginning to show new vitality, but newer ones such as the women's, youth, environmental, and other movements are leading the way to new forms of struggle and empowerment. Popular struggles offer several solutions to the colonial dilemma.

In Chapter 8, Liliana Cotto analyzes the squatter movement. Between 1968 and 1976, the squatter movement gained momentum and then receded, as government both accommodated some popular demands and implemented new laws to prevent the further growth of the movement. The *rescates,* as land invasions are called, were mostly realized by an urban population pressed by housing shortages and the urban crisis. The squatter movement used a diversity of tactics in their struggle, such as pickets, mass mobilizations, civil disobedience, and even violent confrontation with the police. Their struggle evolved into a confrontation with the state and into an ideological challenge to the notion of private property. Eventually, the *rescatadores* (urban squatters) succeeded in obtaining a piece of land and housing for thousands of people, and dozens of communities were formed. The squatter movement made the early 1970s an exciting period in the history of community struggles in Puerto Rico. As Cotto reminds us, we have much to learn from our recent past about popular mobilizations and political realignment in Puerto Rico.

One consequence of the political and popular struggles of the 1970s was the solidification of the feminist movement in Puerto Rico. Puerto Rican feminists, like feminists throughout the third world, face the critical challenge of articulating feminist concerns alongside issues of national liberation. In Chapter 9, Margarita Mergal surveys women's organizing across the island (not all of which is explicitly feminist or pro-independence) arguing that while progressive feminists may work to convey to women their ideals for socialism and independence, they should take care not to impose their views on the feminist organizations they belong to.

Although women show a high level of activism in politics, trade-unionism, and community work, their participation in leadership roles is still hampered by the male-dominated leadership in these organizations and by the patriarchal ideology that still pervades Puerto Rican society. Even progressive organizations, like independence parties and some trade-unions, limit discussion of women's issues and women's participation in decision-making bodies.

Mergal argues that the Puerto Rican feminist movement has been hindered by its lack of identity, political project, and unity. Socio-economic crisis on the island poses a threat to women's survival, turning everyday problems into political ones. With that in mind, Mergal concludes that to "successfully face its challenges, a main objective of feminism should be to achieve a diverse, autonomous movement, capable of bringing together women of different races, classes, and political persuasions."

The Puerto Rican labor movement is in crisis. After a period of strong activism in the early 1970s, unions have been on the defensive and their membership has declined from 20 percent of all workers in 1970 to 6 percent in 1988. Carlos Alá Santiago Rivera argues that the crisis of the labor movement is in part a consequence of its inability to cope with industrial restructuring. Many of the sectors with the largest concentration of unionized workers were severely hit by the economic crisis of the mid-1970s and early 1980s. The emerging growth industries have a strong anti-labor stance and union organizing is very difficult. Moreover, the small number of unions with a significant membership are facing a hard battle against subcontracting and other new employer tactics. But despite these adverse conditions, labor unions have succeeded in organizing the first strong union confederation in the post-war period.

The economic crisis in Puerto Rico has hit hardest those who are most disadvantaged: working people, poor people, those who are unemployed, women, and children. One aspect of the ongoing crisis in Puerto Rico is the crisis of public education, acknowledged as an urgent issue by the island's government and the elite. One positive consequence of any social or economic crisis is that those most affected are urged to participate to solve their problems.

Ana Maria García and José Javier Colón discuss the need of communities in the mostly poor "barrios" to organize themselves and take charge of schools in order to provide their children an education linked to their community's needs, history, culture, and expectations. The authors argue that the government's response to the educational crisis, the Educational Reform Law of 1990, will not solve the problem, since it reproduces part of the problem itself: a top-down bureaucracy and an extremely politicized public school system that alienates both children and parents. The authors argue that the only solution to the crisis lies in linking the public school system to their communities, mostly working class and poor. García and Colón discuss the successful example of the "new school" concept in a community-controlled school in Juan Domingo, a local working-class barrio. The example described shows how a community organized to defend its interests is able to solve those problems that the state bureaucracy is unable to deal with.

Puerto Rican communities in the United States

For Puerto Rican communities in the United States, the plebiscite represents a challenge to their identity. Many do not understand the economic forces that promote the integration of labor markets on a global scale. Though uprooted from their homeland, Puerto Ricans in the barrios have preserved cultural values and political aspirations. In the first article in this section, Frank Bonilla asserts that Puerto Ricans in the U.S. have the right to participate in any major political decision that affects the island. Moreover, Puerto Rican communities will be actively involved in shaping U.S. policies toward Puerto Rico.

Angelo Falcón discusses these issues more extensively in his article on the Puerto Rican community and the plebiscite. Falcon discusses at length a recent survey by the Puerto Rican Policy Institute on this issue. The participation of mainland Puerto Ricans on Puerto Rico's status plebiscite touched a raw nerve in Puerto Rico's politics and identity as a people: are U.S.-based Puerto Ricans to be considered Puerto Ricans? Should they participate in the plebiscite? Many in Puerto Rico felt that they should not participate. Puerto Rico's three main political parties— the only Puerto Rican representatives in the plebiscite process—struggled with this issue. The pro-Commonwealth PPD, in an obviously opportunistic gamble, lately decided to support the participation of mainland Puerto Ricans in the plebiscite; the pro-statehood PNP and the pro-independence PIP opposed steadfastly. On the other hand, as the Institute's survey shows, a majority of U.S. Puerto Ricans wished to participate in the plebiscite. More surprising yet, because of the existing myths on this issue, the survey indicated that Puerto Ricans on the Island and in the U.S. show strikingly similar patterns of political support for the three status alternatives.

Falcón argues that the plebiscite discussion revived a 1970s debate on the "national question" among U.S. Puerto Ricans: are they part of a "divided nation" or do they constitute a "national minority" in the United States? The survey shows there is still no clear-cut answer to this issue. Falcón concludes his article arguing that the "desire of a large majority of Puerto Ricans in the United States to participate in the proposed referendum vote represents the strong ties that continue to exist to Puerto Rico, both because of significant circular migration and family connections. Also involved is the recognition that a change in the Island's political status would have important implications for U.S.-based Puerto Ricans culturally, legally, economically, and politically."

Solidarity has always been an important part of the liberation struggles of colonial territories. The solidarity of the American people with Puerto Rico is no exception. The solidarity movement for the independence of Puerto Rico during the 1970s was but the latest example. Carlos Rodríguez provides a glimpse at the long history of American solidarity with Puerto Rico. He elaborates on an incident involving the famous American painter Rockwell Kent. After a trip to Puerto Rico in the 1930s, Kent decided to publicize the island's struggle for independence. He was angry at the U.S. government for placing the leadership of the Nationalist Party, Pedro Albizu Campos, and his closest associates, on trial for sedition. A first trial, in which most jurors were Puerto Ricans, ended in a hung jury, but a second trial with twelve hand-picked American jurors convicted the Nationalist leaders. Puerto Rican public opinion rejected this blatant injustice. Furious that the American media was not publicizing this persecution by the U.S. government, Kent showed his support by including a simple message of solidarity to the Puerto Rican people in a U.S. government-sponsored mural that he was painting. When the message was made public—it was written in an Alaskan language—it created a furor. Today, as in the 1950s, the solidarity of people in the United States with Puerto Rico is important to a just resolution of the colonial dilemma.

Beyond the colonial dilemma

The Puerto Rican people and the United States government face a colonial dilemma. At first, the plebiscite seemed a viable mechanism to solve the colonial status. But as the Island's politicos and Washington's consuls proceeded with their plans, the plebiscite began to face all the problems that have doomed similar efforts in the past. What is different about this plebiscite process is that, for the first time in history, all three sectors of Puerto Rican politics expressed their views on each status formula, and the Executive and Congress reacted to these. Still the United States seems more interested in maintaining the status quo than in solving the status question. The proposal for an "enhanced Commonwealth" was not well received in Washington, particularly by the Executive. At the same time, even though statehood forces in Puerto Rico have gained momentum since 1968, political support for statehood is fragmented in Washington. And although the independence option was cautiously heard by Washington for the first time in many decades, there is still no wide support for independence in the United States or Puerto Rico. What is certain is that the Puerto Rican people and the United States face a new political challenge.

Facing the 21st century, Puerto Rico is still confronted by serious challenges. Politically, the colonial dilemma is still far from being resolved. Puerto Rico's economy is still facing structural limitations and remains extremely dependent on U.S. programs and policies. The economic and social crisis still affects the lives of a large sector of the population that are faced with poverty, unemployment, and marginalization, and whose levels of drug addiction, alcohol abuse, AIDS, and illiteracy are among the highest when compared to other regions of the United States.

A lesson to be learned from this volume is that Puerto Ricans are facing these challenges, struggling to achieve a better organized and just society. Although they may disagree on the political alternatives for the island's future, Puerto Ricans agree that the colonial status must soon come to an end. And they are calling on the United States to fulfill its responsibility as a colonial power by solving the colonial status. People are dissatisfied with the inability of the traditional *politicos* and the government in solving their most pressing economic and social problems, as well as the colonial issue. Many organizations are emerging in the community, workplace, schools, and universities that are working at the grassroots level to solve these problems.

This anthology gives us a wide perspective on Puerto Rico's politics, economy, society, culture, and history, on its most pressing problems and some alternatives. The solution to Puerto Rico's colonial dilemma cannot be limited to the colonial question, important as it is. Puerto Rico's century-old relationship with the United States involves a whole range of other issues, including culture, national identity, migration, poverty, standard of living, way of life, economic and political dependency, and isolation from Latin America and the Caribbean.

The failure of conventional mechanisms of political negotiation and electoral participation in solving Puerto Rico's colonial dilemma suggests that the solution to colonialism may lie beyond the Congressional corridors in Washington or the established political parties in Puerto Rico. Emerging social movements are beginning to redefine the political spectrum in the island by bringing to the forefront of public concern their struggles for a more just society. Popular struggles have forced existing political institutions to accommodate their demands for political participation and access to economic resources. However, the redefinition of the political discourse and practice is far from completion.

In particular as Wilfredo Mattos-Cintrón argues in Chapter 15, the traditional focus on status politics by pro-independence political organizations is at the expense of the active participation of popular sectors in the political process. The struggle for independence divorced from a social agenda that responds to working class communities and the poor, the labor movement, feminism, students, and other popular sectors is likely to continue to be marginal — contained to a small proportion of the electorate and with limited influence in the political arena.

In a way, independence is the most viable political and economic option. From Washington's point of view, independence does not have the high fiscal costs associated with statehood or the continuation of the Commonwealth. Independence will also solve the political contradiction that a colonial territory represents to the United States in the context of the new international reality where ethnicity seems to be the clear basis for the realignment of nation-states. Independence also offers Puerto Ricans the possibility to reorient and adapt the economic system to the reality of a new global economy. The regionalization of the Puerto Rican economy has run its course since the dynamism of a "936" manufacturing sector has not resulted in lower unemployment and greater economic stability in other sectors of the economy. A pro-independence economic program is consistent with both a domestic realignment of popular sectors emphasizing the development of industries to satisfy basic needs and with the changes in the global economy that will require a reorientation of the export sector.

There is no guarantee, however, that the realignment of social forces during the current political conjuncture will lead to a stronger pro-independence movement. A similar historical period during the 1930s evolved into the Commonwealth status in the 1940s. A stronger pro-independence movement will emerge only when the political organizations that represent this alternative recognize the importance of popular sectors in redefining the political landscape. Or, when popular struggles converge in the formation of their own political vehicle. What is clear, however, is that the convergence of popular struggles and the pro-independence movement will lead to a redefinition of the political status question. We hope this volume is a modest contribution to a better understanding of contemporary Puerto Rico, and that a better understanding of the problem may lead to a long lasting solution.

PART I: POLITICS AND THE STATUS DEBATE

Redefining Puerto Rico's Political Status

Pedro Cabán*

Almost four decades after the U.S. government announced to the United Nations that Puerto Rico had ceased to be a colony, Congress reconsidered the country's political status. In 1989, the 101st Congress initiated a legislative process that was designed to produce a bill to authorize a referendum on the political status of Puerto Rico. Although status-related legislative activity continued into the 102nd Congress, no bill was ever drafted. The House and Senate draft bills would have called on the people of Puerto Rico to express their preference for one of three options: 1) independence, 2) annexation into the Union as the 51st state, or 3) redefinition of the current Commonwealth arrangement. The most significant feature of the proposed legislation was explicit language calling for the implementation of the preferred option.

Although Puerto Rico's political-juridical status has been the subject of congressional scrutiny and debate since as far back as 1898, the current referendum process is unique because it is the first time since 1917 that Congress has taken a lead in defining the nature of Puerto Rico's status. Congressional interest in reworking the colonial formula appears at a particularly dynamic period in world history. Seemingly unrelated geopolitical and international economic developments bear directly on the issue of Puerto Rico's probable decolonization[1] and suggest answers to why the U.S. government has finally decided to revisit the colonial question.

* I would like to thank Angelo Falcón, Edgardo Meléndez, José Sánchez, and Rosalie Morales Kearns for their comments. This is an expanded and updated version of "Reworking the Colonial Formula: Puerto Rico into the Twenty-First Century," which appeared in *Radical America* 23, no. 1 (Jan.-Feb. 1989):9-20.

U.S. colonial policy toward Puerto Rico has historically been propelled by two considerations: utilizing Puerto Rico's strategic location in a region of critical geopolitical significance, and securing a favorable investment climate for U.S. business. Since the end of World War II, Puerto Rico has been promoted as a bulwark against the spread of communism in the Caribbean, and its shores have been used as a base for U.S. military intervention in the region. This perception has gradually changed, however, with the end of the Cold War, the reversals of socialist and social-democratic regimes in Central and Latin America, and widespread popular skepticism about the notion that communism breeds revolution in the region.

Puerto Rico has been an extremely profitable base of operations for U.S. business. Three periods have been particularly important in the country's twentieth-century economic growth, all characterized by export-oriented industries producing for the U.S. market: 1) a sugar-based economy under the control of absentee corporations, 2) U.S.-led labor-intensive manufacturing in apparel and textile products, and 3) most recently, large-scale capital-intensive pharmaceutical and electronics firms and sophisticated financial and communications services under the control of global enterprises. However, with the passing of each phase, the U.S. government has been compelled to assume an ever larger role in sustaining Puerto Rico's economy, playing an increasingly important role in sustaining social welfare, government operations, and industrial production. Moreover, given the nature of the economic growth that is taking place, congressional critics are questioning whether the prevailing relationship is still necessary to attract U.S. investments.[2]

The current congressional debates on the future political status of Puerto Rico occur in the context of a less threatening geopolitical climate but an increasingly volatile international economic scene. Seldom explicitly discussed, but always on the minds of policy-makers, is whether the colony of Puerto Rico is still essential to preserve the geopolitical and economic interests of the United States. Complicating these discussions is the realizaton that Puerto Rico is plagued by a series of social, economic, and political maladies that will likely remain unattended under the prevailing political status. Clearly, events in Washington leave little doubt that the U.S. government considers the prevailing relationship deficient and in need of serious revision. Accordingly, debates between Congress and the Executive Branch have been guided by two sets of concerns—whether decolonization will compromise U.S. national security and undermine the profitability of U.S. business, and whether the prevailing status can be reworked into a more cost-efficient and politically manageable relationship. Crisis in colonial management of Puerto Rico is not new. What is new is Congress's explicit commitment to resolve the vexing problem of Puerto Rico's political status.

In this chapter, I discuss the relationship between Puerto Rico's Commonwealth status and economic growth in the post-war period. I examine the attempts by the PPD, or *Partido Popular Democrático,* repeated since the late 1940s, to gain more autonomous powers for the insular government and the declining relevance of the colonial relationship for U.S. business. I conclude with a review of the legislative process during the 101st Congress and examine the critical issues that framed Congress's debates on the future of Puerto Rico.

The Commonwealth and the economics of colonialism

Puerto Rico's political status is defined by Public Law 600 (PL 600) and the Puerto Rico Federal Relations Act it created. PL 600 went into effect on July 3, 1950, and authorized the government in Puerto Rico to draft a constitution and establish a republican form of government. The PPD, the party in power at the time, was a major force in bringing this project to fruition.

The U.S. Senate Committee that wrote the legislation reasoned "that it is in line with the policy of the Government to provide the largest possible measure of local self-government for people who are under the flag of the United States."[3] The legislation was widely promoted as a fundamental restructuring of the colonial relationship to permit Puerto Ricans to manage their domestic political economy. Yet the same committee emphasized that the new bill did not diminish the island's subordination to the federal government: "The measure would not change Puerto Rico's fundamental political, social, and economic relationship to the United States."[4]

On March 3, 1952, 47 percent of registered voters in Puerto Rico approved a constitution. Approximately 20 percent of the voters rejected that constitution, while independence forces boycotted the referendum. The "Commonwealth," known in Spanish as the *"Estado Libre Asociado" (ELA),* was proclaimed on July 25, 1952, and presented to the world as a new political entity with autonomous powers over domestic affairs—ostensibly the end of colonialism for Puerto Rico. However, the U.S. grant of self-government was provisional, since "…[C]onstitutionally, Congress may repeal Public Law 600, annul the Constitution of Puerto Rico and veto any insular legislation which it deems unwise or improper. From the perspective of constitutional law the compact between Puerto Rico and Congress may be unilaterally altered by the Congress."[5]

While PL 600 was an important element of Puerto Rico's favorable investment climate, it did not affect economic regulations that were originally set up in 1900 through the Foraker Act. In fact, the essential measures that attracted U.S. investments in manufacturing and which locked the country's economy into the metropolitan network of production and trade were in place well before the establishment of the Commonwealth. Exemptions from federal taxation, a common monetary system, inclusion in the U.S. Customs area, provisions for the collection and return of excise taxes, access to U.S. financial markets, special treatment under federal tax laws, insular maritime legislation, partial exemption from the Fair Labor Standards Act, prohibitions against commercial treaties with foreign nations, direct federal transfers to individuals and the public bureaucracy, and application of Taft-Hartley legislation were on the books before 1952. The federal government retained control over monetary and trade policy and kept the original Foraker Act provisions that authorized the colonial administration to establish a tax system.

Nonetheless, PL 600 was significant because it created a set of social institutions and arrangements that enhanced the prospects for long-term corporate investments and profitability. In the process, it established a political and economic environment that accelerated Puerto Rico's integration into the U.S. economy as a low-wage manufacturing center. Although the structure of colonial rule was preserved, the colonial state was given the requisite autonomy to devise planning and social policies consistent with the requirements of a new and more advanced phase of capitalist development.

The creation of the ELA is best understood in the context of domestic and international politico-economic developments in the immediate post-war era, when dominant political forces in the colony, intent on preserving their hegemony, sought alliance with U.S. capital and metropolitan state interests.[6] The national and international attention lavished on Puerto Rico converted that little-known and poverty-stricken country into the center of "freedom and power in the Caribbean."[7]

While the ELA preserved the structure of colonial rule, it also gave government officials in Puerto Rico the necessary autonomy and flexibility to promote a new model of accumulation. For potential investors, Puerto Rico loomed as a new tropical investment paradise, replete with political stability, low wages and a compliant government. Puerto Rico was an ideal investment site for these firms for two reasons. First, Puerto Rico was exempted from federal regulations over industrial labor relations, wage policy, environmental quality, and other areas. Second, ELA retained the most economically attractive features of the colonial relationship—federal tax credits and exemption from taxation, duty-free access to U.S. markets, and monetary stability. In the immediate post-war period Puerto Rico virtually guaranteed U.S. business the *highest* profit rates in the hemisphere.

On January 19, 1953, the United States unilaterally removed Puerto Rico from the United Nations list of non-self-governing territories, and obtained a permanent exemption from having to submit annual reports on the country's social and economic conditions to the Secretary General. Puerto Ricans, the United States told the world, had freely chosen through open democratic elections to retain their long-standing association with the United States. The nature of this compact of mutual association was, and continues to be, legally and politically obscure. However, the ELA was pronounced as being internally self-governing and sovereign over those matters not prohibited by the Constitution of the United States. The PPD joined U.S. policy-makers in a campaign to mystify the country's colonial status. The ELA was part of a strategy to mitigate international criticism of the United States as a colonial power and to authenticate the U.S. crusade for post-war global decolonization. Since 1952, the United States has tried to convince an increasingly skeptical global community that Puerto Rico is not a colony.[8]

The PPD, under the leadership of Luis Muñoz Marín (its founder and first elected governor of Puerto Rico), was a major force behind this symbolic change in the colonial formula. Originally formed in the late 1930s as an anti-imperialist populist movement, the PPD readily dominated Puerto Rico's political scene for nearly three decades. But by 1948, PPD officials abandoned their goal of independence and called upon the people of Puerto Rico to support a program of economic integration into the United States through a refurbished colonial formula. The PPD's decision to abandon independence and intensify the country's subordination to the metropolitan economy was seen in some sectors as a betrayal, which many believe precipitated the nationalist uprisings of the 1950s.

In the bipolar post-war world, conceived of by U.S. legislators in terms of preserving national security in the face of Soviet expansion, there was little patience in Congress for an independent, conceivably social-democratic, regime in the Caribbean. The PPD leadership recognized this and consolidated its emerging hegemony by legitimizing the objectives of a U.S. foreign policy that was predicated on suffocating national liberation struggles throughout the world. In their eyes, Puerto Rico stood as a shining example of the economic and social gains that could be achieved by the third world through dependent capitalist development, and political subordination to the United States.

'Perfecting the Commonwealth'

The redefined colonial relationship did not represent the culmination of the PPD's efforts to rework the terms of Puerto Rico's subordination. On the contrary, it was the foundation upon which the PPD would pressure the federal government for enhanced autonomy in order to "perfect" the Commonwealth relation.

Throughout the 1950s and 1960s, the PPD lobbied the federal government in a failed effort to obtain increased decision-making powers, particularly over those areas that affected economic performance. The PPD had two goals which, if successful, would have also prevented its most serious political opposition, the statehood movement, from emerging as a viable alternative: first, to sustain an internationally favorable investment climate for foreign capital; second, to fortify its own domestic political base. The gradual expansion of Puerto Rico's autonomous powers was seen by the PPD leadership as essential to achieve both goals. With increased decisional capacity over economic matters, Puerto Rico would continue to respond to the needs of U.S. business and thus promote growth. Congressional approval for amendments to the Federal Relations Act would also enhance the standing of the PPD and convince the electorate that ELA was a permanent solution to Puerto Rico's uncertain political identity. With the necessary correctives, the PPD seemed to argue, Puerto Rico would be spared from eventually having to choose between statehood and independence.

Muñoz Marín developed a particular conception of the *Estado Libre Asociado* based on the principles of compact and consent between two equal peoples. According to a State Department study authored by Arthur Borg, Muñoz Marín argued

> In approving the law (PL 600) and submitting it to the Puerto Rican people, Congress was asking them to consent to its taking effect. If they gave it their approval, the argument ran, the result would be that the Puerto Rican constitution and the new Federal Relations Act would be legitimized by the consent of the Puerto Rican people.[9]

By 1959 Muñoz Marín had further developed the concept of "compact." He noted, "The idea of compact determines a basic change in the relationship. It takes away from the very basis of the relationship the nature and onus of colonialism. It cannot be revoked or changed unilaterally."[10] Clearly the problem with all of this was that the formulation was only in Muñoz Marín's mind, since Congress had not legislated away its constitutional powers over territorial matters, and specifically over Puerto Rico. In passing PL 600, Congress was merely expanding the range of Puerto Rico's powers over local self-government.

On March 23, 1959, less than seven years after the proclamation of ELA, Puerto Rico's Resident Commissioner introduced legislation in Congress to alter and clarify PL 600.[11] But the persistent congressional opposition to the implicit claim of sovereignty contained in the bill forced the PPD to substitute a substantially revised bill in September 1959. The new measure was subjected to intense congressional scrutiny, detailed studies by Executive Branch agencies, and wide-ranging debate in public hearings. The public hearings revealed the absence of consensus among Puerto Rico's political leadership on what type of changes should be effected in the colonial relationship. The U.S. government also opposed any changes in legislation that restricted the constitutionally defined prerogatives of the federal government to regulate Puerto Rican affairs. After two years of legislative activity, Congress failed to act on the measure, and it died quietly in early 1961.

Throughout the 1960s, Muñoz Marín pursued his intellectual and political campaign to lay the foundations for an expansion of ELA's autonomous powers. However, even he could not leverage his considerable international prestige and close personal ties with the Kennedy Administration to amend PL 600. But he was able to obtain White House approval for the establishment in 1964 of a U.S.-Puerto Rico Commission. The Commission's work led to one of the most comprehensive reports on Puerto Rico's status, and its members recommended holding a plebiscite. In 1967, amid deteriorating economic conditions, growing popular appeal for the statehood movement, and apparent U.S. impatience with lobbying for more autonomy, Muñoz Marín called for a plebiscite.

Unlike its predecessor in 1952, the 1967 referendum was not an initiative by Congress, and thus had no legal force to affect relations.[12] The PPD anticipated overwhelming popular support for the Commonwealth proposal, which would give it "the authorization to develop the *Estado Libre Asociado*...to the maximum level of self-government."[13] Moreover, the PPD hoped the plebiscite results would solidify its electoral standing and ultimately convince Congress to grant the Commonwealth autonomous powers over critical areas of the political economy. The 1967 plebiscite failed to accomplish any of this; in fact, it intensified the divisions within the PPD, led to the emergence of a younger and more sophisticated leadership in the statehood movement (*Partido Nuevo Progresista*, or PNP), and contributed to the PPD's electoral defeat in 1968.

In 1973 the PPD returned to office, and once again attempted to resurrect its cherished dreams for "perfecting" the Commonwealth. Muñoz Marín obtained presidential approval for a special commission to study U.S.-Puerto Rican relations. That Commission's report was released in October 1975 as the "Compact of Permanent Union" and recommended a thorough restructuring of the colonial relationship. It called for granting Puerto Rico the right to participate in international organizations, jurisdiction over territory held by the United States, control over tariff and immigration policy, the right to enter into commercial treaties, exemption from the Federal Fair Labor Standards Act, authority to regulate environmental quality standards, and other recommendations for increased autonomy.

The report left no doubt that the Commonwealth status deprived the insular administration of the minimal policy tools needed to regulate Puerto Rico's political economy. If the colonial formula were not reworked, the report seemed to argue, Puerto Rico would relinquish its status as a center for capital accumulation. The Compact was a plea by the PPD to the U.S. government to grant the Commonwealth the flexibility it needed to respond to the changing requirements of an emerging new economic order.

What the PPD feared most was that economic deterioration would thwart its aspirations for re-establishing its political hegemony after its defeat in the 1968 elections. But the Compact was not only linked to a new model of capital accumulation and political dominance, it also required a drastic reduction in U.S. authority over its possession—something the federal government rejected then and continues to resist.

During its four years in office (1973-1976), the PPD Administration led by Rafael Hernández Colón did not embark on a campaign to alter the status of the island. Possibly lulled into thinking that the PPD's loss to the statehood party in 1968 was an aberration, Hernández Colón did not view the PNP as a serious electoral threat. Although he set about to reintegrate disaffected sectors of the traditional PPD coalition, his administration was forced to contend with Puerto Rico's most serious recession since the post-war era. In an effort to counter the downturn, Hernández Colón imposed harsh economic measures, with the result that the PPD began to undermine its electoral base. The PPD's inability to extricate the economy from the recession, along with its unpopular austerity programs, set the stage for a victory by the PNP in 1976. However, the elections of 1976 also proved the existence of widespread underlying popular support for the statehood party, and thus reinvigorated the dormant status issue.

After its sobering defeat, PPD strategists re-evaluated the party's electoral strategy in the context of a campaign to enhance the autonomous powers of the Commonwealth. In 1978, the PPD introduced *La Nueva Tesis*, its vision of a new federal relationship for Puerto Rico. Rafael Hernández Colón wrote that in order to confront the changing economic and social demands of the 1980s, Puerto Rico required much greater "political authority over its own life." He called for a number of changes in PL 600, including increased insular control over labor-management relations, salaries and "all the conditions of employment in our economy."[14] *La Nueva Tesis* was closely patterned on the recommendations of the Compact of Permanent Union. However, it contained a withering attack against statehood, arguing that the resulting loss of tax benefits and increased reliance on federal support would create dependency and lead to the destruction of Puerto Rico's nascent middle class.[15]

The PPD was prepared to reactivate the status issue and to make it a focal point of the 1980 elections. For the first time some of its leaders testified before the United Nations Decolonization Committee and met with representatives of the Cuban delegation that had submitted a resolution supporting Puerto Rico's right to self-determination. During the 1980 campaign the PPD came under bitter criticism for its supposed alliance with the Cubans. This collusion with the presumed enemy of Puerto Rico may have been decisive in PPD's subsequent defeat.[16]

Romero Barceló, the incumbent governor, campaigned in part on the premise that if re-elected he would call for a referendum on Puerto Rico's status in 1981. Both parties were staking their electoral futures on the belief that the elections would finally determine Puerto Rico's status preference. Yet the election results were indecisive. Although Romero Barceló was elected governor, his margin of victory was the smallest in any of Puerto Rico's general elections.[17] With such a miniscule mandate, the PNP feared possible rejection of the statehood option if a referendum was held. Not surprisingly, Romero Barceló did not promote a status change during his tenure. However, his administration was characterized by a bitter ideological campaign against those sectors of society promoting autonomy and independence.[18] Independence, socialist, and nationalist forces in Puerto Rico were readily labelled terroristic, and Romero's administration worked assiduously to create the myth that they were closely allied to Cuba. The PPD came under attack and its leadership was portrayed as suspect because of its activities in the United Nations. Since the end of World War II, Puerto Rico's political leadership has effectively promoted fears of communist subversion and Cuban intervention as a means to discredit independence forces. However, what was striking about the Romero period was its virulence against this sector, and its ideological affinity with the Reagan era. Combatting communism in Puerto Rico was, for the PNP, the equivalent of the Reagan Administration's policy of confrontation with the Nicaraguan Sandinistas and El Salvador's FDR-FMLN.

Section 936 and the 'new colonialism'

The post-World War II industrialization policy, known as Operation Bootstrap, succeeded in large part because it guaranteed that Puerto Rico would be a more profitable site than competing regional manufacturing centers in the United States. Until the mid-1960s, this policy responded well to the needs of U.S. capital, which was overwhelmingly labor-intensive and had relatively low capital requirements. Moreover, since these firms imported raw materials and semi-processed commodities from the United States and re-exported their finished products to metropolitan markets, the Puerto Rican economy formed part of the U.S. network of commodity production, trade, and money circulation. Puerto Rico was merely an extension of the metropolitan economy.

However, by the mid-1970s, the traditional structure of production was undergoing profound disruption. Policy-makers learned to their dismay that Puerto Rico was no longer competing solely with decaying regions in the mainland, but with the newly industrializing economies. As a result, the traditional firms, which were losing their competitive advantage, evacuated Puerto Rico with alarming frequency.

Faced with a profound crisis in investor confidence and economic deterioration, planning strategy was altered in response to the investment needs of newer industries. These industries were concentrated in pharmaceuticals, electronics, and specialized medical equipment industries, and were overwhelmingly subsidiaries of multinational corporations. The goal of recreating a more favorable investment climate was behind Hernández Colón's decision in 1974 to form the Committee to Study Puerto Rico's Finances. In 1975, the Committee presented its sobering analysis of the local economy.[19] Its recommendations presaged the Reagan Administration's supply-side philosophy. It called for eliminating those regulations that impeded corporate profitability and for reduced public-sector financing of basic social services. While the Committee endorsed the orthodox palliative that vibrant economic growth would increase the aggregate social wage and lead to an overall material improvement of society, it argued that Puerto Rico lacked many of the policy instruments it needed in order to control the activities of multinational firms.[20] Moreover, its policy recommendations were an explicit rejection of the more balanced growth and socially responsible perspective of the PPD's *La Nueva Tesis*.

By the late 1970s, capital-rich, highly mobile, and technologically sophisticated firms were moving their operations in large numbers to Puerto Rico. They did so to utilize the skilled yet cheap labor, and to take advantage of new industrial incentives. But they were also induced to invest in Puerto Rico by generous federal tax credits. In 1976, Congress amended the tax exemption policy for U.S. firms with branches in Puerto Rico. The revised tax code, known as Section 936 of the U.S. Internal Revenue Code, permits U.S. subsidiaries in Puerto Rico to repatriate profits to the United States and receive a federal tax credit. Under the previous law, firms were taxed if they remitted accumulated profits while they continued to conduct business in

Puerto Rico. Thus, the old system provided an incentive for firms to liquidate their operations at the expiration of the tax exemption period and to transfer their accumulated profits to the booming and lucrative Eurodollar markets. Ostensibly Congress enacted Section 936 to halt these abuses.

The impact of the new tax regime on the economy was dramatic. Multinational firms in the pharmaceuticals, electronics, and precision instruments sector migrated in even larger numbers to the island. These 936 corporations transformed not only Puerto Rico's manufacturing sector, but its financial sector as well. By granting tax exemption on certain types of earned interest deposited in domestic financial markets, Congress encouraged the 936 corporations to retain their assets in Puerto Rico. In essence, Congress created a complementary fund market to provide low-cost capital for investment purposes.

When combined with generous industrial incentives and subsidies, including fiscal inducements, tax exemptions, and low wages, Section 936 converted Puerto Rico into an incredibly profitable investment site for international conglomerates. In 1988, U.S. firms in Puerto Rico realized profits of $8.9 billion, or about 19.7 percent of their declared global profits attributable to direct foreign investment activity.[21] In the process, Puerto Rico's economy became excessively reliant on Section 936 corporations. Rather than repatriating to the United States those profits that were eligible for tax credits and where the net return on investments was not as great as in offshore banking sites, 936 corporations began to deposit their surplus profits in Puerto Rican banks. By 1983, 41 percent of total commercial bank deposits were attributable to these firms and approximately one-third of the labor force was either directly or indirectly dependent on these 936 corporations for employment.[22] As a direct outgrowth of 936, Puerto Rico was increasingly shifting its structure of capital accumulation from manufacturing to financial services. One student of this process notes:

> The financial income of export manufacturing 936 corporations became the fuel of the whole system. Billions of dollars in global profits were transferred to or declared in export manufacturing operations in Puerto Rico through a highly complex and sophisticated international financial network.[23]

The federal government is acutely aware of how important the Section 936 tax credit is to employment and investment in the island, and knows that "a phase-out of Section 936 would cause economic dislocation in Puerto Rico."[24] Nonetheless, in its annual reports on the "possessions corporation system of taxation," the Treasury Department argues that Section 936 is a giveaway for the multinational corporations that results in billions of dollars in lost revenue for the federal government. Since 1976, the Treasury has periodically tried to persuade Congress to rescind the credit as a way of reducing the federal deficit. Only because of a monumental lobbying effort by the PPD, its congressional allies and the Puerto Rico-U.S.A Foundation [25] was the Treasury's 1985 campaign to abolish the credit defeated. But the Treasury, with its revenue-enhancing allies in Congress, has enacted measures that have offset the tax benefits of Section 936.

The implications of this squabbling are theoretically significant. The federal government and U.S. firms are clearly divided as to the benefits and costs of sustaining Puerto Rico as a colony. Certain developments indicate the growing influence of the finance sector on the Puerto Rican economy. U.S. multinational banks and financial and investment firms have rapidly expanded their operations to Puerto Rico and are increasingly financing regional development projects. In addition, the insular government has enacted legislation to convert Puerto Rico into an offshore banking site. This sector of capital is less reliant on Section 936, cheap labor, and the economic benefits of colonialism than the multinational corporations now engaged in production. But periodic congressional review of Section 936 leaves little doubt that the enormous benefits accruing to the manufacturing-finance multinational corporations are also perceived as somehow detrimental to the financial well-being of the U.S. economy.

Puerto Rico has become one of the most profitable assembly, packaging, and testing platforms in the world for multinational firms and has evolved into an important offshore banking site as well. But this high-end economic growth has not mitigated the deplorable social and economic conditions that plague Puerto Rico. Puerto Rico's per capita income is less than one-third that of the United States ($5,157 in 1988, or about 47 percent of the per capita income of Mississippi, the poorest state); unemployment unofficially strikes about 25 percent of the labor force; and labor participation rates are extremely low, about 41 percent.

According to a recent U.S. government report, "Chronic high poverty rates persist in Puerto Rico."[26] In 1979, nearly two-thirds of Puerto Rico's population earned incomes below the federal poverty level. Puerto Rico is acutely dependent upon the federal government to sustain consumption and the operations of the government. In 1988 federal transfers to Puerto Rico reached almost $6 billion, which accounted for 21 percent of the island's personal income and 31 percent of the Commonwealth government's annual receipts. Illiteracy afflicts 11 percent of the population, and thus shatters the prospects for much of the population to participate in the more sophisticated, evolving economy. The Commonwealth spends only $1,400 per student (less than any U.S. state). Because of entrenched unemployment, out-migration has once again increased and was estimated at 280,000 from 1980 to 1988 (about 8.5 percent of the population).

It is against this backdrop of contradictory development outcomes that the current status debate has to be understood. In reality, the U.S. government has kept the colony economically afloat and politically stable. While it developed fiscal tools to promote accumulation, it has had to allocate ever larger amounts of public capital to sustain the material and social reproduction of the colony. Given the nature of late capitalist expansion, which is highly mobile and extremely sensitive to changes in factor costs, this federal intervention to sustain minimal social standards is not surprising.

Puerto Rico's internationalized economy virtually precludes the Commonwealth government from enacting socially responsible policies without jeopardizing the investment climate. The combination of federal incentives and Puerto Rico's giveaways to the multinationals sustains moderate economic growth. This tenuous economic feature of the island's current relationship vis-à-vis the United States has been skillfully exploited by the statehood and independence activists. The colonial model is in crisis and it is they, we are told, who offer a feasible way out of the dilemma.

The Senate and House bills

In the ensuing 22 years since the last plebiscite, status-related activity has been uneventful and largely unnoticed by the public. Status bills were routinely introduced in Congress, and invariably died inconspicuously in various committees. From 1976 to 1983, the pro-statehood PNP controlled the insular government, but lacked a sufficient electoral mandate to risk calling for a referendum on status. When the PPD returned to power in 1984, it did so with a slim margin of victory and with a U.S. president who had endorsed statehood. The time, it seemed, was not propitious for resurrecting the status issue.

Until now, Congress has avoided tinkering with the colonial formula. In part, this is because a more competitive political party system has evolved in Puerto Rico, which Congress has chosen to interpret as indecisiveness among Puerto Ricans about their preferred status. However, since neither the PNP nor the PPD commanded overwhelming electoral support, they didn't push the status issue. Instead, each party attempted to extract more funds from the federal government in order to expand its political base before calling for a referendum.

But the most compelling reason for the U.S. government's inaction up to the present is that a status change opens a virtual Pandora's box of tough policy issues. Puerto Rico has been a boon to U.S. firms and has been a key component of U.S. national security strategy. However, federal budgetary deficits, endemic inefficiency and corruption by the insular administration, entrenched poverty, the internationalized nature of Puerto Rico's dependent economy, continued international criticism of the United States for its colonial policy, and numerous other factors encouraged Washington to revisit the colonial question.

The federal government is intensely preoccupied with how each of the status options affects its geo-political objectives, federal financing, investment strategies, and social conditions on the island. While the colony undoubtedly is still a lucrative venture for certain sectors of U.S. capital and is presumably vital to national defense, it is also a drain on the U.S. Treasury. Puerto Rico's dependence and economic growth shape the contours of its political elites' appeals to the electorate. But each political party also wants to allay the U.S. government's fears about growing budgetary deficits and about jeopardizing national security. The referendum debate has been shaped by these conflicting interests and uncertain projections.

In contrast to almost two decades of inconsequential status activity, 1991 saw a flurry of action, culminating in two bills. The Senate Committee on Energy and Natural Resources approved Senate Bill 712 by a narrow margin of 11 to 8, which indicated substantial skepticism among the senators about the merits of the legislation.[27] The bill, however, was not reported out of the Agricultural Committee when the 101st Congress convened. The House Committee on Interior and Insular Affairs reported the Puerto Rico Self-Determination Act, HR 4765, favorably out of committee. Subsequently HR 4765 was approved by the full House of Representatives.

This most recent episode in the politics of status began in earnest when Senators Johnston and McClure of the Senate Committee on Energy and Natural Resources arrived in Puerto Rico on February 27, 1989. They came to discuss draft legislation for a binding referendum on status with the presidents of the three political parties.[28] Each party president agreed to submit status proposals to the Senate Committee. Three sets of public hearings were held during the summer of 1989 in Washington and San Juan to refine and reconfigure the parties' status proposals. In November 1989, the Senate Finance Committee held hearings in Washington to consider the financial components of the legislation, and planned to draft a report in March 1990.

During the summer hearings, Committee Chairperson Senator Johnston cautioned that the effects of any status change would have to be revenue-neutral, meaning that a change in status could not entail federal expenditures beyond current levels. He noted that because of "the harsh fiscal reality facing Congress," it would "make budget 'neutrality' an objective during its consideration" of the status options. It was Congress's intention, Johnston intoned, to respect the wishes of the people of Puerto Rico and to abide by the referendum results. Johnston also observed that while the United States respected international law as it related to self-determination for the people of Puerto Rico, Congress would be ultimately guided by the Constitution of the United States and applicable Supreme Court rulings.

Each party's proposal was scrutinized and challenged by the Senate Committee and the Bush Administration.[29] Seventeen of the 20 proposals in the PPD project were rejected by the Committee. It rejected any changes in current law that entailed a reduction or constraint in the exercise of congressional and Executive Branch powers over Puerto Rico. State Department representative Mary V. Mochary argued that the enhanced Commonwealth proposal would create an unprecedented political status and "…would grant to Puerto Rico significant attributes of sovereignty which would be incompatible with remaining part of the United States."[30] The State Department objected to delegating to Puerto Rico any authority vested in the Executive Branch by the Constitution. The PPD wanted assurances that Section 936 would be retained indefinitely. However, Treasury Department official Kenneth W. Gideon instructed Congress that it "should make clear that tax benefits such as Section 936 cannot be regarded as benefits that will last indefinitely" but as incentives for investments subject to congressional revision.[31] In short, the U.S. government rejected all PPD proposals designed to grant the Commonwealth limited autonomous powers.

Administration officials reacted most favorably to the statehood proposal, and repeatedly noted that statehood posed the least difficulty with respect to the issues of concern to the Executive Branch. Nonetheless, objections were raised over the use of Spanish in the U.S. District Court, tariffs on imported coffee, the 200-mile jurisdiction of territorial waters and the provision for Congress to enact an omnibus bill that would "ensure that the people of Puerto Rico attain equal social and economic opportunities with the residents of the several states." Objection was also raised to recognizing Spanish as the official language of Puerto Rico. These proposals were quietly dropped from the final version of the bill. While the PNP called for retaining Section 936, the bill provides for a five-year phasing-out period.

Displaying solicitous and studious reflection, the Senate Committee entertained the proposals of the *Partido Independentista Puertorriqueño* (PIP). But despite its seemingly understanding demeanor, Washington officials rejected one of the party's key proposals. They were emphatic that the United States must retain a military presence in an "independent" Puerto Rico. Brigadier General M. J. Byron testified "the Department of Defense considers Puerto Rico as a strategic pivot point of major importance to U.S. national security" and recommended retaining all current key military installations. Although he did not categorically reject the PIP's request for the United States to recognize "the right of the people of Puerto Rico to strive toward the total demilitarization of its territory," Byron cautioned that such a policy would involve degradation of U.S. military capabilities and impose enormous financial costs for the federal government.[32]

More to the point, the State Department witness testified that "owing to the strategic importance of existing military installations and operations in Puerto Rico," the provision calling for the Republic of Puerto Rico to close its territory to any and all military forces of foreign nations was "directly at odds with U.S. global military interests."[33] Given this resistance, the PIP was forced to recognize the legitimate security interests of the United States and said the issue of the military bases was negotiable.

Because of Puerto Rico's excessive reliance on multinational corporations, the PIP called for a 25-year phasing-out period for Section 936. Senate Bill 712, however, terminates the tax credit upon the proclamation of independence and does not provide for alternative tax credits. Also rejected was the PIP proposal for unrestricted free trade between Puerto Rico and the United States. The Senate Committee simply approved a Joint Transition Commission to develop provisions for governing trade relations, and merely stated that Congress will consider negotiating mutual free-trade relations. The notion that Congress should compensate Puerto Rico for over 90 years of occupation was obviously anathema. The United States is willing to provide block grants for a period of nine years, the actual amount of which would be negotiated by the Commission, but it is estimated to be about $3.8 billion annually.

Despite the PIP's inability to extract major economic concessions from the Senate, according to a congressional study Puerto Rico had a brighter economic future as an independent republic than a state. The Congressional Budget Office's report was the first official U.S. government document that acknowledged the economic viability of independence, noting "an independent Puerto Rico may be able to construct a set of incentives—through a combination of tax-sparing treaties and local subsidies—that would approach the attractiveness of current benefits under Section 936."[34] The study observed that "The potential loss of investment under statehood is large, both absolutely and compared with the fiscal benefits of statehood to Puerto Rico."[35]

Throughout the legislative process Congress has rejected any role for the United Nations in monitoring the referendum process. Senator Johnston reasoned that, since the bill conforms to the PIP's proposal on the transfer of sovereignty and self-determination, the United States has complied with the requirements of international law. Senators McClure and Johnston frequently instructed witnesses that Puerto Rico is not a colony and emphasized that the resolution of Puerto Rico's status is strictly a domestic affair and not subject to United Nations mediation. Their views were strongly endorsed by the State Department, which claimed that Puerto Ricans had already exercised self-determination in 1952 and 1967.

The legislative process, as well as the substance of the bill, has been widely criticized as precipitous, inherently anti-democratic, and palpably colonial. Independence forces not affiliated with the PIP have repudiated Senate Bill 712 as an explicit violation of the principles of self-determination. Carlos Gallisá, president of the *Partido Socialista Puertorriqueño* (PSP), provided one of the most dramatic moments in the hearings when he challenged the very legitimacy of the referendum process. Gallisá called upon the Senate Committee to recognize that Puerto Rico is a colony and argued that, if it did not, "then nothing here will be resolved. And we will be repeating the useless exercise of 1967 and the celebration of another sham election such as the previous one."[36] He also called upon Congress to comply with United Nations Resolution 1514 (XV), the "Magna Carta of Decolonization."

Nora Matias Rodríguez, president of the *Colegio de Abogados de Puerto Rico,* testified that Senate Bill 712 should be amended to provide for a constituent assembly that would draw up an alternate proposal that conforms to internationally accepted standards of self-determination. She called the provisions for unrestricted and perpetual access to the territory of Puerto Rico for military purposes a flagrant violation of these standards.[37]

The bill that came out of the Senate Committee contained a provision for making the results of the referendum binding on Congress and committed Congress to implementing the preferred solution (the self-executing provisions of the bill). In addition, the bill contained explicit definitions of the three status options and the economic, political, and social obligations the federal government would assume under statehood, independence, or an enhanced Commonwealth.

The House bill

The House Subcommittee on Insular and International Affairs also held hearings regarding the status of the island in Washington, in various cities in Puerto Rico, and in New York. Rather than subjecting each status option to the kind of rigorous fiscal analysis and political scrutiny conducted by the Senate, the House Subcommittee chose to defer discussions of these and other difficult issues until after the Puerto Rican people had expressed their preferred option. The House favorably reported a bill out of committee that differed markedly from that of the Senate. House majority leader Thomas Foley and Morris Udall, chairman of the House Committee, had openly expressed their opposition to the self-execution provisions of the Senate bill. Puerto Rico's political parties threatened to boycott any referendum that failed to include a self-executing provision, claiming that without such a provision the referendum would be a mere beauty contest, totally at odds with the principles of self-determination. However, the parties grudgingly accepted a non-binding resolution after it became clear that the House would refuse to enact legislation that included self-execution. The House bill further differed in that it did not identify the status options. The electorate was expected to indicate its preference for one of the three options, or "none of the above."

HR 4765 enumerated a three-stage process toward decolonization. The first step was a non-binding vote—a preference contest. Next, the two congressional committees would draft bills on the results of the referendum in consultation with Puerto Rico's parties and the President by March 6, 1992. Finally, the bill provided that the legislation reported by the Joint Committee would become effective once the full Congress approved and in a second vote in Puerto Rico. The House bill also held out the option for further federal government action if the electorate rejected the bill in the second vote.

By the end of October 1990, Puerto Rico's political parties were clamoring for a status referendum bill. While each saw problems with the House and Senate versions, the political leaders were committed to sustaining the referendum process. Only the PPD became skittish about the referendum. Polls conducted by Puerto Rico's largest daily newspaper revealed the deteriorating strength of the Commonwealth forces. By early November 1990, only 34 percent of the electorate endorsed the Commonwealth option, while 41 percent of those polled favored statehood.[38] On November 17, the general leadership of the PPD in an extraordinary meeting essentially voted not to participate in the proposed 1991 referendum unless Congress approved legislation by February 3, 1991. Moreover, the PPD did the unthinkable by demanding that Puerto Rico be excluded from the territoriality clause of the U.S. Constitution, that any status legislation must recognize the sovereignty of the Puerto Rican people. Given the Senate's long-standing and firm opposition to recognizing Puerto Rico's sovereignty, the PPD's decision to boycott the referendum halt contributed to the process. By demanding an explicit recognition of Puerto Rico's sovereignty, the PPD was in reality postulating that it wanted to gain genuine autonomy for Puerto Rico. In the process, it drew much closer to advocating independence than at any time since the late 1930s.

Conclusion

This chapter began with a discussion of the nature of the colonial process and the economic and political factors that led to the establishment of the ELA as a redefined colony. Since 1952, Puerto Rico's economy has been evolving in such a way as to weaken the role the Commonwealth government plays in the capital accumulation process. The U.S. government has historically resisted granting Puerto Rico increased powers to manage its economy, instead enacting policies that encourage U.S. investments while providing direct "band-aid" support to sustain those major sectors of the population discarded by the process of distorted growth.

The legislative process associated with the passage of Senate Bill 712 and House Bill 4765 has been a conspicuous exercise in imperial power. Congress has unilaterally decided that the proposed referendum conforms to standards of international law.

Each of the three status proposals originally submitted by the political parties has been emasculated to conform to the U.S. government's national security concerns, and Congress's deliberations have been excessively influenced by budgetary preoccupations. The Senate and House committees adopted very different strategies in devising their legislation. The Senate publicly aired its position with respect to the parties' proposals. The House, on the other hand, negotiated in private meetings and passed a relatively noncontroversial bill that deferred substantive discussions until the Puerto Rican people had advised Congress on their preference.

The referendum process made clear that the U.S. government is searching for a politically manageable and economical arrangement that will guarantee unrestricted military access to Puerto Rico and preserve the vital economic interests of U.S. firms. In the process, the competing interests of different sectors of capital, the federal bureaucracy, Congress, and Puerto Rico's political leadership (whose participation is required to lend a semblance of legitimacy to the process) have all surfaced. This has hindered the negotiation process.

The proceedings revealed that, while the prevailing colonial formula is unworkable, the U.S. government has no intention of revising the existing legislation to enhance the autonomous powers of the Commonwealth. Until now, the U.S. government has not been able to devise a formula that is satisfactory to all those who have a stake in the status issue. Unless the conflicting array of demands by political and economic forces is resolved, the U.S. may wind up keeping its hobbled colony at least to the end of the century.

Postscript

In the 101st Congress, Senate Bill S712 and House Bill HR4765 were reported out of the respective committees. HR4765 was approved in a floor vote by the full House, but S712 was not reported out of committee before the 101st Congress adjourned. When the 102nd Congress convened, the House Committee introduced its original bill (retitled HR 244); the Senate Energy and Natural Resources Committee proposed an amended bill (S 244) that excluded some controversial provisions of the original measure. But the bill died in committee when proponents for the measure failed to obtain a majority.

The status referendum process revealed a lack of consensus within the federal government on whether to support congressional efforts to enact status-related legislation. Congress was deeply divided on how to conduct the referendum and how to implement the referendum results. Open resistance emerged to any legislation that would have conferred on the Commonwealth autonomous powers in the areas on international commerce, trade, investment, employment, and international relations.

U.S. domestic political consideration, concerns about partisan recomposition of the legislature, antagonism to anticipated ethnic/racial demographic changes, and budgetary considerations all factored into the calculus that led to a rejection of the status referendum legislation. Surprisingly, however, the status hearings had revealed that neither the military nor the national security apparatus publicly perceived that an independent Puerto Rico would compromise U.S. geopolitical interests in the region.

The institutionalization of a highly competitive two-party system, in which statehood proponents hold a slim majority over the advocates for Commonwealth, also presented Congress with a dilemma. Any decolonization proposal had to address the reality that a sizeable portion of the U.S. citizens living in Puerto Rico preferred statehood. Both the statehood PNP and the Commonwealth PPD recognized the implications of this conundrum. The PPD, seeking to convince the U.S. government that Puerto Ricans had an intense national cultural identity that would make annexation unacceptable to the U.S. population, enacted legislation that established Spanish as the official language of Puerto Rico, and sought public approval for changes in the Puerto Rican constitution that codified the sanctity and distinctiveness of Puerto Rican cultural identity. However, the PPD's campaign was repudiated by the electorate, and fortified the position of the statehood forces.

Nonetheless, the recomposition of the political party system generates a new dynamic in the colonial formula. For three decades, from 1940 through 1968, Puerto Rico was essentially a one-party system. The statehood party has attained virtual parity with the PPD, and has at its disposal the resources and technical expertise to generate support among key legislators in Washington. While the party may not overcome what Senator Moynihan called a nativist bias in the Senate, its presence makes any transformation of the current status unlikely. Unless the U.S. government is willing to provide the type of guarantees the independence party proposes for the Republic of Puerto Rico, support for the statehood option will probably remain stable. As long as the electoral basis of statehood remains strong, the prospects for independence are nil.

Colonialism, Citizenship, and Contemporary Statehood

Edgardo Meléndez

The plebiscite of 1989 to 1991 gave U.S. policy-makers a forum at which to debate Puerto Rico's future relationship to the mainland: would it become a state, an independent republic, or remain a Commonwealth? Of these options, statehood has been the most controversial in the United States. Many U.S. liberals feel it is a matter of self-determination and that, if Puerto Ricans so choose, they should be admitted as the 51st state; most U.S. conservatives fear the consequences of incorporating into the U.S. mainstream a Spanish-speaking, Caribbean island with a large mulatto and welfare-dependent population. Whatever Puerto Rico's future political status, both Puerto Ricans and U.S. decision-makers agree that the current political and economic picture of Puerto Rico is not acceptable.

While numerous political, economic, and social factors need to be considered to explain the emergence and development of the Puerto Rican statehood movement, it has been the U.S. colonial presence in Puerto Rico, above all, which accounts for statehood fervor on the island. The most important policies in fomenting statehood have been the granting of U.S. citizenship to Puerto Ricans since 1917 and the increase in transfer payments since the mid-1970s. At the same time, the endurance of Puerto Rican "national" identity and the desire to have control over local affairs have produced a "creole statehood" that is based on the recognition of Puerto Rico as a distinct ethnic enclave.

The plebiscite process, supported by the Puerto Rican elite in Washington, gave island statehooders a first opportunity to present their concrete program for statehood. Despite the fact that many U.S. policy-makers may see statehood as a solution to the colonial dilemma, most of them do not find the definition of creole statehood to be the preferable path.

Statehood and U.S. colonialism

Puerto Rican annexationism is the child of U.S. colonialism. U.S. policy throughout the twentieth century guaranteed its strategic, economic, and political interests on the island and throughout the Caribbean. The United States has followed a "status quo" policy in Puerto Rico for over 90 years, allowing only minor reforms. Yet U.S. policies in Puerto Rico have been implemented in an ad hoc, piecemeal fashion, trying to solve short-term, immediate problems in the colonial administration.[1] Overall, the United States lacks a guiding objective in its policies towards the island. This inconsistency has fueled a tension that remains constant between the ruling metropolis and Puerto Ricans.

Since the United States lacks a colonial policy towards Puerto Rico—U.S. legislators deny the colonial relationship—or the administrative institutions to effectively manage the colony, U.S. policies on the island have had contradictory results throughout the century. Two sets of policies exist side-by-side on the island: exclusion of Puerto Ricans from the U.S. (the colonial regime) and inclusion within the metropolitan state (U.S. citizenship). Policies of exclusion (such as are enforced by the Foraker and Jones Acts discussed below, and the Commonwealth itself) comprise the structures of colonialism and keep Puerto Ricans out of the structures of the federal government. On the other hand, policies of inclusion (such as citizenship and federal welfare programs) have inserted Puerto Ricans, at least in a formal way, into the structures of the metropolitan state.

The Foraker Act, approved by Congress in 1900, essentially implanted the colonial regime that now exists in Puerto Rico. The act placed Puerto Rico within the U.S. tariff system, as a concession to U.S. sugar and commercial interests eager to invest in the newly acquired territory. However, the U.S. Constitution was not transferred to Puerto Rico and U.S. citizenship was not granted to Puerto Ricans until 1917.[2]

The island's colonial status was further demarcated with the so-called insular cases, where the U.S. Supreme Court decided that Puerto Rico was a "non-incorporated territory" of the United States. These decisions established that although Puerto Ricans were officially U.S. citizens, Puerto Rico had no right to become a state, unlike "incorporated territories," and that its affairs were to be decided by the will of Congress. The island was declared an economic possession of the United States only, without any of the constitutional and political rights enjoyed by other territories.[3]

The policy of granting U.S. citizenship to Puerto Ricans has had the most far-reaching consequences for U.S.-Puerto Rican relations and for politics on the island. Initially rejected by the Puerto Rican Legislature, the Jones Act of 1917 imposed citizenship upon Puerto Ricans as a means to stop the rise of independence fervor at the time and to provide cannon-fodder for the U.S. army's World War I efforts. The Jones Act did not change the colonial status of Puerto Rico, since Puerto Rico remained a "non-incorporated territory." In fact, U.S. citizenship was granted with the clear understanding that it in no way represented a step towards statehood.[4] The result is a glaring contradiction: Puerto Ricans are integrated into the U.S. polity as citizens, but Puerto Rico as a territory is not part of the federation.

Colonialism and citizenship remain at the heart of the relationship between the United States and Puerto Rico. Citizenship became the axis around which statehood ideology and politics evolved; Puerto Rican annexationists call citizenship "the gateway to statehood." They argue that only statehood can guarantee all the rights of citizenship. Contemporary annexationist ideology is characterized by the fusion of the anti-colonialist sentiment of the masses with the appeal for U.S. citizenship. For some Puerto Ricans, annexation, a logical consequence of U.S. colonialism in Puerto Rico, provides the solution to the Puerto Rican colonial dilemma: only by admitting Puerto Rico as a state, they argue, can the United States and Puerto Rico solve the colonial problem in a dignified way.

Colonialism and citizenship have set up the framework for greater economic and political integration to the United States. Since the beginning of the century, Puerto Rico's colonial subordination facilitated the economic integration to the mainland economy. Political integration has thus led to the ever-increasing formulation and execution of public policy by the federal government and by a greater dependency of the colony on federal funds. Puerto Rico's economic and political integration to the United States has intensified since the creation of the Commonwealth in 1952, an important factor in explaining the resurgence and growth of the statehood movement since that time.

Perhaps nothing better reflects the process of Puerto Rico's economic and political integration to the United States than the injection of federal funds both to maintain social and economic stability and to safeguard U.S. political interests in Puerto Rico. The first massive transfer of funds provided welfare relief to the great mass of people impoverished by the Great Depression. Thus, the United States kept up the viability of the colonial regime and defused independence fervor. The Commonwealth has always needed federal funds to sustain the population and its own cost of operations.[5] Since the 1970s, federal funds have provided nearly one-third of Puerto Rico's personal income and nearly one-third of the Commonwealth budget; significantly, these transfers have also been a great stimulus to the demand for U.S. products on the island.[6]

The transfer of federal funds to Puerto Rico is another example of the sometimes ad hoc character and lack of clear goals by U.S. policy-makers towards Puerto Rico. No one in Washington foresaw, for example, that the food stamp program in Puerto Rico would soon comprise one-fifth of the federal program, or that, when Congress later cut the program drastically, it would have dire economic consequences on the island. The rising numbers of economically marginal and poor individuals created by Puerto Rico's economic crisis during the last two decades have come to depend on federal programs for their economic survival. The Puerto Rican poor support statehood, not because of an ideological or cultural bond to the United States, but because they believe statehood will guarantee their economic security.

STATEHOOD AS AN ALTERNATIVE

The United States never really considered statehood for Puerto Rico as a viable option until the 1970s. Until then, U.S. legislators had steadfastly rejected statehood for Puerto Rico. The imposition of a colonial regime in 1900 without incorporation or citizenship was a clear rejection of the statehood demands of the Puerto Rican elite. Although citizenship was imposed in 1917, Congress clearly stipulated that this action carried no promise of statehood. Statehood activists thus faced a great contradiction: their desire for integration into the U.S. federation, around which they elaborated their political program, was rejected by the metropolis. This is one reason why for nearly two decades after 1917 the pro-statehood Republican Party proposed independence—in case the United States did not accept Puerto Rico's statehood.

Autonomy for local affairs became the alternative promoted by the United States to reform the colonial regime during the 1940s. Two reports from the U.S. government rejected statehood and independence for Puerto Rico as options favorable to the United States. One of these reports characterized statehood as "a worn-out political issue."[7] In 1953, after Commonwealth status was recognized by the United Nations as a form of self-determination, President Eisenhower offered independence to Puerto Rico if Puerto Ricans so desired it. The local Republican Party, which had supported Eisenhower in the previous election, was forced to repudiate his rejection of statehood.[8]

The 1966 report of the presidentially-appointed United States-Puerto Rico Commission on the Status of Puerto Rico, a majority of whose members were members of Congress, for the first time recognized statehood as a valid and acceptable alternative to the United States, along with Commonwealth and independence. The report concluded that once Puerto Rico satisfies the traditional requirements for admission to the federation, particularly a majority vote for statehood, Congress would consider statehood for the island.[9] The 1967 plebiscite marks a breakthrough event for the statehood movement in Puerto Rico. Enticed by the Commission's report, statehood forces created a new organization and gained 34 percent of the plebiscite votes, their highest ever. The New Progressive Party (PNP), formed immediately after the plebiscite, won the 1968 elections and thereby ended three decades of PPD political dominance. Since then, the PNP has alternated in power with the PPD and is today the most solid political force in Puerto Rico.

The United States began to consider statehood as an alternative in the mid-1970s, when Washington was searching for options to the economic and political crisis of the Commonwealth. A plethora of studies and reports by U.S. government agencies have analyzed the statehood option after President Ford's statements in favor of statehood in 1976.[10] Several conclusions emerged from these reports. First, the Commonwealth solution was no longer economically or politically viable for Puerto Rico and the United States. Second, any alternative status was to satisfy U.S. economic, political, and strategic interests in Puerto Rico. And third, the alternative chosen had to be the least economically and politically "costly" for the United States. The generalized conclusion of these reports was that statehood is the best alternative for the United States, although there were concerns with the economic and political "costs" of this option.[11] Consequently, statehood has become the option most favored by the U.S. decision-makers to replace the Commonwealth; it has been openly supported by the Ford, Carter, Reagan, and Bush administrations.

But while sectors in Washington have been viewing statehood as an alternative, statehooders in Puerto Rico have been promoting their own brand of statehood. The problem is that U.S. decision-makers never really paid any attention to the demands of statehooders, while the latter presented a view of statehood that does not fit U.S. expectations.

Puerto Rican definitions of statehood

Annexationist sentiment emerged among sectors of the creole elite who were dissatisfied with the Spanish economic and political regime on the island during the 19th century. The U.S. occupation of Puerto Rico radically transformed the island's economy and politics. The U.S.-imposed regime facilitated the swift expansion of capitalism and of U.S. capital on the island. Those who favored the economic and political presence of the United States in Puerto Rico organized the Republican Party. The party's leading sectors—

the sugar bourgeoisie and the professional middle class—became the local supporters of the U.S. colonial regime and of the expansion of U.S. capital on the island.[12]

The statehood movement experienced a period of crisis from the mid-1920s to the 1950s. The leading sectors of the Republican Party clashed over the party's goals, even on the desirability of statehood. The ideal of statehood itself was seriously questioned by some Republicans, mostly because of Washington's constant rejection of Puerto Rican statehood and its preservation of the colonial regime.

The economic crisis of the 1930s further aggravated statehood politics. The middle and working classes moved away from the conservative policies of the Republican leadership headed by the sugar bourgeoisie and gave their support to the rising and reformist Popular Democratic Party. The U.S. government and the PPD implemented a series of economic, social, and political reforms from the 1930s to the 1950s, including Operation Bootstrap and Commonwealth, that were adverse to the republican ideology and interests. Statehood and republicanism became symbols of opposition to change. Statehood lost its early idealist content and became identified with the extremely conservative politics of the republican bourgeoisie. Statehood experienced its lowest political support ever during this period.[13]

The expansion of industrial capitalism in the post-war period drastically transformed Puerto Rican society and politics. Changes in the social class structure provided the basis for a new constituency for statehood. The decay of the sugar industry and the expansion of industrialization fomented the rise of new sectors of the local bourgeoisie and the economic and political demise of the sugar bourgeoisie. The industrial bourgeoisie, in particular, challenged the sugar bourgeoisie's dominance over the statehood ideology and program. A new and more affluent middle class—one very much attached to the U.S. way of life and values—emerged in the private and public sectors. Particularly during the last two decades, growing sectors of the Puerto Rican bourgeoisie and middle class have increased their ties to U.S. capital and the federal government in Puerto Rico. Industrialization in Puerto Rico also created a significant sector of poor and unemployed people, marginal to the capitalist production in the island. This sector is extremely dependent on state transfers for their subsistence; and state transfers in Puerto Rico are provided almost exclusively by the federal government. The entry of the new middle and working classes into statehood politics radically transformed the statehood program and ideology.[14]

The formation of the New Progressive Party and its electoral victory in 1968 ushered in a new era for statehood politics in Puerto Rico. For the first time ever, a statehood party enjoys popular support and alternates in local government with the PPD. The leading sectors of the PNP—bourgeoisie and new middle classes—have been able to present a liberal program that secures the poor's support for statehood. PNP politics have been characterized by rising popular support and a stable and solid multi-class political constituency, the elaboration of a political program to achieve statehood in the shortest possible time, and the use of the Commonwealth government to advance statehood in Puerto Rico and the United States.[15]

The PNP is the ideological and programmatic heir of the twentieth-century Puerto Rican statehood movement. The PNP program has incorporated the two most important conceptions of annexationist ideology in Puerto Rico: "statehood as sovereignty" and "statehood as equality." Both conceptions developed in response to important issues that Puerto Rican annexationism has faced during the twentieth century. "Statehood as sovereignty" seeks to define the role of Puerto Rico within the U.S. federation. By promising a "sovereign" Puerto Rican state, this conception assures Puerto Ricans they will have control over local affairs, including the power to protect the cultural and ethnic identity of Puerto Ricans. "Statehood as equality" seeks to define the relationship of Puerto Ricans with the U.S. state, particularly in the economic and social areas. It offers economic security by arguing that only statehood can guarantee social and economic equality within the United States.

STATEHOOD AS SOVEREIGNTY

"Statehood as sovereignty" was the first conception developed by Puerto Rican annexationists at the beginning of the century. At that time, the Republican Party defined statehood as "independence for local affairs." By doing this, the party's leading sectors were seeking to guarantee the control of the local economic and political spaces for the creole elite; they expected a minimal interference in local affairs by the metropolitan state. In fact, for several decades the demand for the independence of Puerto Rico co-existed side-by-side with the demand for statehood in the republican program as a means to guarantee their power over local affairs.

The concept of sovereignty also addresses the problem of how to adjust the ethnic-cultural differences of Puerto Ricans. Puerto Ricans' lack of cultural assimilation represents a great obstacle to annexation; language and other factors have historically sustained Puerto Rican national identity. Throughout the century, annexationists have argued that U.S. federalism allows state governments the power to protect the cultural identity of their diverse ethnic populations. Already discussed in the founding assembly of the Republican Party in 1899, the concept of *patria regional* (regional fatherland) has evolved to the present day as a solution to this problem. The conception of a regional fatherland established the difference between the fatherland region, ethnically and culturally determined, and the "Nation," the central State to which all Puerto Ricans must be loyal.[16]

This concept was further elaborated upon during the 1940s, when statehooders argued that the United States was a "melting pot" of diverse nationalities where the State did not intervene in the definition of the cultural identity of the diverse ethnic groups. They incorrectly contended that U.S. federalism guaranteed the ethnic-cultural diversity of its component units, as if the United States were a "multinational federation," which it is not.[17] Out of this notion comes the contemporary conception of *estadidad jíbara* (creole statehood), introduced by former PNP president and governor Luis A. Ferré during the 1960s. To Ferré, "Puerto Rico is the fatherland, the United States is the Nation." Creole statehood argues that U.S. federalism will protect the cultural and linguistic identity of Puerto Ricans. The PNP has promised Puerto Ricans that Spanish will remain the dominant language under statehood.[18]

STATEHOOD AS EQUALITY

Statehood as equality, elaborated during the 1940s, posits U.S. citizenship as the "gateway" to statehood. Annexationists argue that statehood became a "right" of citizenship once Puerto Ricans were made U.S. citizens and that statehood is the only means to guarantee Puerto Ricans full equality under U.S. citizenship. The concept of statehood as equality gained more relevance after the emergence of the U.S. welfare system in the 1960s. Given the increasing number of poor and unemployed people in Puerto Rico since that era, statehooders argue that only statehood can guarantee Puerto Ricans their full participation in federal programs. Departing from these ideas, the PNP under the leadership of Carlos Romero Barceló argued that only statehood guarantees full political equality—represented by presidential vote and congressional representation, which is necessary to obtain full social and economic equality (that is, to receive all the benefits of the U.S. welfare state).[19]

Romero's PNP created an extremely effective base of popular support for statehood by joining "statehood as equality" to the demand for *estadidad ahora* (Statehood Now!). Under the leadership of Ferré, the PNP had an evolutionary view: statehood was to be achieved after a long process of education and adaptation, after annexationists convinced Puerto Ricans of the benefits of statehood. Contrary to Ferré's evolutionary statehood strategy, Romero argued that Puerto Rico was ready to become a state as soon as Puerto Ricans demanded it. Joining the anti-colonialist fervor of the masses to the annexationist rhetoric, under Romero the PNP presented statehood as the only dignified way for the United States to eliminate Puerto Rican's second-class citizenship and to end Puerto Rico's colonial status. According to Romero, statehood would allow Puerto Ricans to exercise their right to self-determination and would end colonialism by completely integrating the island to the metropolis. Romero made popular the belief that once Puerto Ricans opted for statehood, Congress would have no alternative but to grant it.[20]

The PNP was extremely successful in increasing support for statehood in Puerto Rico during the last two decades. Combining the two conceptions of statehood into one program was crucial in solidifying mass support. Statehood as equality has also been used to legitimate the Puerto Rican demand for statehood in the United States, since it is presented as a demand for equality from the second-class citizens of the U.S. colony of Puerto Rico.

The PNP has been very effective in combining the desire for greater liberty and equality among the masses that characterize the decolonizing movements of the twentieth century with the demand for complete integration to the metropolis. The crucial question now is whether the United States is willing to accept Puerto Rican statehood as defined by Puerto Ricans. The 1989-91 plebiscite process presents the opportunity to examine this question.

Creole statehood and the plebiscite process

The PNP's statehood proposal presented to Congress what the party had been promising Puerto Ricans for 20 years: Puerto Rico would become a "sovereign state" with "creole statehood" and full equality. As presented in the first draft (June 1989) Senate Bill 712, the Energy and Natural Resources Committee bill that called for a plebiscite on Puerto Rico's political status, the PNP demanded payment of Puerto Rico's public debt by the United States; the transfer of federal taxes to Puerto Rico for "X" number of years (20 years expected); the permanence of Section 936 for "X" number of years (20 years expected); tariffs to protect Puerto Rican coffee; the return of excise taxes on alcohol to Puerto Rico; the retention of Spanish as an official language; the transfer of federal land to Puerto Rico; and a 200-mile economic zone for Puerto Rico.[21]

The definition of statehood in the second version of Senate Bill 712 (September 1989) was not what the PNP expected; this version of the plebiscite bill incorporated the criticisms made to the bill by the Executive Branch, other sectors of Congress, and particular interest groups. Excluded were the notions of a "sovereign state," of "creole statehood," and of statehood as full equality. The September version of Senate Bill 712 excluded the demands for a 200-mile economic zone, for U.S. payment of Puerto Rico's public debt, for tariffs to protect coffee, and for language and culture protection. The transfer of federal lands to the new state is not to be considered until five years after statehood. The economic transition demanded by the PNP was greatly reduced in scope: federal excise taxes would immediately be applied and federal income taxes would be effective after 1994, while Section 936 exemptions would be reduced by 20 percent a year after 1994 and eliminated in 1998. The following items were approved as a statehood grant: the return of alcohol taxes and custom duties to Puerto Rico; the return of excise taxes until 1998; and the return of all federal income taxes in 1994 and 1995.[22]

In spite of its overt support for statehood, the Bush Administration slashed the PNP's statehood proposal. For the first time ever, the PNP's program, which was so successful in solidifying support for statehood in Puerto Rico, came under furious attack in Washington. Notions central to the PNP's statehood program—like statehood as the guarantee to full equality, Spanish as an official language, the economic transition, and the sovereign state—can no longer be taken for granted in Puerto Rico. To make some gains out of the plebiscite process, the PNP shifted its strategy: it rejected Senate Bill 712 and supported the House version, which included no status definitions and no promise from Congress to accept the Puerto Ricans' decision.[23]

The notion that statehood will guarantee social and economic equality was rejected by Edward Dennis from the Justice Department. Title II (statehood) in the first draft of Senate Bill 712 would have required Congress to approve an "omnibus act" to "ensure that the people of Puerto Rico attain equal social and economic opportunities with the residents of the several states."[24] Dennis characterized this not only as unrealistic, but even as possibly unconstitutional:

> It is impossible to foresee all of the implications of such a vague provision. But it is doubtful whether Congress truly could "ensure" that the people of Puerto Rico—or any other group—enjoy equal "social and economic opportunities," presumably in all spheres of life. The Constitution and laws can guarantee equality under the law, and forbid invidious discrimination. We doubt whether any legal code effectively could ensure equal social and economic opportunities.[25]

In effect, the Executive Branch told Puerto Ricans that the U.S. government cannot guarantee them full equality, that "political equality" need not be translated into social and economic justice.

The PNP's language proposal—central to the rhetoric of creole statehood—was extensively debated and questioned in the Senate hearings. After strongly defending the PNP's position that Spanish be recognized as the official language of Puerto Rico, Romero agreed to the harshly worded recommendation of Senator Johnston that it be taken out of the proposal. Representatives of "U.S. English" and "English First" campaigns demanded that English be the official language of Puerto Rico under statehood. Senator McClure, co-sponsor of Senate Bill 712 and supporter of statehood, insisted on having English as the official language included in the bill.[26]

The issue of taxes during the statehood transition (as discussed under Section 936 and IRS laws) was extensively debated during the hearings. In an effort to protect the statehood proposal, the Bush Administration argued that the status alternatives should be discussed without considering their economic implications or cost. This strategy backfired. The Senate Energy and Natural Resources (ENR) Committee accused the Bush Administration of torpedoing the plebiscite process and demanded clear figures on the economic costs of each alternative. A November 1989 report prepared for the Senate Committee by the Congressional Budget Office indicated that statehood was by far the costliest alternative economically: the transition to statehood would cost the federal government $3.25 billion by 1995, while the Commonwealth represented no increase and independence would mean a real decrease in federal transfers.[27]

The economic costs of statehood became the central issue of debate in the plebiscite process after the Senate hearings. The Senate ENR Committee report acknowledged that this was a major consideration in revising the PNP's economic transition demands. Responding to criticism that Senate Bill 712 was "too imbalanced" towards statehood, the Committee argued that future consideration of Puerto Rico's status should be guided by three principles: 1) that there should be an "even playing field" between the three alternatives; 2) that there should be a smooth transition to statehood and independence; and 3) that "economic adjustment should be revenue neutral to the extent possible, in that it does not cost the Treasury additional dollars over a period of time."[28] "Revenue neutrality" turned out to be the Sword of Damocles over the statehood option. The major opposition to the Senate Bill within the Senate ENR Committee came precisely on the issue of the economic costs of statehood in an era of budget deficits.[29]

Legislative concern about statehood's economic implications was further fueled by an April 1990 report by the Congressional Budget Office (demanded by the Senate Finance Committee). The report painted the worst-case scenario for statehood feared by the Puerto Rican bourgeoisie and the PNP: a real decrease in economic growth, a sharp drop in investments and a massive loss of jobs after the termination of Section 936, an increase in the tax load, and a reduction in the social services provided by the local government.[30] This CBO report dealt a fatal blow to the PNP's argument that statehood, by providing political stability, would raise the investment rate and bring economic growth.

Will Puerto Rico become the 51st state?

This is the question many people are asking in the United States and Puerto Rico. There are no definitive answers yet, but there are some clear indications of the obstacles Puerto Rican statehood will face in the United States and Puerto Rico. It seems quite clear by now that there is still no consensus in the United States to grant statehood to Puerto Rico.

Many special interests groups have begun to question the idea of a change in Puerto Rico's political status, fearing particularly the possible economic and political consequences of statehood. A most important sector that has taken a hard line against the plebiscite and statehood are the 936 corporations. In Puerto Rico, all sectors of the Puerto Rican bourgeoisie have called for the permanence of Section 936 under any status, which has been already denied for statehood.

Statehood faces other political obstacles in the United States as well. There is increasing opposition in Congress to the self-executing and the simple-majority clauses; if kept in the bill, these clauses could impose upon Congress a Puerto Rican state that may lack the support of a substantive majority. There are also mounting fears in Washington of the enormous costs that statehood will impose on the U.S. Treasury. Furthermore, opposition to statehood in the United States has emerged from a source no one ever expected: the Republican right-wing. If Pat Buchanan's statements voiced a widespread concern in the Republican Party, the PNP may have lost the last stronghold of support for statehood in the United States.[31]

The Senate ENR committee hearings on February 1991 confirmed the PNP's worst fears: a formal rejection of statehood for Puerto Rico by Congress. For all that matters, opposition to statehood killed the plebiscite bill. Senator Wallop (R-WY), the committee's new minority leader, argued in those hearings that statehood was an issue to be decided by the 50 states, not by Puerto Ricans. Senator Nickles (R-OK) argued that Puerto Rico's Hispanic culture and language, along with high poverty levels and welfare dependence are strong barriers to statehood. Senator Conrad (D-ND) stated that "we may create a Quebec if we bring Puerto Rico in as a state." *The Washington Post* summed up the opposition's argument as follows: "Referendum opponents had said they feared such a vote would bring the impoverished, Spanish-speaking Caribbean island closer to statehood, an option that Congress would not grant regardless of what choice the island's voters selected."[32] The Committee's Republican members (and some Democrats) voted against the bill, resisting even the highly publicized pressure brought to bear by President Bush himself.

U.S. Military Installations in Puerto Rico: Controlling the Caribbean

Humberto García Muñiz

> With Guantánamo, there's always uncertainty in the long term, it could always be subject to some discounting. Even in Panama there's an agreement that at some time has to be renegotiated. But the one unqualified American military presence in the Caribbean is Puerto Rico, the one certain place.
>
> *Rear Admiral William O'Connor,*
> *Commander of U.S. Naval Forces, Caribbean*[1]

Since the military conquest of Cuba and Puerto Rico in 1898, the United States—in the pursuit of its strategic, economic, and ideological power—has controlled the Caribbean. Nearly a century later the U.S. military presence has expanded into a regional network of installations of varied sizes and purposes reinforcing U.S. dominance in the region, U.S. control of the North and South Atlantic, and preparations for nuclear warfare. As the United States moves to reconsolidate its control over the hemisphere in response to increasing economic pressures and under the guise of the "War against Drugs," its installations in the Caribbean, particularly in Puerto Rico, are seen by national security managers in Washington as "irreplaceable."

In 1991 this structure of power included more than 50 installations spread through the islands of Antigua, Bahamas, Bermuda, Cuba, Puerto Rico, and the U.S. Virgin Islands—and more than 5,000 military personnel.[2] Roosevelt Roads and other installations ensconced in Puerto Rico are by far the most important elements of this structure, with half of the U.S. military personnel in the Caribbean.[3] Guantánamo, on the southeast tip of Cuba, is the oldest U.S. overseas base, a vestige of Cuba's semi-colonial relationship with the United States which made it the only country in the hemisphere in the singular situation of having both U.S. and Soviet installations. The other facilities, located in Antigua, Bahamas, and Bermuda, are the legacy of British acquiescence to U.S. military control of the Anglophone Caribbean subregion since the early 1900s, leading to a presence from the Second World War onwards.

The purpose of this essay is to describe and analyze the scope of U.S. military installations in Puerto Rico, where their presence is deeper and more complex than elsewhere in the Caribbean. It will cover first a brief historical background of the evolution of U.S. base structure in Puerto Rico, with reference to its social and political impact. It will then proceed with an analysis of the U.S. military command arrangement in the Caribbean. This will be followed by a review of U.S. military installations in Puerto Rico, their role in conventional and nuclear warfare as well as for internal security (i.e. repression) and interventions in the Caribbean region, and a succinct examination of the Vieques situation. It will conclude with a discussion of the future of U.S. military installations in Puerto Rico.

Historical overview

The United States commenced its overseas empire late in the nineteenth century, after it had completed and consolidated its continental expansion. As a result of its invasion of Puerto Rico during the Spanish-American War, the United States acquired the island as its first formal Caribbean colony; its second, the U.S. Virgin Islands, was purchased in 1917 from Denmark.

The first forward-basing U.S. naval station in the Caribbean was built in San Juan during the early 1900s.[4] It lasted until 1912 when it was decided that Guantánamo would be the main naval installation in the region. Culebra, off the east coast of Puerto Rico, was the center of U.S. military activity in Puerto Rico. Numerous naval exercises of the Atlantic fleet took place in Culebra's waters from 1901 to 1914. From Culebra the Caribbean Squadron was deployed to Venezuela, the Dominican Republic, and Panama during the critical years of 1903 and 1904. In 1902, Camp Roosevelt was built in Culebra. Two years later it was upgraded to a naval station, whose main function was as a landing field. The expansion entailed the first uprooting by U.S. military services of a Caribbean community, as the residents of San Ildefonso were forced to relocate in a new settlement named Dewey.[5]

In addition to these traditional naval installations, a facility of a technical nature, a radio transmitter, was built in Culebra in 1903, which permitted communication with San Juan and Cayey (Puerto Rico), Key West (Florida), Guantánamo, Colón (Panama), St. Thomas, Barbados, and Trinidad. Puerto

Rico's first wireless station was constructed a year later at San Juan, which could communicate not only with the stations at Culebra, Guantánamo, Key West, Haiti, and St. Martin, but also with ships on the high seas. In 1918 a powerful transmitter built at Cayey, together with the San Juan receiver station, was described as "Uncles Sam's ears at San Juan while his voice comes from Cayey."[6]

During the Second World War, for all practical purposes, the Caribbean fell under the occupation of the U.S. armed forces.[7] U.S. goals were in large part defensive, seeking to prevent German possession of any island or territory from which the Panama Canal, the continental United States, or commercial and military sea lanes could be attacked. Old military installations in Cuba, Puerto Rico, and St. Thomas were upgraded. Of the numerous new installations constructed in this period, Roosevelt Roads in Puerto Rico was the most important. It was built to house the entire British navy in the event of a Nazi invasion of Britain.

The building of some of these installations resulted in the uprooting of communities in Vieques Island (off the east coast of Puerto Rico) and in Aguadilla (in the northwestern end of Puerto Rico). In 1941 the navy expropriated 26,000 of the 33,000 acres of land in Vieques, 76 percent of the island's land area. As the short-lived economic boom from military construction and the sugar-based economy finally died, Vieques was in a most desperate situation:

> The richest and most fertile lands were expropriated by the Navy....Families lost their houses, cows, horses and farmland and had to make do with a makeshift roof, a handful of money... Those with subsistence plots or who lived on the property of others...lacked even air to breath.[8]

The relocation of the entire population of Vieques to St. Croix was discussed in 1947 within U.S. government circles, and presented to the Puerto Rican colonial government, but no official action was taken.[9] In time, however, migration from Culebra and Vieques to St. Croix accelerated, changing the social, racial, ethnic, and linguistic configuration of this island as well as the political scenario of the U.S. Virgin Islands.[10] The land in the hands of the U.S. military was considered a "unique problem" by the planning board due to the scarcity of urban and rural land and the increasing population.[11]

After the Second World War, Guantánamo, several bases in Puerto Rico, and Chaguaramas in Trinidad and Tobago were the only installations in the Caribbean kept active, though downgraded. By the 1950s changes in the international order—particularly the emergence of a bipolar world—and technological breakthroughs affected the U.S. basing structure in Puerto Rico.

In 1957, due to "its crucial location and the rapid changes in naval weaponry," Roosevelt Roads became the hub for the Atlantic fleet's guided missile operations.[12] The revival of Roosevelt Roads was part of a global expansion of the U.S. installation structure "following the Communist attack in Korea and was given greater impetus by that attack."[13] Elsewhere in Puerto Rico, Camp García was officially activated in Vieques by the Marine Corps, becoming a training base for the Atlantic marine force in 1959. The only important air force installation in Puerto Rico, Ramey Field, which was part of the Strategic Air Command, became redundant with the development of intercontinental ballistic missiles (ICBMs) and was closed in the 1970s.

LANTCOM and SOUTHCOM

Today U.S. installations in Puerto Rico (See Table 1) are part of the navy-controlled U.S. Atlantic Command's (LANTCOM) area of responsibility. LANTCOM, a unified command headquartered in Norfolk, Virginia, has responsibility for all joint U.S. military actions in the Atlantic Ocean from the North Pole to the South Pole, including the Caribbean Sea; the Norwegian, Greenland, and Barents Seas; the waters around Africa extending to the Cape of Good Hope; and the Pacific Ocean west of Central America. LANTCOM has assigned elements from all three services, but the navy's Atlantic fleet is by far the largest component (312 active and reserve ships, 1,100 aircraft, 29 fleet ballistic missile submarines, and more than a quarter-million personnel).[14] In mid-1989 U.S. forces, Caribbean, a subunified command of LANTCOM, was disabled, with all its responsibilities falling to LANTCOM's headquarters in Norfolk as they had been prior to 1980.[15]

Before the collapse of the Cold War, LANTCOM's declared military strategy was organized around an offensive forward deployment on NATO's northern flank. Under the maritime strategy LANTCOM threatened first-strike destruction of the Soviet Union's nuclear navy based on the Kola Peninsula and sought to ensure control of the Atlantic sea lines of communication (SLOCs). Thus, it would guarantee the flow of supplies and military equipment for the reinforcement and maintenance of forces in Europe. Even before the Sandinista government took over Nicaragua and the U.S. military's increased attention to consolidating a U.S.-dominated American trade zone, the United States was particularly sensitive to the possibility of Soviet-backed Cuba interdicting U.S. shipping lines of supply, due to its strategic position and alleged military capabilities.

With headquarters at Quarry Heights, Panama, the Southern Command (SOUTHCOM) is responsible for the defense of the Panama Canal and the coordination of military activities in South and Central American countries.

Table 3-1

Major Military Installations in Puerto Rico, 1980s

Department	Installation	Authorized manpower full-time permanently assigned Military/Civil/Total/Total Personnel				Total Acreage	Major Activity/ Function
ARMY (National Guard)	Camp Santiago (1987)	2	39	41	1,146	11,431	National Guard Training
ARMY	Fort Buchanan (1985)	468	1,065	1,533	2,448	828	Reserve Component Training
NAVY	Naval Station Roosevelt Roads (1989)	2,671	1,289	3,960	5,004	32,161 (includes Vieques)	Operating Base
NAVY	Naval Fleet Training Area, Vieques (1985)	–	–	–	–	25,552	Training
NAVY	Naval Security Group Sabana Seca (1987)	398	72	470	481	2,618	Communications
AIR FORCE	Puerto Rico Int'l Airport/Air Guard Station (1989)	2	299	301	1,164	44	156 Tactical Command Fighter Group

Source: U.S. Department of Defense, *Base Structure Reports, 1980-1989.*
Note: Years in parentheses indicate last report where information has been published.

Under the terms of the Panama treaties of 1977, army-dominated SOUTHCOM is supposedly bound to leave its facilities in 1999 as the responsibility for the operation and security of the canal would be turned over to the Panamanian government. Nonetheless, after the U.S. military invasion of Panama in 1989 and the takeover of the Panamanian government by a puppet regime, it would not be surprising if the terms of the treaty are renegotiated as it seems that SOUTHCOM has no place to move except to the continental United States.

In this post–Cold War era, the strategic orientation of the U.S. military establishment is changing from an East-West axis concentrating on "high-intensity conflict" to the third world focusing on "low-intensity conflict" (insurgencies or minor military forces, organized terrorism, paramilitary crime, sabotage) as well as "mid-intensity conflicts" (major regional contests).[16] The establishment of the U.S. Special Operations Command in 1986 and of the U.S. Transportation Command a year later were a step in this direction. A discussion simmered within U.S. political-military circles (reflecting inter-service rivalry) during the 1980s on the adequacy of splitting military command responsibilities for the southern half of the Western Hemisphere, which might lead to changes in the U.S. command structure in the Western Hemisphere in the 1990s with the changing conditions in the international arena.[17]

The division between LANTCOM's Caribbean and SOUTHCOM's Central American areas of responsibility does not imply a lack of communication, coordination, or joint efforts between commands. For example, in 1984 before the rhetoric of the "war on drugs" was used to rationalize U.S. domination of the Caribbean, Alvaro Magaña, interim president of El Salvador, casually revealed that in Roosevelt Roads a police school established by the FBI had been offering monthly courses for two years to participants from El Salvador, the Dominican Republic, Costa Rica, Honduras, and Puerto Rico.[18]

Most, but not all, examples of cooperation between the internal security apparatus and military installations in the Caribbean originate in Puerto Rico.[19] The FBI is notorious for its failure to aggressively investigate before, during, and after not only the murder of two *independentistas* in Cerro Maravilla by Puerto Rican intelligence police in 1978, but also its own role in the whole process and the cover-up. An FBI-Roosevelt Roads link was again in evidence in 1985 when 11 alleged members of a pro-independence group, the *Macheteros,* were taken to the base on navy helicopters for their extradiction flight to Connecticut. One of the accused, Filiberto Ojeda, was imprisoned on that military base in September 1988, for new charges related to his arrest in 1985.

Conventional warfare scenarios

In conventional terms, Roosevelt Roads is seen as crucial in providing necessary port, airfield, and logistics facilities to support fleet and naval operations during Atlantic area contingencies, in operations to control the SLOCs between the United States and Latin America, and in facilitating force projection to South America and Africa. It has played an important role in U.S. interventions in Central America and the Caribbean, such as in Guatemala in 1954; in the Dominican Republic in 1965; and the final rehearsal for the invasion of Grenada, which took place in Vieques (code-named Universal Trek I-83) just four months before that poorly executed military operation. During the Grenada invasion tactical air command F-15s were positioned in the base to provide surveillance and defense against possible interference by Cuban forces.

The most important command at Roosevelt Roads is Naval Forces, Caribbean (NFC) which has authority over all naval activities in the Caribbean. These operations are supported by Fleet Air Caribbean (FAIR), also headquartered at Roosevelt Roads, which exercises command of aircraft and aircraft operations in the Caribbean. FAIR also exercises control over the Atlantic Fleet Weapons Training Facility (AFWTF), which has its control center in Roosevelt Roads and includes Vieques and the U.S. Virgin Islands. AFWTF has been described as "irreplaceable" by the navy because it provides evaluation of new weapons systems, personnel training, and integrated training operations necessary for fleet readiness.[20] Roosevelt Roads is also the coordinating center for four annual military exercises, of which Operation Springboard (the navy's Caribbean wartime maneuver) and Operation Readex are the most important.

As in other Caribbean nations, U.S. army presence in Puerto Rico is modest. Located in the south central part of the island, Camp Santiago falls under the U.S. national guard, but is also utilized by army and reserve troops. Its value has increased appreciably since the closure of Fort Brooke in the 1970s and with the transfer of the School of the Americas to Fort Benning, Georgia, in 1985. Following the New Jewel coup in Grenada in 1979, Camp Santiago added a regional dimension as annual exercises in this training facility were held between the U.S. national guard in Puerto Rico and military forces from the Dominican Republic, Jamaica, and Barbados.[21]

The U.S. army's only other installation in Puerto Rico is Fort Buchanan, located in the south shore of San Juan Bay and today almost entirely surrounded by the San Juan metropolitan area. Its role is purely internal: providing administrative, logistical, and training support and supervision to the U.S. national guard in Puerto Rico, the reserve and ROTC; conducting army intelligence activities; providing commissary and exchange benefits to retired personnel and their dependents as well as to veterans; and coordinating the recruitment program of the U.S. armed forces in Puerto Rico.[22] The necessity of this installation is questioned from time to time but has been retained, in part due to an outcry from the Puerto Rico military-related community, about 100,000 people. The Pentagon has been reluctant to close the base because its strategic location in the metropolitan area of San Juan is seen as a deterrent "to any aggressive action or civil disorder from the enemies of government." It is perfect for mobilization purposes "in case of sabotage, subversive actions, and open aggressions by anti-government groups in the San Juan area."[23]

Nuclear dimensions

Several exclusively nuclear warfare missions are based at Roosevelt Roads. In 1984, a detailed study by William Arkin noted that the United States does not store nuclear weapons in Puerto Rico, but concluded that "[t]here is evidence of the U.S. intention to bring nuclear weapons into Puerto Rico in a crisis or during wartime."[24] In case of the destruction of U.S. bases on the mainland, Roosevelt Roads has been designated as an alternate command center for missile submarines in the Atlantic.

After an analysis of the nuclear infrastructure established in Puerto Rico, Arkin indicates that U.S. military policy violated the Treaty of Tlatelolco proscription of nuclear weapons in Latin America and the Caribbean (of which the United States is a signatory) in four areas: 1) in preparations and planning for the command and control of nuclear missile carrying submarines from Roosevelt Roads, 2) in plans to activate a base for nuclear anti-submarine weapons at Roosevelt Roads to carry out anti-submarine warfare, 3) in training and testing of nuclear weapon systems within Puerto Rico and elsewhere in the Caribbean, 4) in command of and communications for nuclear weapons facilities in Puerto Rico and the Caribbean. In 1985, Arkin made public a document entitled "Nuclear Weapons Deployment Plans," which delineated U.S. contingency plans to deploy nuclear weapons not only in Puerto Rico but also in Bermuda, Canada, and Iceland.[25]

Five communication facilities in Puerto Rico have nuclear weapons related functions, in some cases in addition to their conventional warfare roles. The three main long-range communications stations in Puerto Rico are the low-frequency transmitter at Aguada, the high-frequency (HF) transmitter at Isabela, and the HF receiver at Sabana Seca (used also for intelligence collection). The transmitter in Aguada, one of about 20 communication facilities in the world that back up six major very low-frequency transmitters, is a primary means of communicating from land to submerged submarines and, with the transmitter at Isabela, would be the principal means in Puerto Rico to communicate with submarines and ships. A "Mystic Star" transmitter at Fort Allen and a receiver at Salinas—which, as part of the U.S. president's special communications network, is used for communications with airborne command posts, including the National Emergency Command Post, and the LANTCOM's airborne center—could both send orders to fire nuclear weapons.

Vieques: A 'suppurating sore'

"Common defense" with the United States has meant in reality that Puerto Rico shares the consequences of a unilaterally imposed U.S. defense policy. Puerto Rican elected colonial administrators can rely only on informal means to express their opinions. For example, in the early 1960s the U.S. military was still trying to acquire the whole of Vieques and Culebra, now as one of the military responses to the Cuban Revolution. For this purpose, the Secretary of Defense wrote to then governor of Puerto Rico, Luis Muñoz Marín, on

a) The need for Vieques Island, including the necessity to relocate all 7,500 residents, providing a secure location for overt and covert training and/or staging of U.S. or foreign forces.

b) The need for Culebra Island, including the necessity to relocate all 570 residents in order to provide a suitable impact area for the rapidly increasing missile training of our fleet and naval air units.[26]

This attempt by the navy was thwarted by Muñoz Marín, who wrote a strong letter to President Kennedy arguing that "[t]he political, social and human effects of the Department's plans…will be so profoundly destructive that the project should be abandoned unless it is not merely desirable, but clearly, critically, and urgently necessary for the defense of the Nation."[27]

The Vieques controversy, described by Raymond Carr as "a 'suppurating sore'…a signal of American insensitivity," is a case in point.[28] In October 1975, President Nixon ordered the navy to leave Culebra, responding to the community's united front against the navy's presence. The island was led by its mayor Ramón Feliciano, and the Luis A. Ferré and Rafael Hernández Colón administrations lent lukewarm support to Richard Copaken's campaign against the navy.[29] The immediate and predictable result was the navy's increased shelling, bombardment, and practice landings on nearby Vieques.[30]

The Vieques issue contrasts with the Culebra controversy on several important points. The larger Vieques community was politically divided: at the initiative of then governor Carlos Romero Barceló, the case was diverted to the district federal courts (controlled by judges who are pro-U.S. zealots) that concentrated on important yet secondary environmental issues. In addition, the changes in the regional and international scenario (due mainly to the coup by the New Jewel Movement in Grenada, the Sandinista victory in Nicaragua, and the fall of the Shah in Iran) strengthened the U.S. militaristic approach towards the region, reinforcing the already intransigent position of the navy. This led in turn to an official change in the Commonwealth's stance, and the navy's attitude (at least publicly) became less arrogant and more understanding.[31] Finally, the navy versus Vieques conflict became a highly politicized issue due to the alleged murder of Angel Rodríguez Cristóbal (one of the numerous trespassers into land claimed by the navy) in the Tallahassee Federal Correction Institution; the reprisal killing of two navy men in a bus coming from the Sabana Seca facility; the charging of the navy public relations specialist Lt. Alex de la Zerda with the bombing of the Bar Association; and the destruction of nine U.S. national guard planes in early 1981 stationed in Muñiz base, adjacent to the Muñoz Marín International Airport.

All pending litigation was brought to an end in October 1983, when the navy and the Commonwealth signed an accord that placed a limit on the live-shelling area on Vieques Island, included environmental conservation concessions, and a pledge by the navy to seek the creation of more jobs in Vieques by trying to attract more industries. A few days after the signing of the accord, top executives of nine of the largest U.S. corporations and an important contingent of procurement officers from the Department of Defense visited Vieques and said they would seek means to generate enough jobs in defense subcontracts to wipe out the island's unemployment. After some initial success, it was clear by 1987 that the Pentagon-designed and -guaranteed Vieques Economic Adjustment Program had failed: Vieques had only one company with one project for $1.2 million.[32] However, the Navy's economic plan had been successful for a time in neutralizing social movements that opposed U.S. presence in Vieques.[33]

In February 1989 the conservative, pro-U.S., most widely read dailies *El Vocero* and *El Nuevo Día* criticized the neglect of Vieques ("...the major consequence of the annual artillery volleys of the Navy is deafness...the official deafness that ignores the just claims of the *viequenses*") and noted that navy relations with the community had fallen to a new low ("It seems that the relations between the Navy and the *viequenses* have deteriorated to the point of disintegration").[34] Navy men and U.S. federal marshals attempted in April the eviction of Carmelo Félix Matta from land that allegedly belonged to Camp García. This led to the burning by about 100 angry *viequenses* in Lope de Vega's Fuenteovejuna's fashion of two navy vehicles.[35] By late May, 300 families had taken over 880 acres of alleged navy land. After the devastation of Vieques by Hurricane Hugo in September of that year forced these families to look for protection, the navy built a fence in the lands that had been rescued.

Notwithstanding the power of the navy and the futile attempts of the colonial government on duty to defuse the issue, opposition to the navy in Vieques will be steadfast in years to come, not necessarily for political reasons but for reasons of survival. Antonio Figueroa, one of the leaders, says: "My big fear is that the navy will think this is an act of aggression against them. It is not. It is an act of self-defense, of survival for the people of Vieques."[36] As in Culebra, it is a matter of time before the *viequenses* agree among themselves that the presence of the navy, a military force of an alien culture, is responsible for truncating the life of their community, for the depopulation of the island (in 1920, 11,651; in 1940, 10,362; and in 1980, 7,662), and for its underdevelopment.[37]

The future of U.S. military installations in Puerto Rico

The future of the U.S. military installations in Puerto Rico is linked with the changing international order, technological advances, and with developments in the United States and in Puerto Rico. Since early 1989, Puerto Rico has been immersed in a referendum on status, whose parameters are to be determined by Congress and which unfortunately will not necessarily end in the decolonization of the island. In congressional hearings held in mid-1989, the continuation of several U.S. military installations in Puerto Rico surfaced as one of the key issues. The pro-Commonwealth side continued in their support for the "common defense," even though it notes the "lack of any effective participation of Puerto Ricans in the shaping of defense policies for the United States, crucial as they are for their own survival."[38] Statehooders not only accepted the military presence, but also offered to cede the lands where the installations are located to the federal government. Only the Puerto Rican Independence Party questioned the presence of the U.S. military, calling for Puerto Rico as a nuclear-free zone and for total demilitarization in order to devote all Puerto Rican efforts and resources to the island's social and economic development.

As expected, the Department of Defense noted that "the independence option would have the most significant implications...but under any option we would...retain and use" the entire Roosevelt Roads complex, the Vieques facilities, the Naval Security Group at Sabana Seca, the Punta Borinquen and

Punta Salinas radar sites, access to the Muñoz Marín International Airport/Muñiz Air National Guard Base, and Borinquen International Airport, and the Camp Santiago training area.[39] The retention of these installations is based on their alleged importance in the event of regional and/or global conflict, the need for U.S. presence and support (including training) of friends and allies in the eastern Caribbean (specifically the regional security system of the eastern Caribbean) and the Caribbean Basin as a whole, and for the U.S. drug eradication campaign.

Regardless of the outcome of the referendum, if it is ever held, the U.S. military aim is to retain its installations in Puerto Rico. In addition to the geopolitical-strategic-military value assigned by the U.S. military establishment to Puerto Rico, bureaucratic politics are also a factor to be weighed as the U.S. armed services (especially the navy) are very powerful in Washington. In a recent exercise of base realignments and closures, naval installations, including those in Puerto Rico, were not even considered because the navy "stonewalled and got away with it."[40]

In the post-Cold War world, with the weakening of Cuba's links with the Soviet Union, the gaining of power by UNO in Nicaragua, and the consolidation of the puppet regime of Endara in Panama, the United States has strengthened its preeminence in the Caribbean. In these times in which access, defined as bases and overflight rights, is getting scarcer worldwide, Puerto Rico and other Caribbean islands may be the exception to the rule.[41] In no instance has the United States been compelled to close an installation of value in any Caribbean country. Indeed the permit costs, meaning those fees paid for the privilege and authority to build, maintain, and improve U.S. military installations on another state's territory, have always been very favorable to the United States.

Still, changes in the international system—or within a nation-state in the Caribbean—as well as technological developments could affect U.S. basing structures in the region. There are several factors to be taken into account in any consideration of the future basing structure in Puerto Rico and in other Caribbean islands. First, the panel appointed by the House Committee on the Armed Services to evaluate the controversy remained unconvinced of Vieques's indispensability for the navy and urged the finding of an alternate site.[42] Moreover, the limited role played by Roosevelt Roads in the Grenada invasion, in contrast to the major one of the southern mainland installations (particularly Norfolk) indicate that proximity as well as increased ranges of those ships make fewer installations in the Caribbean necessary. The Strategic Homeporting Plan, which entails the placing of ships in different ports, is a step in this direction: "Homeporting in the Gulf is needed to protect our

SLOCs...to the European Theater and will also enhance our responsiveness to potential Caribbean/Central American conflicts."[43]

Also, technological advances should in the next few years continue to prove some facilities redundant, as low-cost satellites in space can replace the communications and intelligence-gathering functions of overseas installations, very long-endurance aircraft can be built for surveillance, and standard merchant container ships could be used to support specially configured units, with the container carrying the necessary military equipment.

In conclusion, U.S. military installations in Puerto Rico, as in the Caribbean, are the results of colonialism. The presence of these bases and facilities have affected the economic, social, and political life on the island, particularly in the case of Vieques, resulting in the dispossession and stunting of that community. The multidimensional role of Roosevelt Roads, together with other installations on the island, make Puerto Rico the center of U.S. military presence in the Caribbean. Puerto Rico is the major naval and staging base for conducting training, fleet deployments to the region, and testing weapons ranges. It also provides port, airfield, and logistics facilities to support naval operations during contingencies. Roosevelt Roads is a training ground for surrogate security forces from Central America and the Caribbean and also serves as a base for military interventions in these same regions. Puerto Rico, a "host" of a nuclear weapons-related infrastructure to be activated in time of crisis, including a number of communications facilities in different parts of the island, has to face the ever-present danger of nuclear accidents or of a nuclear attack in case of war due to the nuclear infrastructure present in Puerto Rico, which will affect also neighboring Caribbean islands.

The National Question in Puerto Rico

Juan Manuel Carrión

The Caribbean has been the quintessential colonial region of the capitalist world system. The trans-European expansion that marked the birth of this world system came together with the birth of modern colonialism. Significantly, the first colonies were established in the Caribbean and colonialism persists there up to the present. Throughout a history that encompasses five centuries, colonialism has evolved, taking new forms, in the same way that capitalism and class rule have evolved.

Puerto Rico is perhaps the best example of this evolution. For four centuries it was a colony of Spain. Acquired when Spain was the preeminent power in the world, Puerto Rico suffered all the vicissitudes of that country's centuries-long decadence. In 1898, by an act of war, Puerto Rico lost a backward colonial master and obtained a very modern one, the United States, a hegemonic power in its early stages of power ascent. By the nineteenth century, the first sketches of a would-be nation were taking shape, after a long process of ethnic formation and differentiation that began under Spanish domination. With the beginning of U.S. rule, powerful new ingredients were added to an age-old mix, with confusing results. Significantly, a nationalist movement that had been struggling for independence from Spain collapsed with the U.S. invasion, only to be reborn in the early part of this century under very different conditions.[1]

Puerto Rican nationalism and the struggle for independence in this century has been deeply affected by the particularities of U.S. colonial and imperial power. Even in the first half of this century, when U.S. colonial control of Puerto Rico was more crude, using governors appointed by Washington and other symbols of direct metropolitan control, colonialism on the island was not the same as in most parts of the world. Repression and exploitation were rampant, but also present were the peculiar effects of having the major bourgeois democratic state of the world system as the colonial master, a power not typically colonial in its imperial expansion. Colonial control of Puerto Rico was, more often than not, pushed to the sidelines in "benign" imperial neglect. When, in 1952, the so-called Commonwealth of Puerto Rico was established, colonial control remained with its fundamental features unchanged. Its outward manifestations were masked by delegation to Puerto Rican hands of the administration of the colony, by direct election of the governor. The United States also allowed the Puerto Rican flag to fly side-by-side with the Stars and Stripes.

Colonialism in Puerto Rico has continuously adapted itself to world systemic and internal changes, and to the pressures exerted by the anti-colonial struggles, without losing any of the fundamental mechanisms and devices of colonial control.

The parameters of the national question in Puerto Rico

Puerto Rico is a U.S. colony. Even the U.S. Supreme Court has expressed the opinion that Puerto Rico belongs to, but is not a part of the United States. Since colonialism in Puerto Rico is profusely discussed throughout this book, it is not necessary to replicate the common arguments.[2] More importantly, in Puerto Rico, the colonial problem is a *national* problem because of the historical presence of a nationalist movement and of nationalist sentiments (although heterogeneous) among the population. In analyzing Puerto Rican nationalism, different socio-economic elements, such as class conflict, in their structurally conditioning effects must be taken into account. But the issue in the final analysis is that of forging a people into a nation.

Nationalist sentiments are not monolithic throughout class-divided Puerto Rican society. Historically, collective national identities have been partially shaped by the class struggles that have taken place within the political parameters that U.S. colonialism has imposed. Though a class analysis is an indispensable part of the full-scale understanding of Puerto Rican nationalism, it is necessary to consider other social factors that affect the development of socially determined, collective identities.

National conflicts always take place within parameters that are set by the class struggle, but the class struggle is never pure, and in many cases it is difficult to perceive class separate from status group conflicts. Cultural and historical factors affect the presence and effectiveness of nationalist movements, going beyond the explanatory capacity of an economic-political analysis.

There is a Puerto Rican nation in spite of, and because of, almost five centuries of colonialism. Its presence can be attested to by the existing features of a culture that, although it has roots in different external cultural experiences, is unique. There is an island-wide, relatively homogeneous culture with Caribbean, Hispanic features that are clearly distinct from the culture of the metropolitan society, in spite of almost a century of U.S. domination and persistent attempts at cultural assimilation. The persistence of an ethnically and culturally strong nation in Puerto Rico has not been a natural and spontaneous occurrence. Instead, it has involved organized resistance.

The national struggle for survival has been actively led, though not exclusively, by the pro-independence movement. While the political and electoral manifestations of Puerto Rican nationalism are relatively weak, a very strong current of cultural nationalism affects all formal political pronouncements, even those of the pro-statehood forces. When the pro-statehood movement argues that Puerto Rico will be a Spanish-speaking state and that culture is a non-negotiable issue, movement activists recognize the strength of Puerto Rican cultural nationalism, even though they might not believe in it.

One of the ironies of Caribbean history is that Puerto Rico, a society with definitive national features and a 150-year-old independence movement, is still a colony, while other island societies, such as Jamaica, are already independent. The particularities of U.S. colonial power in Puerto Rico are an indispensable part of the explanation for this. Neo-colonialism and other forms of indirect control, rather than true colonialism, have been a much more common projection of U.S. power in the third world. U.S. imperialism, significantly, has lacked feudal or semi-feudal residues. It has been an almost completely pure bourgeois project, in which U.S.-style democracy has been exported, promoted as synonymous with U.S. capitalism. The U.S. empire has been, typically, an "informal" empire, built around economic structures with military reinforcement. In this regard, Puerto Rico, being a more "classic" colony, is an anomaly.

Problems of Puerto Rican nationalism

Throughout this century, the Puerto Rican national formation has had to confront some basic problems that persist even while present conditions are affecting and changing their specific features.

The anti-national, pro-U.S. identifications of the early Socialist Party and of the black Puerto Rican followers of the pro-statehood Republican Party are clear-cut evidence of persistent national divisions within the people of Puerto Rico. Early twentieth-century nationalism had socially conservative elements, detrimental to any appeal to the working class. On the other hand,

U.S. colonialism, by introducing social and political reforms akin to metropolitan institutions, was able to present itself as a progressive social force that was in the interest of the proletariat to support. In this way, U.S. colonialism played on already existing national divisions. The persistence of these national differences does not overrule the sentiments and identifications that predominate among the Puerto Rican people, but points out their limitations and contradictions.

A Puerto Rican nation clearly exists, and Puerto Rican culture is alive and vibrant. The strength of Puerto Rican culture can be seen in its expression in different fields: literature, music, the visual arts, even a small but growing cinema. For example, in 1989, the film *"Lo que le pasó a Santiago,"* directed by Jacobo Morales, received an Academy Award nomination for Best Foreign Language Film. But new and unresolved issues in the colonially induced crisis of identity lurk behind all expressions of Puerto Rican culture. Intellectual and literary debates of recent years give some indication of the critical importance of the shape of old and new fissures in the national formation. Old-fashioned Puerto Rican nationalism, even in its radical interpretations, tried to cover up some of the inherent differences and divisions within the Puerto Rican people. In their writings, pro-independence intellectuals, such as A.G. Quintero Rivera and José Luis González, have discussed the importance of class and racial conflicts in Puerto Rican history, and their conflicting relationship to a nationalist project that has been mainly petit bourgeois.[3]

Ethnicity has been, in many cases, the source of modern nationalism. A.D. Smith, in his recent book *The Ethnic Origins of Nations,* discusses the links between "people" or "ethnie" and nation.[4] But not all ethnies are, or become, nations. A people are a nation in only two cases, when there is a state that purports to represent and defend the cultural identity and collective interests of the group in question, or when a people, lacking their own state, have a socially expressed movement that seeks to establish a sovereign state for such a people. In the second case, the existence of a nationalist movement is the decisive factor in determining whether a nation exists. If a people with their own cultural characteristics lack a historically significant nationalist movement, then we can refer to them as an ethnic group but not a nation.[5] The possible transition from ethnie to nation is in all cases problematic.

In Puerto Rico, the transition from "ethnic" to "nation" has been affected by the characteristics and behavior of the U.S. state apparatus. The economic, social, and political integration of the colony into the United States has been felt differently by the various sectors of Puerto Rican society. Because of class and racial divisions, the benefits and negative effects of U.S. colonialism, in terms of degrees of collective social improvements and options for local political empowerment, were not the same throughout Puerto Rican society.

Initially, at least, the U.S. invasion brought about a "bourgeois democratic revolution" favorable to the working class, and many of the social conquests of the U.S. proletariat were extended to Puerto Rico.[6]

The democratic rhetoric of the U.S. has been a strong assimilationist mechanism in the service of colonial control. One of the particular elements of U.S. colonialism in Puerto Rico has been its contradictory assimilationist-cooptative/racist rejectionist attitudes and their translation into institutional behavior vis-à-vis the Puerto Rican population. On the one hand, Washington has sought to "americanize" the island's population, while at the same time, Puerto Ricans have felt the rejection of a metropolitan policy strongly influenced by racist and ethnocentric beliefs.

For Puerto Rico, recent changes in the U.S. nation formation are potentially capable of increasing the assimilationist pull of the metropolis, in spite of U.S. nativist sentiments against the absorption of Puerto Rico. The assimilationist pull of the metropolis increases daily, in spite of the counter tendencies of Puerto Rican nationalist reaffirmation. Ironically, the gravest danger might reside in connection with the most liberal and progressive sector of U.S. mainstream politics, for example Jesse Jackson. Becoming "American" would be more palatable to a non-Anglo Saxon interpretation of the U.S. national identity, one that would respect and accept Puerto Rico's distinct cultural identity, together with an extension of full citizenship rights. Historically, that has not been the case, and it is doubtful whether it could ever happen without threatening the long-accepted basis of national unity in the United States.

Puerto Rican nationalism is, depending on whether you emphasize culture or politics, strong or weak. The movement for cultural preservation has been more persistent and linear in its development, while political nationalism has been on a roller coaster, and become more complex and confusing every day. The growth and increasing complexity of the Puerto Rican economy since the start of U.S. rule has drawn the island closer to the United States, while at the same time strengthening the national formation by fostering a more intense island-wide socio-economic integration and modernization of basic social institutions. The self-recognition of a basic ethnicity in Puerto Rico is as strong as ever. The significant improvement in the socio-economic situation over the last 90 years is an important factor in making this possible.

Puerto Rico's national cultural identity has been worked out more evenly than its political and electoral expressions. Throughout this century, several major political parties claiming independence as a goal have grown and declined, or changed their political orientation. From 1913 to 1922 the Union Party, the largest party on the island, said that independence was its final goal. In 1922, it abandoned this goal, but during the 1930s under the new name of the Liberal Party, it readopted the independence banner and enjoyed the largest base of support. In the early 1940s the new Popular Democratic Party (PPD), made up of the younger, more reform-and-independence oriented sector of the former Liberals, came to power. By the late 1940s and early 1950s, though, after the PPD renounced its nationalist orientation, the Puerto Rican Independence Party (PIP) was formed and became the second strongest on the island. Since then, the electoral strength of the independence movement has undergone many ups and downs (see Chapter 16).

The major drawback of the nationalist movement has been its historically persistent weakness vis-à-vis the strength of colonial bourgeois hegemony. Colonial hegemony is maintained in part by export-oriented development strategies and a relationship of forced dependency through federal welfare handouts. In addition, U.S. democratic rhetoric and the imposition by the Puerto Rican political establishment of U.S. electoral procedures as the working definition of democracy, and their tacit acceptance by the population, have done much to support U.S. hegemony.[7]

Today it seems as if a plateau has been reached. The nationalist movement, though small, is strong enough to have veto power over pro-statehood projects at the same time the pro-statehood movement seems to have reached an electoral majority. The nationalist movement, although electorally weak, presents the pro-statehood forces, and the U.S. government, with the prospect of intense and permanent factional struggles in an increasingly heterogeneous U.S. society. The sometimes violent Puerto Rican nationalist movement has been the source of the most persistent "terrorism" problem within U.S. territorial borders.

The Puerto Rican national question in the 1980s

The 1980s began with a pro-independence movement still strong from its resurgence in the late 1960s, but marked by contradictions that exploded during this decade. Luis Muñoz Marín died in 1980, and with him an era ended. Muñoz was the founder of the present colonial arrangement, an erstwhile "Nationalist" and, eventually, a major foe of independence. In 1980, the island's pro-statehood party, the New Progressive Party (PNP), won the election by a narrow margin that caused accusations of fraud. Lurking behind the 1980 campaign was the 1978 "Cerro Maravilla Affair," in which two young pro-independence militants were assassinated in what was later publicly demonstrated as a case of police entrapment and cover-up. The scandal led to the PNP defeat in the elections of 1984. The 1980 campaign also marked the last, and highly disastrous, participation in elections of the marxist-leninist Puerto Rican Socialist Party (PSP). At the beginning of the 1980s, clandestine armed actions by nationalist groups such as the *Macheteros* were reaching a crescendo. Their most notorious action was the 1981 night commando attack on the Muñiz air national guard base in San Juan, in which nine combat planes were destroyed. By 1985, the FBI was claiming credit for destroying the clandestine armed wing of the nationalist movement after the successful arrest of scores of people.

The presidential election of Ronald Reagan in 1980 had an immediate impact upon Puerto Rico. The pro-statehood feelings within the administration in Washington coincided with the stagnation of federal handouts to the island, these being a form of patronage helpful to local pro-U.S. political forces. Different Puerto Rican government administrations tried to attune their policies to U.S. regional hegemonic interests by jumping on the Reagan bandwagon through participation in the ill-fated Caribbean Basin Initiative.[8] During this time, the Puerto Rican government also increased the power and influence of U.S. finance capital on the island in the form of the so-called 936 companies. Finally, the contours of the Puerto Rican pro-independence movement changed as did the world system during the 1980s. The U.S. government dedicated much of its efforts to beating the "Vietnam Syndrome" through active sponsorship of counter-revolutionary insurgencies in the third world. The "crisis of socialism" and the response of Gorbachev have had unsettling effects for a nationalist movement that in the recent past thought marxism and socialism were the solution to its woes.

The end of a cycle

In the early 1960s, the Puerto Rican nationalist movement experimented with new styles of struggle and the pro-independence political discourse changed. The founding of the Pro-Independence Movement (MPI) in 1959 and its transformation into the PSP in 1971 were significant events in this process. Some important ideological changes occurred in the main electoral party of the movement, the PIP. But by the late 1980s, many factors pointed to the exhaustion of the early 1960s "new struggle for independence." Juan Mari Brás, long-time leader of the MPI and PSP, claimed in a recent book that the cycle in the nationalist movement that he helped to start in the 1960s has perhaps ended.[9]

One of the features of the "new struggle for independence" was a militancy inspired by the Nationalist Party of Pedro Albizu Campos, considered by some the most important Nationalist leader of the century. Distinct from Albizu's radicalism, this new radicalism put forth a unique social analysis of Puerto Rican reality. The anti-imperialism of Albizu was combined with a marxist-inspired concern for class struggle. Unlike the PIP and other traditional bourgeois nationalist organizations, concern for electoral participation was pushed aside in favor of "extra-parliamentary" struggle, but not in the suicidal, individualistic fashion of Albizu's party. There was a new emphasis, instead, on massive demonstrations, picket lines, and other forms of non-violent resistance without renouncing the right, in the case of self-defense, to take up arms.

Although these extra-parliamentary struggles were in many ways, highly successful, their limitations became increasingly clear. The new movement was able to "gain the street," and open new spaces for public pro-independence activity, fomenting a process of "expansionary democracy" for a movement that had never clearly enjoyed the benefits of Puerto Rico's colonially sponsored bourgeois democracy.[10] The limitations of this strategy became evident in the 1980s, when the system unleashed new forms of co-optation and/or repression.

In addition, the strength of the colonial arrangement became surprisingly evident, in spite of the political challenges and decades of social and economic crisis. Even with persistent, massive unemployment and chronic economic difficulties, the application to Puerto Rico of welfare-state measures, such as food stamps and the continuous emigration as a social safety valve softened the social impact of the crisis.

The contradictions between the nationalist and socialist ideologies of the "New Struggle for Independence," intensified in the 1980s. In some ways, socialism as a political ideology and the working class as a historical subject were seen by some sectors of Puerto Rican nationalism as the necessary tools to break the impasse in the struggle for independence. The great expectations and immense hopes of the 1970s gave way to disillusionment and frustration. By the early 1980s, the PIP was softening its democratic socialist rhetoric and the PSP was breaking apart due to ideological disputes between those who favored a more orthodox marxist-leninist "workers' party," and those who wanted to return to a class-pluralist position, encapsulated in the idea of making the party a "national liberation movement."

The crisis in radical nationalism fomented other developments. The so-called *melonismo*, that is, *independentistas* voting for the PPD, which favors the current colonial arrangement, was justified with the view that the main enemy of the "fatherland" was the pro-statehood movement, represented by the PNP. The historical links between the pro-independence movement and the bourgeois "autonomist" option (evident in the history of such parties as the Unionist, Liberal, and early PPD) plus the relative stagnation in the electoral growth of the PIP in the 1980s helped push these illusory compromise solutions. Finally, the success of FBI repression against pro-independence armed struggle helped to nurture new defeatist attitudes among some sectors of the nationalist movement.

The cycle that began in the 1960s and end in the 1980s does not conclude in a completely negative way. An important victory has been achieved in opening the space for public debate on nationalism. A decriminalization of the long persecuted pro-independence movement has occurred in recent years, partly as a result of the Cerro Maravilla affair, and that is no small achievement. It is no longer *a priori* criminally suspect to be in favor of independence. At the University of Puerto Rico, the Federation of Pro-Independence Students (FUPI), a traditional victim of government repression, has been recognized as a legitimate organization. In the legislature, PIP representatives, such as David Noriega, have acquired important "bourgeois respectability" by their attacks on government corruption and their combative defense of the common folk and the downtrodden. This new legality is very fragile indeed, but it is an achievement that cannot be scorned.

Conclusion

Behind the complacency that sometimes seems to dominate U.S. colonial rule over Puerto Rico lurks a will of national affirmation that refuses to die. The persistent appeal and "power of convocation" of the movement was evident in the massive pro-independence demonstration in June 1989, provoked by the then possible 1991 status plebiscite.

Presently, the capitalist world system is going through important changes in all spheres: a scientific-technological revolution with economic consequences for the world division of labor; a transformation of the structural features of the inter-state system that was the inheritance of World War II; and the important changes that are taking place in the former Soviet Union and Eastern Europe. The whole process presents special problems for the expression and development of the anti-systemic movements of historical capitalism. Symptomatic of these changes, the struggle for independence in Puerto Rico is going through some very difficult times, while age-old definitions and viewpoints are being discarded. But the achievement of the past decades of a strong national cultural identity point to a future for Puerto Rican nationalism. What we see is a momentary impasse, not a regression in the development of nationalism.

PART II: PUERTO RICO'S ECONOMY & ITS NEW ROLE IN THE CARIBBEAN

Politics and Economic Reforms in Post-war Puerto Rico

Edwin Meléndez

When the November 1984 elections brought Governor Rafael Hernández-Colón and the *Populares* back to power in Puerto Rico, many islanders breathed a short sigh of relief. The election results seemed to herald a shift away from Carlos Romero-Barceló's pro-statehood New Progressive Party (PNP, *Partido Nuevo Progresista*) which had administered Puerto Rico since 1976, and from their conservative economic policies. The situation, however, was not clear cut. Hernández-Colón faced not only the debris of eight years of PNP rule but also the echoes of his party's post-war policies. The Popular Democratic Party (PPD, from the Spanish *Partido Popular Democrático)*, now in their sixth year after returning to power, seem to have exhausted their options for economic reform.

The inability of Hernández-Colón and the PPD to formulate a coherent alternative to the conservative and pro-annexation economic program of the Romero-Barceló administration is more significant given the 1991 status debate. Pro-statehood forces are gaining popular support on the island and political momentum in Washington. Here I argue that the PNP was elected to office for proposing an economic program that was perceived as an alternative to populism. The PNP program confronted the economic crisis, and the advance of the statehood movement was momentarily interrupted. However, the PPD seems to have *wasted* an opportunity to reverse the trend in popular support for statehood and their economic program is in part responsible for that. After providing a brief summary of populism and the economic conditions that brought the PNP to office, I will outline the PNP economic program and the adverse conditions that affected its implementation. Finally I discuss the PPD's economic reforms and their political implications.

The post-war expansion

The mid-1970s recession brought the end of the populist model of development. Net fixed investment—a good index of the success of capital accumulation—decreased from 30 percent of the island's gross product in 1971 to 15 percent at the end of the decade.[1] Unemployment jumped during the same period from a record post-war low of 11 percent to more than 20 percent.[2] Because of the stagnant economy, real per capita income declined for the first time in the post-war period.[3] This was obviously the end of the so-called "Puerto Rican economic miracle." To understand the demise of the populist regime of accumulation we must first look at its beginning.

The island's economic expansion immediately following the Second World War cannot, of course, be isolated from that of the United States or the rest of the world. It was based on four pillars. U.S. hegemony over international markets, riding on the long post-war wave of economic expansion, was the first pillar holding up the "miracle." The development model was based on exports, and it worked in Puerto Rico because products from the island could compete successfully in U.S. markets. International competitors were weak relative to domestic producers. The U.S. post-war expansion also allowed the massive migration of Puerto Ricans to the United States. Migration served as an escape valve for the social pressure of persistent high unemployment and extreme poverty.

The second pillar was the influx of foreign industrial capital to the island's economy. Annual flows of direct foreign investment—most of it from U.S. corporations in search of cheap labor and favorable business terms— grew from $276.8 million in 1950 to $14 billion in 1980.[4] Production on the island became vertically integrated into the multinational corporate structure. Both unemployment and output expanded. Since this type of enclave operation brought capital-intensive technology, unemployment did not decline in proportion to the expansion of output. In 1980, direct investment in Puerto Rico represented 35 percent of total U.S. investments in Latin America (not counting finance capital) and 44 percent of profits.[5] Investment in Puerto Rico is, as we can see, important to U.S. business.

The third pillar of the post-war expansion was industrial peace. A stable gain in real wages was the most important contributing factor to the low level of labor militancy. Industrial peace was also the result of the PPD's ability to control the labor movement, the imposition of the Taft-Hartley Law in 1947, and the dominance of the AFL-CIO unions. The carrot-stick strategy worked well. In the 1947-50 period, 46,206 workers went on strike each year, a record high. But between 1956 and 1962, only 7,631 workers struck each year.[6]

The fourth pillar was heavy state support for capital accumulation. Foreign investors enjoyed many direct and indirect subsidies in their operations: corporate tax exemptions, labor-force training, cheap physical plant facilities and utilities (energy, water, communications, and roads), and operational loans. These state subsidies, along with cheap labor, led the profit rate in Puerto Rico to become several times higher than that in the United States. A higher profit rate, in turn, induced new flows of capital and a high rate of reinvestment of foreign profits in the island.

One important consequence of this post-war regime of accumulation was a high degree of integration of the Puerto Rican economy into the U.S. system. Labor, capital, and commodity markets became almost "part of" the U.S. economy. Simultaneously, local industrial capital played only a minor role in an accumulation process controlled by foreign capital. By 1975, the multinational share of the total capital stock was 58 percent, but in some industries they had almost 100 percent. A high proportion of absentee ownership was (and is) particularly alarming in core industries such as drugs, petrochemicals, petroleum refining, chemicals, fabricated metals, machinery, and electrical machinery.[7] The "Puerto Rican miracle" developed on a shaky basis, highly susceptible to external economic fluctuations. Foreign capitalists' investment decisions had become a major determinant of macroeconomic stability.

The crisis of populism

The annexationist PNP, the political movement that advocates the island becoming the 51st State of the Union, proposed and carried out during its eight-year administration (1977-84) an economic program that restructured every major element of the populist regime. Each pillar that held up the structure of capital accumulation—promoted by the PPD in alliance with multinational capital—eroded. Paradoxically, foreign capital and the logic of capital accumulation in a small and open economy became the principal culprit in the demise of the Puerto Rican miracle.[8]

For the first time in the post-war years, the logic of foreign capital investments changed and the surplus drainage phenomenon appeared— more foreign capital was leaving than was coming into the island. The decrease in the rate of reinvestment of foreign capital was at the root of economic instability in the late 1970s and early 1980s. This was the natural consequence of an economy dominated by foreign capital at a time when the worldwide post-war boom was playing itself out. Eventually the outflow of profits generated by past investments was more than the inflow of external capital. [9]

The rise of a new labor movement in the early 1970s challenged industrial peace. Since the long post-war expansion had reduced unemployment, workers felt an increase in their bargaining power. When the steady gains in workers' income stopped and gains in productivity were no longer met with wage increases, workers reacted with a wave of militancy not seen since the early 1950s. A new breed of militant labor leaders—mostly from the independent trade-union sector—broke the hegemony of the PPD and AFL-CIO unions.

The Commonwealth government was unable to respond to the crisis. A rising public debt constrained fiscal policies, as populism's early subsidizing of industry took its toll. Public debt grew from $4.69 billion in 1970 (35 percent of gross product) to $7.13 billion (71 percent) in 1975. In one year from 1974 to 1975, the interest rate for the Commonwealth's 20-year maturity bonds rose from 5.75 percent to 9.00 percent.

Federal subsidies somewhat relieved the constraints imposed by lower credit margins at higher costs. In a short period, Puerto Rico received the largest share of non-military aid from the United States. Between 1975 and 1979, federal government transfers to individuals, subsidies to the Commonwealth and municipalities, and net operating expenditures of federal agencies in Puerto Rico amounted to $15 billion.[10]

The erosion of the populist structure of accumulation resulted from its own internal contradiction. The multinationals' expectation of higher profits in other countries and of increased social instability in Puerto Rico induced them to withdraw resources from the local economy. Their withdrawal, as if part of a self-fulfilling prophesy, pushed the end of populism.

Annexationism

The erosion of populism is the context in which we can understand the pro-statehood political movement and its conservative economic program. In periods of crisis, workers' living standards deteriorate, the profit rate falls, and bankruptcy threatens small businesses. Eventually, every social class and social group agrees on the need for change.

The annexationists' blueprint proposed a two-pronged strategy to solve the economic crisis. First, to complete the economic absorption of the island's economy into that of the United States; and second, to change the island's political structure to correspond to such change. To assess the viability of such a program, we must ask ourselves two key questions: could the program boost profitability, capitalist expectations, and a higher reinvestment of the surplus into the island economy? Could the conservative program allow for viable class alliances and social stability?

The first element of Romero-Barceló's economic program was to defeat labor's uprising. He promised to end the previous Hernández-Colón Administration's "chaotic" situation by pursuing strong anti-labor policies. In bitter confrontations with the strongest public-sector unions, and helped by a high unemployment rate and the weakness of the political opposition, Romero-Barceló disciplined workers. Especially during the early years of his Administration, labor conflicts lasted longer and workers were clearly defeated. Because of the government offensive and the recession, labor productivity went up, the growth rate of wages decreased, and profit rates reversed their decline.[11]

Romero-Barceló also based his economic program on an even larger role for multinational capital. One proposed focus was on subsidizing high-tech investment in both industry and agriculture. By 1982, the chemical and machine industries accounted for 36 percent of aggregate net income and over half of the manufacturing income. The expansion of capital-intensive industries led to increased output growth; during the economic expansion of 1977-79, for example, output grew at a rate of 5 percent.[12]

Ronald Reagan's blueprint for restoring U.S. hegemony in the world market had two important consequences for the island. The militaristic U.S. response to Central American revolutionary movements allowed Romero-Barceló to link the island's increasingly prominent geopolitical role to military expenditures. Military spending did not grow as rapidly as Romero-Barceló's administration expected, but in crucial regions, such as Vieques, military and related expenditures have been significant and politically pivotal. U.S. expansionism also increased the economic significance of Puerto Rico in the region. The Caribbean Basin Initiative proposed using the island as an intermediary in regional trade and capital movement.

Contradictions in annexationism

The electoral defeat of Romero-Barceló in 1984 may be interpreted both as a popular repudiation of PNP strategy and as a result of the contradictory nature of the party's economic program. With regard to the latter, the PNP paid a high price. The attack on labor not only led to higher political instability but to more cohesive political opposition. Mass support for the PNP among workers shrank. Even so, support remained strong among those employed in multinational corporations, in the patronage-based government bureaucracy, and among poor people dependent on federal government transfers. Thus, the PNP's electoral support depended on the mechanisms that had been set up to deal with the economic crisis, particularly in large urban areas. Eventually the instability and dissatisfaction generated by the economic crisis were overwhelming. Unemployment, which by Reagan's mid-term recession had reached a record 23 percent, eventually became a critical issue in the 1984 gubernatorial campaign.

Although the multinational sector of the economy, backed by generous federal tax regulations, had theoretically created a pool of economic resources from which a stable accumulation could proceed, the promised expansion of high-tech employment was not substantial or rapid enough to have any significant impact on unemployment. Real gross fixed investment remained below its 1975 peak throughout Romero-Barceló's tenure, and that lower investment affected employment trends. When Romero-Barceló was elected in his first term—it coincided with the trough of the 1970s business cycle—there were 678,000 persons employed and the unemployment rate was 19.4 percent. Employment peaked at 759,000 in 1981 but the unemployment rate remained at 18.0 percent.[13] This is, at best, a poor showing. A growing GNP did not result in significant expansion in employment or a reduction in unemployment.

During Romero-Barceló's tenure the island increased its dependence on federal funds. By 1980, Puerto Rico was receiving $4.25 billion—28.5 percent of its GNP, for an increase of 8.5 percent since 1975. In 1983, federal disbursements reached $4.6 billion, a significant figure even when compared to continental states. For instance, the federal government provided 22 percent of total receipts for the average state in 1980; the figure for Puerto Rico was 31 percent. Romero-Barceló reduced the public debt during his first term but it jumped to $8.5 billion during the 1982-83 recession.[14]

Reaganomics produced a nightmare for the conservative program. Cuts in federal welfare programs and "laissez-faire" policies were a hard pill for a weak economy to swallow. Puerto Rico's trade-dependence ratio, which had been 100 percent in 1950-54, reached 161 percent in 1981.[16] Since recovery on the island lagged behind the U.S. recovery, Romero-Barceló entered the election year amidst the worst possible economic scenario.

All in all, Romero-Barceló's political and economic programs were in contradiction. The PNP economic program could have been a long-term solution for the stability of dependent capitalism in Puerto Rico. But in the short term it was clearly unable to raise the level of economic activity and, during its eight years, it did little to address the problems of high unemployment, political polarization, and social instability. The restructuring of U.S. capitalism aggravated the problem. Two simultaneous needs trapped annexationism: restructuring capital accumulation and legitimating a capitalist system in crisis.

The 'new' populares and the 936 economy

Romero-Barceló's defeat in 1984 did not necessarily represent the defeat of conservatism nor the end of annexationism. The new PPD administration (1985-present) did not depart significantly from the PNP economic program. Hernández-Colón's first term (1972-76) in many ways presaged Romero-Barceló's programs. Strong anti-labor rhetoric and state policies unconditionally supporting multinational capital did not arrive in 1977 with annexationism. Conversely, the new PPD administration inherited the legacy of annexationism.

After the 1984 elections, Hernández-Colón and the PPD leadership attempted to project a new style. Their eight years in the opposition softened their anti-labor stance and induced them to propose some economic reforms. Unemployment became, at least in rhetoric, their top priority. Within the PPD, there was opposition to conservative policies. Not only did the party's autonomist sector, along with local industrial capital, small producers, and so forth, support moderation in the new Administration, but the labor movement and pro-independence forces, perhaps the most affected by the Romero-Barceló Administration, were in tacit alliance with the PPD.

Besides broad political support for a less polarizing political administration and diminished support for conservative economic policies (i.e., the opposition agreed on what they did not want but not so much on what they wanted), the PPD benefitted from a defeated and weak labor movement and the economic upswing in the United States. Romero-Barceló's long and bitter confrontations had defeated radical leaders, who remained popular among workers, and militant labor unions, whose militancy was constrained by the then prevailing climate of industrial relations. The level of unionization declined from more than 20 percent in the early 1970s to less than 10 percent in the 1980s. Likewise, the number of workers on strike declined from an average of more than 20,000 a year in the early 1970s to less than 2,000 throughout the 1980s.[16]

The U.S. economic expansion gave a needed booster shot to the Puerto Rican economy after 1984. Between 1985 and 1988, real GNP grew at an annual average rate of 3.3 percent and unemployment declined from 21.4 percent to 15.9 percent. During this period, real per capita income grew at an annual rate of 3.8 percent—the highest rate since the early 1970s.[17] But despite favorable political and economic conditions, the Hernández-Colón Administration lacked a clear sense of direction.

The economic program of the PPD remained a combination of old Fomento arguments about the benefits of foreign capital and a continuation of more recent conservative reforms. For example, the Government Development Bank organized a seminar on economic development and strategic planning to discuss the new "economic strategies" of the Administration. At this 1986 conference, the Puerto Rican economy was portrayed as a region of the United States undergoing a process of industrial adjustment. Puerto Rico was evolving toward a post-industrial society in which the creation of employment no longer depended on cheap labor. Rather, new jobs would be created in high-tech or capital-intensive manufacturing and corporate business services. Tax incentives and other instruments of public policy should support, and often expand, job creation in these new axes of economic growth.[18]

Major economic policy initiatives, such as Puerto Rico's participation in the Caribbean Basin Initiative, have conformed to the post-industrial society views (see Chapters 6 and 7). This program provides low-cost financing to corporations that invest in joint production facilities in Caribbean countries. In the first three years of operation, the government financed 43 new projects throughout the Caribbean and Central America.[19] In addition to the fact that twin-plants investment has been modest, the real problem is the implicit growth strategy. Once more, economic development is based on foreign investments geared to U.S. markets, while the potential reconstruction of traditional manufacturing and agriculture is ignored.

The debate on Section 936 of the U.S. Internal Revenue Code has dominated public policy discussion since the last year of the Romero-Barceló Administration (see Chapter 7). Section 936 survived the Tax Reform Act of 1986 because Hernández-Colón promised Congress that Puerto Rico would loan as much as $840 million in Section 936 funds to the Caribbean. The Section 936 debate is far from over; loans for twin-plant investments during the first three years of the program operation amount to less than $20 million. Another compelling reason for eliminating Section 936 is that U.S. tax payers are not getting a good deal. Multinational corporations enjoy the benefits of billions of dollars in tax exemptions, while businesses with no interests in Puerto Rico and U.S. families send billions of dollars in federal transfers to the island.

Puerto Ricans may not be getting a good deal either. Exactly how many jobs are generated by the federal tax exemption is in dispute. Pro-Section 936 economists estimate than more than 200,000 jobs depend directly or indirectly on Section 936 corporations. Others cut this figure in half, and question how many jobs would really be lost if Section 936 were eliminated. In one way, Section 936 affects multinational corporations' (MNC) decisions to invest in Puerto Rico. In another way, MNCs also exploit human and natural resources and receive other direct and indirect subsidies from the Commonwealth. Above all, MNC decisions to repatriate profits and not to reinvest in the island, as I have argued before, are at the heart of macroeconomic instability.

Perhaps the most controversial reform attempted by the Hernández-Colón Administration is the privatization of public authorities, a revival of the regressive theme of Romero-Barceló's 1976 electoral campaign. Public corporations produce essential utilities and services, ranging from electrical power and marine transportation to bus services and housing. These authorities account for a large share of gross domestic product and constitute the only productive sector in which domestic (i.e., public) capital is significant. Since the strongest labor unions are organized in public corporations and these authorities provide essential services, the PPD received the same response as the Romero-Barceló Administration. Opposition to privatization of public authorities is the only issue that has galvanized broad-based support among unions, consumer advocates, and other popular sectors. In Puerto Rican history, public services for private profit have produced inefficient operations, higher prices, and continuous labor disputes.

Conclusions

The "New Populares" have wasted a good opportunity to reform the economic system. They have had a windfall to the same extent that Romero-Barceló was a "crisis" manager. Instead, they confused the temporary effects of a long business cycle economic recovery in the United States with the arrival of a new miracle.

Available data suggests that relative profitability on the island has improved in the last few years, due to the effect of Section 936 tax incentives, a higher capacity utilization rate, and stable unit labor cost. Despite this fact, the rate of reinvestment of foreign corporations' profits in Puerto Rico continues to be sluggish.[20]

We have learned from our recent past that in an open economy, highly dependent on foreign capital and export markets, little else matters. The logic of capital accumulation dictates that multinational corporations will invest in Puerto Rico based on their economic interest. The next external shock, perhaps already underway, will find an even weaker economic structure.

Conservative economic policies, implemented by all administrations, have been unable to stabilize the economy since the economic crisis of the mid-1970s. Both the PNP and the PPD relied on tax incentives to induce new investments, weakened the labor movement, increased reliance on foreign investment and export growth, and ignored the potential impact of insular industrial and agricultural development. In fact, contrary to conventional wisdom, market mechanisms (that is, higher profits) have failed to induce long-term economic stability. Alternative policy initiatives should focus on internal sources of growth. For instance, special credit programs, research and marketing support, and tax incentives could target domestic producers with import substitution or export diversification potential. In addition, current production subsidies and tax incentives targeting foreign investment and exports should be revised to increase internal employment and earnings.

In the concluding remarks of his controversial book, Raymond Carr reasoned that "the immediate problem of Puerto Rico is not the state of its political relations with the United States but the state of its economy."[21] Like many others, he separates the economic from the political. Yet, "colonialism by consent" (as he describes the Puerto Rican relation to the United States) is colonialism. Webster's Dictionary defines colonialism as "the system or policy by which a country maintains foreign colonies, especially in order to exploit them economically." Unequivocally, the immediate problem of Puerto Rico is the state of its political relations with the United States, especially concerning economic exploitation. Authentic popular and progressive economic reforms may offer an alternative path to long-term economic prosperity. But popular sectors—labor, farmers, small business, the poor—must comprehend the relationship between the economic and the political. Only then will the issue of Puerto Rico's relationship with the United States be resolved.

Export-Oriented Industrialization and the Demand for Female Labor:

Puerto Rican Women in the Manufacturing Sector, 1952-1980

Palmira N. Ríos

The gendered division of labor is manifested in the differential distribution of men and women in the labor force. If men and women are concentrated in gender-typed industries and occupations, they are operating in different labor markets and, hence, they are relatively non-competitive.[1] Changes in the labor force participation of men and women are the result of differences in the rates of growth of specific industries and occupations, since women enter and men stay in the labor force in proportion to the rates of growth of sectors in which they are typically employed. In other words, changes in the relative participation of women and men in the labor force are not solely determined by general changes in the economy, but by changes in the demand for labor in female-typed and male-typed industries and occupations.

Several studies have noted the high proportion of women working in Puerto Rico's manufacturing establishments.[2] There is extensive evidence that manufacturing activities historically played a key role in the proletarianization of Puerto Rican women.[3] Although women do not represent the majority of the Puerto Rican manufacturing work force, their share of total manufacturing employment is greater than their share of all jobs in the Puerto Rican economy. While women represented 36.5 percent of Puerto Rico's total work force in 1980, they represented 48.3 percent of the manufacturing work force.

As in other developing countries, industrialization in Puerto Rico did not exclude women from the paid labor force or marginalize them in the informal economy.[4] Rather, the expansion of manufacturing activities in those countries that resulted from the restructuring of the global economy and the emergence of a new international division of labor generated a strong demand for women workers.[5] Where job opportunities for men workers have declined, developing countries have experienced a growing feminization of their labor forces.

This article analyzes the gender-typing of industries by Puerto Rico's export-oriented industrialization program and the resultant persistently high proportion of women in Puerto Rican manufacturing from 1952 to 1980. In spite of an official public policy to promote more jobs for Puerto Rican men, the industries attracted by export-oriented incentives rely extensively on women workers.

Operación Manos a la Obra (Operation Bootstrap)

In 1950, the government of Puerto Rico launched *Operación Manos a la Obra* (Operation Bootstrap), a modernization program that aimed to industrialize the economy and improve the welfare of the population. Operation Bootstrap relied on incentives to private investors, both local and foreign, in order to finance the industrialization of the Puerto Rican economy. The principal features of Operation Bootstrap are well-known: tax exemptions to new industries, subsidized factory space, recruitment of trained personnel, and assistance in obtaining loans. The government of Puerto Rico also made a commitment to develop the island's economic infrastructure by building the transportation, energy, and communications systems, and improving the educational and health systems of the island. Puerto Rico offered other important incentives: a large labor pool, a government willing to accommodate the demands of foreign capital, and financial and military protection to investments assured by the island's colonial relationship with the United States. Consequently, that Caribbean nation became a modern industrial society within a short period of time.

The expansion of the manufacturing sector under Operation Bootstrap followed three distinct stages. Most of the industries established during the first stage of this program (1950-1963) were labor-intensive light manufacturing, such as apparel and textiles. The second stage (1967-1977) was characterized by the growth of capital-intensive heavy industry, such as petrochemicals and pharmaceuticals. The third and current stage has been characterized by the rapid expansion of high-technology industries, such as electronics and the production of professional and scientific instruments.

Throughout the Operation Bootstrap period, employment in manufacturing increased at a moderate rate, and its share of total employment remained stable at 20 percent. Manufacturing generated about 30 percent of all net *new* jobs created by the Puerto Rican economy between 1950 and 1980. During the 1960s, the manufacturing sector overtook agriculture as the leading employer in the island, a position now held by the professional and related services sector.

Between 1950 and 1980, the labor force participation rate of Puerto Rican men declined significantly, from 70.6 to 54.4 percent. Although Puerto Rican women's labor force participation rate dropped between 1950 and 1960, it has increased steadily since and by 1980 it reached a new height of 29.1 percent. Moreover, women's share of total employment increased from 23.4 to 36.5 percent. Consequently, the Puerto Rican labor market experienced a growing feminization of its ranks during the past three decades.

During the same period, women's employment in manufacturing grew at a lower rate than the overall growth of the total manufacturing labor force. While women's jobs increased by 149 percent, total manufacturing employment increased slightly faster at 157 percent. The proportion of women in manufacturing went from 49.9 percent in 1952 to 48.3 percent in 1980.

The changing gender composition of manufacturing

The distribution of women in Puerto Rico's manufacturing sector differs from that of men. During 1952-1980, the Puerto Rican manufacturing workforce experienced significant changes in size and composition, and the employment of women reflected many of those changes. In 1952, the two leading sources of manufacturing jobs were the apparel and food industries. Two non-durable light industries, apparel and tobacco, employed 75 percent of all women in the manufacturing sector. The food industry was the principal source of manufacturing jobs for Puerto Rican men, an industry still today dominated by men.

Almost three decades later, men and women are still concentrated in different manufacturing sectors, although the electronics and apparel sectors are important sources of employment for both. Men are still found in larger numbers in the food industry, and new industrial sectors, such as the chemical and petroleum industries employ significant numbers of men. In 1980, the apparel, electronics, and the professional and scientific instruments industries employed 63.1 percent of all women in the manufacturing sector. Moreover, five industrial sectors had a majority of women workers: apparel, leather, textiles, electronics, and professional and scientific instruments.

Table 6-1. Puerto Rican Labor Force Participation Rates by Gender and Women as a Percentage of the Total Employed Population, 1950 to 1980.

	Labor Force Participation Rate		Women as Percentage of
	Men	Women	Total Employment
1950	70.6	21.2	23.4
1960	65.8	20.0	24.4
1970	58.8	24.5	30.8
1980	54.4	29.1	36.5

[Note: 1970 and 1980 refer to population 16 years and older, otherwise the data refers to population 14 years and older.]

Source: U.S. Bureau of the Census, *Census of Population, Puerto Rico.* 1980, 1970, and 1950.

A closer examination of employment changes between 1952 and 1980 indicate why women have a strong presence in the manufacturing sector. They have been concentrated in the industry with the largest number of jobs (apparel), as well as in some of the fastest growing sectors (electronics and professional and scientific instruments). However, the expansion of female employment, with the exception of the 1970-1980 decade, trailed the expansion of the manufacturing sector. Therefore, women's share of total employment dropped slightly.

In the decades examined, the female manufacturing labor market suffered in three ways: (1) a dramatic drop in tobacco manufacturing, an industry that historically played a role in incorporating women into the labor force;[6] (2) a sluggish apparel labor market; and (3) a below-average presence in some key capital-intensive sectors, such as the chemical industry. Puerto Rico's success in attracting heavy industries with many male-typed jobs and competition with other sectors of the economy certainly should be considered in explaining the slow rate of growth of women's employment in this sector. Women, however, were the beneficiaries of the post-1975 recovery of the manufacturing labor market. The post-recession recovery was led by four capital-intensive industries (electronic, chemical, machinery, and professional and scientific instruments), two of which have a majority of women workers. The electronic industry alone added over 8,000 jobs from 1975 to 1980.

Table 6-2: Employment in Puerto Rico's Manufacturing Industries and Percentage of Women in Major Industry Group, 1952-1980

	1952		1955		1960		1965		1970		1975		1980	
	Total	Women	Total	Women	Total	Women	Total	Women	Total	Women	Total	Women	Total	Women
All industries	60,056	49.9	71,691	52.5	81,740	47.2	111,953	47.3	136,737	48.5	136,617	49.0	154,643	48.3
Food products	14,130	6.5	13,747	9.6	15,883	10.7	19,877	13.5	20,580	15.8	22,950	23.6	23,368	24.5
Tobacco	10,800	81.9	11,929	80.6	5,628	74.0	8,446	59.9	6,120	59.8	4,980	52.1	2,104	45.8
Textile	3,103	41.7	3,971	56.3	5,018	47.8	5,987	47.7	8,904	53.8	4,898	56.8	3,356	52.2
Apparel	15,176	90.0	18,736	89.7	22,409	88.4	30,809	87.4	36,819	86.5	36,075	86.6	33,575	83.9
Wood products	3,031	4.3	3,139	4.9	3,454	6.6	4,729	6.8	5,089	7.7	3,891	11.6	3,573	12.5
Paper, printing, publishing	1,578	11.7	1,962	11.8	2,538	12.6	3,255	13.1	3,950	16.7	3,812	15.6	5,051	18.4
Chemical and allied	989	15.8	1,630	14.3	1,921	17.0	2,477	19.7	4,890	22.5	10,615	27.5	15,606	32.8
Petroleum, rubber, etc	N/A	—	N/A	—	2,359	18.5	4,072	24.9	6,964	26.0	5,364	21.4	7,726	24.5
Leather products	1,972	75.5	2,272	62.2	3,881	63.1	8,018	64.9	8,309	70.6	5,161	71.2	6,642	68.0
Stone, clay, and glass	3,035	11.4	3,884	9.6	4,458	7.5	5,856	5.7	6,838	5.6	6,169	8.5	4,816	11.9
Metal products	279	5.3	2,385	10.8	2,670	10.1	4,208	8.4	6,066	7.6	5,597	7.0	5,349	9.5
Machinery, except electrical	1,082	4.0	N/A	—	1,049	6.6	1,725	6.7	1,937	8.6	3,469	28.1	7,931	39.9
Electrical machinery	748	55.7	2,087	58.9	4,502	49.6	6,310	52.5	10,716	54.0	9,919	55.1	18,024	58.0
Professional instruments	525	60.0	1,195	52.4	1,772	67.7	2,383	63.3	5,246	68.7	10,829	65.9	13,607	63.1
Miscellaneous	3,608	60.4	4,754	66.8	4,198	62.8	3,801	63.2	4,309	58.8	2,888	56.9	3,915	47.7

SOURCE: Department of Labor (P.R.; 1953, 1956, 1961, 1966, 1971, 1976, 1981).

Characteristics of Puerto Rican female-dominated industries

Five manufacturing sectors have a majority of women workers. They are apparel, textiles, leather products, electrical machinery, and professional and scientific instruments. In 1980, these female-dominated industries employed 48.6 percent of all manufacturing workers, but 71.5 percent of all women workers in the manufacturing sector. An analysis of the type of manufacturing activity, proportion of production workers, size of establishments, average level of wages and rate of profit, ownership, and product destination provide strong evidence that Puerto Rican women were an integral component of Puerto Rico's export-oriented manufacturing strategy.

At first sight, female-dominated industries seem to defy simple classification. They can not be classified as labor-intensive, non-durable industries because electrical machinery and professional and scientific instruments are durable goods, and their production is capital-intensive. The common denominator of female-dominated industries is assembly-type operations. Even the sophisticated operations of the professional and scientific instruments industry, such as making heart pacemakers are, essentially, the assembly of very small units.

Female-dominated industries employ a high proportion of production workers. In 1980, the average proportion of manufacturing workers engaged directly in production activities was 80.5 percent. All female-dominated industries were above that average: leather, 93.9 percent; apparel 93.4 percent; textile 91.4 percent; electrical 86.5 percent; professional and scientific instruments, 85.2 percent. Only two other industrial sectors had an above average proportion of production workers, the tobacco (93.2 percent) and the miscellaneous (87.5 percent) industries.

Female-dominated manufacturing establishments have a high number of employees. While manufacturing establishments employed on the average 65.4 workers, in 1980 four female-dominated industries were among the the top five industries with 100 or more employees per establishment. The industries with the largest concentration of workers were: leather (166.0), professional and scientific instruments (151.1), electrical machinery (125.1), textile (111.8), and tobacco (100.1). The sixth largest establishments, with an average of 99.9 employees per establishment, were apparel manufacturers.

Real wages in female-dominated industries in 1980 were below or barely above average. The average weekly manufacturing salary in 1980 was $70.29. Only one female-dominated industry (electrical) was among the five industries that paid the highest wages. Three female-dominated industries (apparel, textiles, and leather goods) were among the five industries with the lowest salaries. The highest salaries were paid by the chemical ($102.44), machinery ($80.70), metal ($80.44), electrical ($76.49), and paper goods ($75.51) industries. The lowest salaries were paid by the tobacco ($64.26), lumber ($56.19), leather ($57.28), textile ($55.85), and apparel ($54.12) industries. The corsets and related garments industry, which employed 26.3 percent of all women in the apparel sector, paid even lower salaries—an average of $52.87 per week. The average weekly salary in the professional and scientific instruments industry ($73.99) was only slightly above average.

Female-dominated industries were mostly foreign-owned or subsidiaries of U.S. industries, and they produced for the U.S. and foreign markets. Although data on ownership is very hard to find, the evidence available indicates that the proportion of foreign and U.S. ownership among female-dominated industries in 1979 was leather, 88.0 percent; electrical, 82.0 percent; professional and scientific instruments, 82.5 percent; apparel, 53.6 percent. The textile industry is mostly foreign-owned also, but no specific figures are available.[7] The Economic Development Administration (EDA) reports that some firms in the professional and scientific instruments, electrical, and apparel industry are in the Fortune 1000 list. Other industries with a high proportion of foreign-owned establishments were the pharmaceutical (90 percent), paper (78 percent), food (71 percent), and machinery (56 percent) industries. The lumber, rubber, and metal industries had greater or equal proportions of native owners.

In summary, the data available strongly indicate that Puerto Rican women were not employed by declining manufacturing industries. Quite the contrary, the majority of the women in Puerto Rico's manufacturing sector are working in large assembly-line factories that are foreign-owned and produce for the export market. Women are also concentrated in relatively low-paid industries with lower rates of profits. Puerto Rican women did not remain on the sidelines of the export-oriented industrialization process but were key actors in this development strategy. In actuality, I would argue, low-paid women workers are the key to the survival of these highly competitive industries in the new global economy.

Gender and development policies

In any country with strong patriarchal traditions in which a growing number of men cannot find a foothold in the labor force, one should not be surprised by expressions of concern over economic development policies that seem to benefit women over men. Many Puerto Rican government officials have expressed their concern with a development strategy that seemed to be ineffective in alleviating male unemployment.[8] Some officials have recognized that there is a relationship between the island's manufacturing structure and the gender composition of its labor force.

Various government documents, both public and private, indicate that consciously gender-based considerations played a role in the formulation of development policies in Puerto Rico. There is documentation that the Commonwealth of Puerto Rico assigned a top priority status to the reduction of male unemployment and that it was not concerned with female unemployment. For example, in 1960, the women's share of the labor force dropped to its lowest level in the post-World War II period. A report published by the Government Bank for the Development of Puerto Rico interpreted that figure as an indicator of progress. In their view, the declining proportion of women workers was an indicator that more men were able to find well-paid jobs, which in turn allowed more women to become full-time homemakers.[9]

This policy was restated a decade later by the Economic Development Administration when it made the following argument:

> Another cardinal objective of the industrialization program is to create jobs for men. Undoubtedly, a society in which a greater part of the jobs are held by women, unless it be a matriarchal society, creates serious social problems when the woman works and the man is unemployed. Not only does it affect the matrimonial institution of a society in which traditionally the male is the principal provider but it also affects the development of the family when the mother is not able to give proper attention to the home and children. The problem requires attention on a high priority since projections of the work force for 1975 anticipate a greater growth in the number of males than females.[10]

A similar argument appeared in the *29th Economic Program* (1973-1976) issued by the planning board of Puerto Rico. The report stated that "female unemployment is not necessarily associated with poverty nor with great human suffering since, in most cases, it does not fall upon the head of household. Therefore, in the development of a public policy to reduce unemployment, the masculine factor should occupy a top priority."[11] Accordingly, tax incentives were tailored to meet the needs of men's labor market. In 1963, the Puerto Rican Legislature approved a Law of Industrial Incentives which aimed to promote, among other things, manufacturing establishments that would employ men.[12]

The story of petrochemical complex

Although the story of Puerto Rico's petrochemical complex is well-documented, few studies have paid attention to the role that gender considerations played in the formulation of the capital-intensive strategy. The success of Operation Bootstrap was such that by 1963, plants promoted by the Economic Development Agency employed almost 70,000 workers. However, about 60 percent of the new jobs were held by women, leaving most of male unemployment unaffected.[13] The belief that Operation Bootstrap was not helping much in reducing the high unemployment rate of Puerto Rican men forced policy-makers to review their strategy. Hubert Barton, a key officer in the Economic Development Agency, recognized that Puerto Rico's manufacturing sector did not represent a cross-section of the American manufacturing sector. Puerto Rican manufacturing industries were concentrated in a relatively narrow range of industries that covered almost one-third of the spectrum of industries found in the United States and other industrialized countries.[14] The specialization in the assembling of goods, especially non-durable goods, explained the continuing demand for women workers.[15]

As early as 1957, at the annual meeting of the Puerto Rico Economic Association (a meeting in which Teodoro Moscoso, the head of the Economic Development Agency, was a discussant), Barton articulated the rationale for a new course in the industrialization program. Heavy industries, Barton argued, would generate a large number of jobs, increase the general levels of wages, and decelerate the growth of non-integrated, labor-intensive industries.[16] Furthermore, heavy industries represented "largely male employment, in contrast to the present situation among Fomento plants which employ two-thirds women."[17] Barton recognized that the gender-typing that he observed was not the product of Puerto Rican practices; it was the general practice of those types of industries both in Puerto Rico and the United States. In a 1966 report, Barton said:

> This concentration in the non-durable goods industry accounts for the high proportion of women in Puerto Rican manufacturing. Nearly half of the factory workers in Puerto Rico are women while in the United States women account for only about a quarter of total factory employment. Industry by industry, the sex ratios are similar but Puerto Rican employment is concentrated in apparel, especially women's underwear and brassieres, and in leather goods industry, in electronics, all of which employ a high proportion of women in the United States as well as in Puerto Rico.[18]

The economic development strategy that followed promoted different kinds of industries, those in which men typically worked. Consequently, by the mid-1960s, Puerto Rico inaugurated a new strategy for economic development. The Economic Development Administration actively promoted capital-intensive industries like petrochemicals and pharmaceuticals and sought investors to exploit the island's copper mines. The petrochemical refineries were conceived as a first step in the development of a vast industrial complex based on the manufacturing of petroleum derivatives. The Economic Development Administration envisioned the establishment of a chain of interdependent establishments that would produce everything locally, from tires to textiles and plastic products. The strategy included the building of a special dock in Guayanilla where oil tankers could deliver the black gold. Officials estimated that the multiplying effect of the proposed industrial network would generate approximately 200,000 new jobs. They also hoped that this industrial complex would increase the level of wages and give more stability to Puerto Rico's industrial sector.[19]

That strategy enjoyed mixed success. Special quotas granted to Puerto Rico by the U.S. Department of the Interior facilitated the expansion of corporations like the Caribbean Gulf Refining Company, the Commonwealth Oil Refining Company, Phillips Petroleum, and Sun Oil. However, political opposition to the petrochemical complex, fueled by environmental and nationalist concerns, and increases in the price of crude oil dictated by the Organization of Petroleum Exporting Countries (OPEC) slowed the implementation of this policy and led to a crisis in Puerto Rico's petroleum industry. Consequently, government officials set their sights on the high-technology and service industries as an alternative strategy. Ironically, the high-technology industry was yet another sector in which women were typically employed.

It should be pointed out that there is no evidence of a conspiracy to drive women out of the labor force. The creation of jobs for women was not a priority because women's jobs usually are unstable and pay low wages. A development strategy that relied on such traditional female-typed industries would have been precarious, at best. While Barton believed that capital-intensive industries could exert a positive effect on women's wages,[20] the bottom line was that government officials seemd to fear only the political consequences of male joblessness.

Restructuring the world economy

The disproportionate presence of women in Puerto Rico's manufacturing sector is not an aberration or a chance occurrence but an inherent feature of a development strategy that has been part of the post-World War II restructuring of the world economy. Although the hierarchy of the old economic order has survived these changes, this process of global economic restructuring represents a qualitatively different mode of reproducing the most advanced labor processes worldwide and integrating new markets into the global economy.[21]

The restructuring of the world economy consolidated a single world market of capital, labor, and commodities. It also redefined the role of developing nations in the world economy. Several studies have pointed out that a new international division of labor is replacing the traditional function of developing nations as suppliers of raw materials.[22] Underdeveloped nations are rapidly becoming sites of manufacturing activities. While advanced nations are specializing in research and development, financing, specialized services, and administration, developing nations are increasingly specializing in the manufacturing of goods for the world market.[23] The proliferation of offshore export processing zones (or free-trade zones) represents a new mode of insertion of developing nations into the world economy.

The main reason behind the expansion of manufacturing activities in developing nations is that, in many cases, they provide a more profitable environment than traditional sites. Labor costs are usually lower and, in many cases, workers are not organized, giving management greater flexibility and control over the production process. It is not that production in traditional sites is not profitable but that, in many cases, it is less profitable than in the developing countries.[24]

The relocation of manufacturing establishments was not just the consequence of economic decisions. Technological innovations made the project of coordinating a global system of production a reality by making it possible to break down complex manufacturing activities into simple tasks that could be distributed worldwide and that were easily learned by unskilled workers. Innovations in transportation and communications also facilitated the relocation of manufacturing establishments to non-traditional sites. Hence, the global assembly line was born. The implementation of export-oriented development programs throughout the developing world and liberal tariff codes were additional incentives.

Out of these processes emerged a more mobile and flexible capitalist organization of production. The new international division of labor represents a global mechanism of incorporating new segments of the population into the labor force, creating in the process an international labor market.[25] That new worker is often a woman.[26]

Puerto Rico and the new international division of labor

Although there is a growing literature on the new international division of labor, it has ignored Puerto Rico's role as the pioneer of this historical phenomenon. Most studies date the origins to the mid-1960s when Fairchild opened his first off-shore electronic plant in Hong Kong.[27] I would argue that Operation Bootstrap paved the way for the new international division of labor and that its basic components were tested in Puerto Rico before being exported to other developing nations. Operation Bootstrap proved, a decade before Fairchild started operations in Hong Kong, that developing nations could be feasible and profitable sites for modern manufacturing.

Puerto Rico represented a relatively safe testing ground. The Commonwealth of Puerto Rico established a free-trade relationship with the United States and was subject to U.S. tariff, monetary, fiscal, and commercial navigation regulations. As a U.S. territory, it offered U.S. and other foreign investors financial and military security that no other developing nation could match at that time. Furthermore, U.S. manufacturers were familiar with the island and its workers since U.S. manufacturing establishments, garment in particular, have been operating in Puerto Rico since early in the twentieth century.

The success of Operation Bootstrap in proving that workers in developing countries could successfuly adjust to the modern factory was well publicized throughout the world by Puerto Rican and U.S. agencies and by academics. Puerto Rico was presented as the model for the developing world, an example of development with democracy. With the establishment of a communist regime on the nearby island of Cuba in 1959, the Puerto Rican model entered into the Cold War rhetoric: democracy's answer to communism.

Many of the architects of Operation Bootstrap played an important role in the formulation of similar programs in other developing nations. Governor Luis Muñoz Marín became an international spokesman for Operation Bootstrap. Teodoro Moscoso—who was head of the Agency for Economic Development from 1942-61, U.S. Ambassador to Venezuela in 1961-62, and U.S. Coordinator of the Alliance for Progress in 1962-64—served as consultant to various governments implementing Operation Bootstrap-like programs. Hubert Barton, another developer of Operation Bootstrap, also served as advisor to several Caribbean nations.

Variations on the Puerto Rican model are functioning today in the Caribbean, in Mexico, in Ireland, and throughout Southeast Asia. Fernández-Kelly (1985) estimates that there are 200 export-processing zones that employ approximately 3 million workers. Although most are engaged in garment, textiles, and electronic manufacturing, new industries are entering into this type of production. The latest entry is the data-processing industry, which is relocating its data-entry activities to countries like Barbados, the Dominican Republic, and Ireland.

As in the case of Puerto Rico, the spread of export-processing zones throughout the developing world plays an important role in the incorporation of women into the labor force. There is extensive evidence of the feminization of the export-processing labor market.[28] Women, mostly young and single, represent between 85 and 90 percent of the export-processing work force.[29] Countries in which they work are Mexico,[30] the Dominican Republic,[31] Haiti,[32] Barbados,[33] Jamaica,[34] Curaçao,[35] St. Lucia,[36] Morocco,[37] Hong Kong,[38] Malaysia,[39] Singapore,[40] Taiwan, Indonesia, and the Philippines.[41]

Conclusion

Gender-segregated employment patterns are shaped as much by economic as by political, social, and cultural constraints. Economic development strategies are not gender-neutral in their intentions nor in their consequences. The Puerto Rican experience demonstrates that the social organization of the workplace can pit the interests of employers against those of policy-makers. The continuing demand for women workers by Puerto Rican manufacturing establishments was an unintended and unanticipated by-product of Operation Bootstrap. It did not pass unrecognized. Policy-makers were aware that the island's specialization in the assembling of goods and in low-wage manufacturing was attracting women into the paid labor market. That strategy did not help much to alleviate male joblessness in Puerto Rico, a major political problem. The tension between the economic development strategies of a regional economy and the restructuring of the global economy set the stage for new forms of policy intervention to change the gender composition of the labor market. Puerto Rico's capital-intensive strategy was a deliberate attempt to benefit Puerto Rican men by promoting industries in which men typically worked. By pursuing a development strategy that deliberately benefited men, government officials recognized the pervasive character of the gendered division of labor and signaled their unwillingness to tamper with the patriarchal order. The failure of this strategy in changing the gender composition of the manufacturing workforce exemplifies the inherent difficulties facing policy-makers in developing nations, since discouraging the growth of industries that typically hire women would slow their incorporation into the modern industrial world.

Puerto Rico's New Role in the Caribbean

The High-Finance/*Maquiladora* Strategy

James L. Dietz and Emilio Pantojas-García

Puerto Rico's role in the international economy began to be transformed dramatically after the oil-induced recession of 1973-75. The evolution has been from a predominantly export-platform economy based on capital imports to its recent emergence as a secure tax haven, as an international financial center, and as a regional base of operations for vertically integrated North American transnational corporations (TNCs) operating in the Caribbean. The so-called "Puerto Rican model" in which U.S. assembly plants are promoted is no longer at the center of the Puerto Rican economic strategy. It has been progressively supplanted by what can be called the "high finance/*maquiladora* strategy," which is becoming the new Puerto Rican development model at the same time as the old model is exported to Puerto Rico's neighbors at an accelerating pace.

The underpinnings that have made possible this structural transformation of Puerto Rico's economic strategy and hence its evolving status within the international and regional division of labor can be most clearly distinguished in Section 936 of the U.S. Internal Revenue Code (U.S. IRC) passed in 1976, in the Puerto Rican industrial and tax incentive acts of 1978 and 1987, and in the provisions of the Caribbean Basin Economic Recovery Act of 1983 (CBERA) that enacted the pivotal Caribbean Basin Initiative (CBI). This body of legislation, formulated in Washington and San Juan, further enhanced and extended Puerto Rico's well-known tax holiday standing and extended its free-trade zone advantages to the rest of the Caribbean. In the process, and not surprisingly or incidentally, the already profitable financial, commercial, and manufacturing activities of qualifying firms locating in Puerto Rico have been made even more extraordinarily lucrative.

Throughout this transformative period, the Puerto Rican government has assumed an ever more active, visible, and aggressive presence in shaping the new economic structures. As just one example of this, in 1985, Puerto Rico inaugurated its Caribbean Development Program (CDP) which, according to the Economic Development Administration (Fomento), has the objective of promoting economic development in Puerto Rico and the Caribbean by utilizing the incentives embedded in the CBI, in Puerto Rico's tax incentive laws, and in Section 936. With the creation of this program, the importance of which is still not fully appreciated, Puerto Rico began the process of converting itself from being a mere competitor for U.S. investment with other Caribbean nations and instead became the promoter, financier, and central complementary production site for a growing number of U.S. manufacturing, financial, and service companies locating in other countries of the region. It is this high finance/*maquiladora* economic strategy that has secured for Puerto Rico its new and more interventionist role in the Caribbean.

Just as the island's critical function as a U.S. military bastion in the region has been maintained and strengthened alongside the major changes occurring in the world order since the 1970s, so too has Puerto Rico's economic and political power as an intermediary for United States policy in the Caribbean progressively been expanded and intensified over the same period. It has been the Puerto Rican government and allied groups of industrialists and financial interests, however, and not just Washington policy-makers, that have fashioned Puerto Rico's increasing central prominence in regional economic affairs.

Crisis and restructuring

Puerto Rico's export-platform economy was founded in the 1950s on three key comparative advantages instrumental to attracting U.S. enterprises and capital to the economy: (1) unlimited, free access to the U.S. market; (2) a common currency (meaning no exchange-rate distortions or costs); and (3) Commonwealth and federal tax exemption. Other complementary benefits included relatively cheap labor and raw materials and occasional exceptional treatment on trade restrictions applicable to imports to the U.S. customs union (such as import quotas on foreign oil in the mid-1960s).

The world economic crisis of 1973-76 accelerated tendencies that already had been eroding these comparative advantages. The comparative wage advantage for U.S. companies locating in Puerto Rico relative to neighboring countries had been continually deteriorating as minimum wages on the island tracked those in the United States. Although the absolute wage differential between Puerto Rico and the United States remained significant (in fact it was growing), Puerto Rico's average wage substantially exceeded that of its international competitors, including other Caribbean nations. A growing number of countries were able to closely match Puerto Rican productivity levels, at least partly due to the greater mobility of international capital and technology within the structure of TNCs, so that cheap labor *per se* counted for less and less as an incentive in any specific production location decision.[1] Now, relative labor costs among competing locations with roughly comparable levels of productivity became an important indicator, among many, affecting TNC decisions to produce off shore.

Puerto Rico's comparative wage disadvantage was compounded in the early 1970s by increases in the cost of maritime transportation that further raised export and import prices. The three principal U.S. shipping companies operating between Puerto Rico and the United States (Transamerican Trailer Transport [TTT], Seatrain Lines, and Sea-Land Service) increased their rates in 1972 by 18 percent per trailer load and 28 percent for less-than-a-trailer load. The oil price hikes after 1973 due to the Arab embargo set off a series of additional rate increases that even the purchase of the assets of the three U.S. companies and the creation of a public corporation to operate the island's shipping business *(Navieras de Puerto Rico)* could not arrest.[2]

Increased energy generation costs resulting from higher oil prices created yet another comparative disadvantage for export-oriented industrial producers in Puerto Rico, an external shock compounded by the lack of attention to infrastructure development by the Commonwealth government. By 1976, the average annual electricity bill for industrial establishments in Puerto Rico was 31 to 120 percent higher than in the United States (with the exception of the mid-Atlantic region). On average, the cost of energy to industries in Puerto Rico was between $700 and $3,390 a year higher, depending on consumption levels.[3] The forces that ultimately pushed the Puerto Rican economy and its development model to crisis in the 1970s were grounded both in inherent factors that limited the viability of the export-processing model and in the international economy.[4] Profitability had declined throughout the world economy in those industries that had led post-war prosperity, with durable consumer goods production (autos, steel, and the like) becoming progressively less profitable in the core countries. Competition from the so-called NICs (newly industrializing countries), high labor costs, and market saturation were some of the most cited causes for this downturn in profits.[5]

Puerto Rico was no exception to this trend. The aggregate rate of profit had, in fact, been declining steadily since the 1960s. Still, in some sectors such as chemicals, electronics, scientific instruments, and machinery, profitability remained higher than in the United States.[6] By the mid-1970s, however, the combination of the worldwide economic crisis in productive activities and the specific comparative disadvantages of the export-manufacturing model Puerto Rico had followed since the 1950s made imperative a reassessment of Puerto Rico's overall economic strategy.

The result of this reappraisal, first undertaken systematically under the direction of the pro-Commonwealth *Partido Popular Democrático* (Popular Democratic Party, PPD), was a determination that productive, that is, manufacturing, investment could not remain as the engine of the growth process. Of the three original sources of comparative advantage, only Puerto Rico's locational tax advantage continued to be consequential to U.S. TNCs. The PPD's strategic consideration became how Puerto Rico might regain its former relatively privileged position within the international circuit of production and exchange of U.S. capital at a time when deteriorating comparative productive advantages for export manufacturing worked against Puerto Rico. The solution seemed to be in taking somewhat different advantage of the unique tax and financial advantages available to Puerto Rico as a consequence of its territorial relation with the United States, and in the crafting of novel incentives appropriate to the competitive conditions characteristic of the international economy which opened up after 1973. In this process of revamping the economic model, initiatives emanating from both Washington and San Juan were equally indispensable.

The drive toward restructuring

To alleviate the hardships caused by lifting the special oil-import quotas and to meet specific problems caused by the existing legislation on the federal treatment of profits earned in Puerto Rico, Congress revised its policy covering the tax-free repatriation of profits from U.S. firms operating on the island by creating Section 936. Section 936 constituted the first component of a series of initiatives that would contribute to the redefinition of the Puerto Rican model. Section 936 provided new incentives for investments in Puerto Rico (and other territorial "possessions") by eliminating the limitation on tax-free profit repatriation of accumulated profits by liquidated subsidiaries, as the previous Section 931 had stipulated. Under Section 936, U.S. subsidiaries located in Puerto Rico (legally termed "possession corporations," but popularly known as 936 corporations) could repatriate profits free of federal taxes to parent companies in the United States on a current basis, that is, quarterly, yearly, or at any other time.

In order to prevent any sudden loss of its financial capital base, the Puerto Rican government imposed a 10 percent "tollgate tax" on such repatriated profits. Then, having imposed this tax, the Puerto Rican government made it possible to avoid full payment either by reinvesting profits locally, that is, not repatriating them or by depositing them in special certificates offered by Puerto Rican financial institutions, thus making such profits eligible for (partial) tollgate tax exemption at the time of repatriation. By doing so, 936 companies were able to reduce the effective tollgate tax to 5 percent or less, depending upon how long the funds were actually left on deposit.

The subsequent proliferation of 936 corporation deposits resulted in a windfall of liquidity for banks. By 1977, $1.6 billion of the $5 billion of accumulated profits of possession corporations had been deposited in qualifying financial investments, and about 50 percent of these were held by Citibank and Chase Manhattan.[7] By September 1989, 936 deposits had risen to over $10 billion, comprising over a third of all deposits. Though the volume of such deposits has declined slightly in the early 1990s due to some changes in local legislation on how 936 funds must be utilized, there is no question that such funds remain integral to the evolving financial strategy of Puerto Rico.[8]

The second component of the shift away from the manufacturing export base was contained in the Industrial Incentive Act of 1978 referred to as Law 26. Policy-makers within the pro-statehood *Partido Nuevo Progresista* (New Progressive Party, PNP), which superseded the PPD in power in 1977, succeeded in enacting a law that subtly, but significantly, redefined industrial tax exemption. Complete local tax exemption, the hallmark of the PPD's Operation Bootstrap manufacturing export strategy since the 1950s, was replaced with a diminishing tax exemption scale.[9] This law was consistent with what PNP policy-makers believed to be a necessary transitional phase on the road toward statehood. At this point, federal tax exemption would end completely and companies in Puerto Rico would confront a non-zero federal tax burden (though local tax exemption modifications would then be conceivable, and perhaps desirable again, in an effort to retain overall tax advantages for remaining firms).

The more significant component of Law 26 for the transformation of the economic strategy, however, was the appending of export *service* industries to the list of eligible tax-exempt activities, which until then had been exclusively oriented toward manufacturing. Law 26 stipulated that services produced for external markets were eligible to enjoy a 50 percent tax exemption (later increased to 75 percent) on income, property, excise, and municipal taxes, as well as license fees. Services eligible for such exemption, however, had to be provided for foreign markets, including the United States. Some of the eligible services listed in the law were: international commercial distribution facilities; investment banking; public relations; consulting services; insurance; film-making and processing; repair services; laboratory services of various kinds (dental, photographic, optical); and computer services.[10]

The inclusion of export-service production among the industries eligible for tax-exempt status turned out to be a critical redefinition of the future economic strategy. It provided an augmented focus for the promotion of new industries in the economy, and though the export orientation of the previous model remained intact, the shift toward services geared toward the needs of international TNCs in the region was pivotal for creating a new mode of development.[11]

Although it would be difficult, and perhaps foolish, to argue that the passage of Section 936 and Law 26 were part of some envisaged master plan of economic restructuring shared by an enlightened elite, it is undeniable that, consciously crafted or not, these two laws helped to form the legal framework for an economic strategy based on *high-finance, knowledge-intensive* industries that emerged as a coherent corollary to the former model dependent on manufacturing exports for its dynamism. Most important, this shift in strategy seemed to offer a way out of the crisis of the early 1970s as it converged with trends in the international economy. PNP strategists argued strongly that Puerto Rico's future was to be found in an even more open and further internationalized economy that would "become the gateway through which European companies will penetrate the Latin American market and will, at the same time enable U.S. goods produced both in the [United States] and in Puerto Rico to reach the markets of Central and South America."[12] Core, high-tech industries geared to the international market and supported by regional and international services were to be the backbone of the Puerto Rican economy of the post-1970s, an economy increasingly inserted into the wider regional and international economy.

In the short term, however, the new economic strategy did not translate into immediate economic gains; the U.S.-induced, anti-inflation recession of 1980-82 pulled down the growth trend of world production, adversely affecting Puerto Rico's growth rate. The real average annual growth rate of gross domestic product (GDP) between 1980 and 1983 was -0.4 percent. Personal income declined even more rapidly, at a rate of -0.6 percent a year over the same period, the first decline since the late 1940s. Unemployment rose from 17 percent in 1980 to an all time high of 23.5 percent in 1983.[13]

Fearing failure of the new thrust toward becoming a regional economic center in the Caribbean for U.S. TNCs, PNP strategists thus welcomed and embraced, though at first not wholeheartedly, the Reagan Administration's 1983 Caribbean Basin Initiative, both as a way to restructure Puerto Rico's role in the region and to create a more dynamic basis of accumulation and growth for the island.

The Caribbean Basin Initiative

The most significant provision of the original CBI was its one-way, duty-free treatment of a wide range of goods entering U.S. customs from designated beneficiary countries in the Caribbean and Central America. Products eligible for duty-free treatment were required, however, to meet a minimum content requirement to qualify for CBI duty-free entry to the United States.

This content requirement dictates that a minimum of 35 percent of total value of production input be created in one or more designated beneficiary countries. In making this determination, but only in this instance, Puerto Rico is included as a designated beneficiary of the CBI, and the value of labor or material input from Puerto Rico may be included to fill any percentage of this value-added requirement.[14] Since up to 15 percent of the minimum content requirement also may be added in the United States, a designated Caribbean beneficiary country conceivably can qualify for duty-free treatment with minimal local content if a significant portion of production takes place in Puerto Rico.

This content-requirement allowance has facilitated Puerto Rico's effort to benefit from the CBI by bending its design to fit its emerging regional economic strategy. This has been achieved by making full use of the substantial incentives provided by Section 936 and via the creation of the complementary or twin-plant program discussed below.[15] In fact, it can be argued that it has been the twin-plant program, and Puerto Rico's emergent role as a champion of more transnational investment in the Caribbean, that has provided the *final* component to the transformation of the former economic model into its present form.

The CBI provided the opportunity to reinsert the Puerto Rican economy prominently into the circuit of U.S. capital through the "twin plant," or *maquiladora,* concept promoted by the Caribbean Development Program or CDP. The prototype for the twin-plant program in Puerto Rico had been developed by the accounting firm of Coopers & Lybrand which, with a grant from the U.S. Agency for International Development, had conducted a feasibility study specifically concerned with the viability of locating the labor-intensive segment of production of the electronic and apparel industries in low-wage countries in the Eastern Caribbean and the finishing and packaging processes in Puerto Rico. The twin-plant program was designed to further segment the international process of production of TNCs so as to reduce labor costs (by sourcing relatively simple assembly operations in low-wage economies), while preserving and expanding the more productive, higher wage, and more technological portions of the production process within Puerto Rico.

At the same time, this twinning strategy would enable TNCs to shift profits from Caribbean subsidiaries to the reduced-tax environment offered by Puerto Rico. It became clear that the relatively low value-added requirement for CBI duty-free eligibility of electronic products would make advantageous ventures in that industry, while the absence of quota restrictions for textile imports from Puerto Rico to the United States would provide a significant advantage for apparel assembly firms co-producing with a Puerto Rican twin. The added incentive for 936 corporations to realize their global profits in Puerto Rico rather than in their Caribbean subsidiaries would enable federal tax-free profit repatriation to the United States of a larger share of global earnings for TNCs in both industries.[16]

The twin-plant program was officially announced in 1985 when the CDP was created. Interestingly, the details of the CDP had been conceived by, and the program was to be overseen by, its former opponents the PPD, which originally had feared the CBI would destroy Puerto Rico's special access to the U.S. economy. Now, however, the PPD was in the forefront of promoting the CBI and the twin-plant component of the development strategy. In his inaugural address on January 2, 1985, PPD Governor Rafael Hernández Colón also announced the creation of a scheme to use a part of the huge pool of 936 funds deposited in Puerto Rican banks to finance investment in the Caribbean. This marked a 180-degree turn by the PPD leadership, which, ironically, was not only embracing what had originally been a PNP initiative, but was now giving the entire program another push.

This radical change in the position of the PPD leadership was at least partly serendipitous, resulting from a desperate move to counter the Reagan Administration's threat to eliminate Section 936 as part of a more comprehensive federal tax reform bill. In exchange for leaving Section 936 intact, Hernández Colón promised to put the Puerto Rican government's promotional and financial resources on the line in an effort to breathe life into a flagging CBI through the creation of twin-plant operations in neighboring Caribbean countries and through the financing of approved development projects in those nations. It was argued that this effort would both increase exports from the Caribbean to the United States, an important goal of the CBI, while directly contributing to the growth and development of the Caribbean nations. The latter was believed necessary as a means to reduce social tensions for more comprehensive reform. Neither of these twin goals of the CBI had met with much success, and the PPD's offer struck a responsive chord in Washington, which feared the CBI was headed for an embarrassing, costly, and perhaps socially destabilizing failure.

The PPD government offered to pledge to guarantee an annual investment of $100 million in 936 funds in CBI countries if Section 936 were retained without substantial alterations. This promise was supported by eighteen 936 corporations that acknowledged they would make investments in the Caribbean amounting to $66 million if Section 936 tax privileges were continued in the tax revision. The support of Caribbean leaders like Eugenia Charles, Herbert Baize, and Edward Seaga, at the time prime ministers of Dominica, Grenada, and Jamaica respectively, was also secured, and what would become known as the "936/CBI strategy" was poised to go into operation. All that was necessary for the high-finance/*maquiladora* model to be put in place was the retention of Section 936.

Ultimately, an agreement was reached with the Reagan Administration and Congress based on a memorandum presented to representatives of the National Security Council by the government of Puerto Rico. And, in 1986, the federal tax reform law finally approved by Congress contained relatively few alterations to Section 936. One notable modification to this section (subsection 936(d)(4) of the U.S. IRC), however, provided the legal base for the twin-plant program. This subsection stipulated the principal conditions for the use of 936 funds in the Caribbean and placed in the hands of the U.S. Treasury the final determination on the eligibility of projects to be financed with Puerto Rico's 936 funds. This made it impossible for the PPD to make good on its promise to finance $100 million in investment; in the early 1990s, new general guidelines helped Puerto Rico not only to meet the $100 million lending goal but to exceed it.[17]

The government of Puerto Rico and its agencies, for their part, proceeded to amend the necessary local laws and regulations required to put the newly proposed CDP in motion. This included the creation of the Caribbean Development Office (in 1986) to implement the 936/CBI program and to promote twin plants between Puerto Rico and the rest of the Caribbean, as well as to finance qualifying investments.[18] In January 1990, the Caribbean Basin Projects Financing Authority, a government entity, was created to provide an additional vehicle, other than commercial banks and private financial institutions, for facilitating investment of 936 funds in the region. The 1988 Point Four Program, an outreach and promotional tool, the Caribbean Scholarship Program, and a number of cooperative technology schemes, among others, also have been created by the government of Puerto

Rico to extend the possibilities of investment created by the 936/CBI program throughout the Caribbean.[19]

The Puerto Rican government thus has become the leading promoter of the CBI and of U.S. investment in the region, investment that is now to be linked, whenever possible, to twin plants in Puerto Rico that form but part of the vertically integrated global production process of the TNCs. It was firmly believed that this expanded strategy and capacity to promote Caribbean-wide investment decisions for TNCs would help Puerto Rico gain a central role in the restructuring of regional economic relations, to the benefit, it was argued, of Puerto Rico and the Caribbean Basin nations.

Puerto Rico, U.S. TNCs, and the Caribbean

Without the renewal of Section 936, Puerto Rico might have become no more than a marginally attractive location for TNCs. But Section 936, combined with the possibilities provided by CDP and the CBI, created a significant incentive for locating in Puerto Rico among those TNCs with both international productive capabilities and the financial capacity to transfer costs and earnings. The island has become a unique tax haven as the expansion of intermediate processing and the proliferation of financial activities by TNCs has been stimulated. This process was somewhat interrupted by the uncertainties generated by the status debate and the proposed plebiscite in 1991, as discussed in other chapters in this volume, though when the plebiscite was not held this barrier was removed.

Unlike the Bahamas, Bermuda, or the Cayman Islands, however, Puerto Rico is not a tax shelter for financial manipulations made mainly through banks or paper corporations. Most U.S. federal financial regulations and corporate laws apply to Puerto Rico, making it extremely difficult to engage in marginally legal practices possible in other foreign, off-shore tax havens. To enjoy the advantage of federal tax-free profit repatriation from operating in Puerto Rico, companies must be engaged in a qualifying business in Puerto Rico: 80 percent of gross income of a 936 subsidiary must originate from sources within the possession, and at least 50 percent of this gross income must be derived from the active conduct of trade or business, that is, at least half of any income must be from productive activities rather than purely financial investments. In other words, to be able to shelter financial ("passive") income, a company has to have the capacity to produce in Puerto Rico manufactured goods or services for the international market, and/or the ability to transfer to a production subsidiary on the island profits from productive operations in other parts of the world. Clearly, export-processing industries, including services with international financial income sources were targeted to become the major beneficiaries of this new strategy.

Aside from those manufacturing export companies able to segment their production regionally, the other major beneficiaries of the new Caribbean strategy have been financial and professional service companies. Larger quantities of liquid assets and profits were channeled to Puerto Rico and then to banks operating there to reduce the tollgate tax burden prior to profit repatriation. The available pool of U.S. and locally trained accountants, lawyers, and other professional services needed to manage these large sums provided an exceptional opportunity for the substantial expansion of such services.

The original enactment of Section 936 in 1976 had accelerated the restructuring and internationalization of the Puerto Rican financial system. The 1973-76 recession had resulted in the bankruptcy of a number of local banks, and one Canadian and three Spanish banks absorbed four local banks. This takeover and buy-out process continued beyond the recession with another six local banks being assimilated by two Spanish, one Puerto Rican, and three American banks between 1978 and 1983. By 1983, ten locally owned banks had disappeared, and three Spanish and another three American international banks had opened operations in Puerto Rico. By 1980, the Banco de Santander, Banco Central, Banco Occidental (Bilbao Vizcaya), Continental Illinois Bank, Bank of America, and Bank of Boston had made their entrance into the rapidly internationalizing Puerto Rican commercial banking sector, perhaps the single sector that has gained most from the regional thrust of the altered economic strategy.[20]

Brokerage houses also proliferated on the local financial scene, attracted by the large quantities of 936 money. Until 1976, only a handful of these houses operated on the island; Merrill Lynch, Payne Webber, Prudential Bache, Citibank, and Chase Manhattan Bank had limited operations. After 1976, E.F. Hutton, Kidder Peabody, Drexel Burnham, Dean Whitter Reynolds, and First Boston Corp. all began operations, and existing companies expanded their operations.[21] Likewise, investment banking and other such financial intermediaries proliferated.

Section 936 thrusted Puerto Rico into the world of high finance. And, although neither the federal nor the colonial government would admit it, Section 936 made Puerto Rico a major tax haven for manufacturing TNCs within the legal and financial system of the United States, an exceptional situation which the Internal Revenue Service refers to simply as "a tax loophole," as if it were just like any other. The financial income of export manufacturing 936 corporations has become the fuel for a large and complex transnational financial labyrinth created by companies to avoid paying taxes not only in the United States but in other parts of the world as well, as billions of dollars in global profits are transferred to, or declared as part of, the income of operations in Puerto Rico. So central has Puerto Rico become to many TNCs that, in 1986, U.S. corporations derived more profits from their Puerto Rican operations than were received from either Canada or the United Kingdom, both of which have much larger economies and a larger volume of U.S. investment.[22]

Maquiladoras and the Caribbean Development Program

Puerto Rico's Caribbean Development Program is important not just for the expected benefits for the island; it is also the key to accelerating the transformation of the Caribbean Basin into a huge tax and duty-free export-processing zone and financial center that allows the legal, tax-free repatriation of profits on productive operations to the United States. Whereas before profits had to be shifted around, laundered, or accumulated in locations such as the Bahamas, Bermuda, Panama, or the Cayman Islands, now it is relatively straightforward and *perfectly legal* to repatriate profits to the United States passed through operations located in Puerto Rico, without paying more than token taxes.

From its inception in 1986 to July 1990, the 936/CBI program had promoted investments in the amount of $410.3 million, funding 80 projects, including twin plants and other investments (such as infrastructure). The Dominican Republic was the most important location for twin plants, accounting for 39 projects. Costa Rica had 11, and Jamaica was third in importance with 8 projects. Trinidad and Tobago accounted for the most investments of any country, $177.3 million, or 43.2 percent of the total, but had only four projects, with the bulk of the investment being 936 funds in the petroleum industry.[22]

Most of the projects that have been promoted by the CDP are assembly manufacturing operations, or *maquiladoras,* which import their intermediate products and export the final output, primarily to the United States. These are operations that tend to generate low-paying jobs located predominantly in free-trade zones. Their employment effect can be substantial for a small economy, but there seems to have been little effect on aggregate unemployment. In total, the Caribbean Development Office claims that the CDP has created, or is in the process of creating, 15,367 new jobs in the CBI countries and 2,996 in Puerto Rico. The impact of the *maquiladoras* is generally strongest, however, not as growth poles for the creation of forward and backward linkages and employment in the CBI countries, but in generating foreign exchange needed for debt financing.[24] Electronics, pharmaceutical, and apparel companies have been the main beneficiaries of the CDP, though some utilities and petroleum companies also have benefitted. Companies such as Baxter, Eli Lilly, Avon, Pfizer, Johnson and Johnson, Abbott, Westinghouse, and Maidenform, among others, have established twin-plant operations between Puerto Rico and other Caribbean Basin nations in response to the strong incentives of the 936/CBI strategy and Fomento's promotional activities.[25] Some smaller independent producers also have joined, and are benefiting from the TNC windfall by engaging in subcontracting operations throughout the Caribbean.

Conclusion

In the international division of labor that emerged in the late 1980s, the Caribbean Basin was becoming an export platform for U.S. manufacturing in electronics, textiles, pharmaceuticals, sporting goods, and other light manufactures, an increasing quantity of which enters the U.S. market via Puerto Rico, where it passes through final processing in local twin plants.[26] Within this order, Puerto Rico is fast becoming the administrative and financial center for the regional free-trade zone created by the CBI, spurring the initiatives of the Puerto Rican government to alter the base of the former capital-import, export-processing strategy that had shaped the economy until the mid-1970s.

The Puerto Rican government argues that turning intermediary is the only way to sustain growth, by at least retaining, and hopefully attracting more of, the top end of the production process of TNCs to Puerto Rico, even as the low end of labor-intensive production is increasingly moved to lower-wage economies. Unfortunately the Caribbean and Central American countries facing financial duress act as if they have no alternative but to acquiesce to the 936/CBI strategy and the expansion of *maquiladora* production within their borders. The more disturbing question, though, is if the CBI is not simply another step in the formation of a Pan-American free market under the aegis of the United States. If it is, Puerto Rico seems to be carving for itself the role of foreman of the Caribbean, a position within the regional and international division of labor that may be doing it more harm than good.[27]

PART III: EMERGING SOCIAL MOVEMENTS

The *Rescate* Movement:
An Alternative Way Of Doing Politics

Liliana Cotto

This article addresses the relationship between the State and urban popular sectors through a concrete analysis of the Puerto Rican government's response to land invasions, or *rescates*.[1] I have used newspapers and government documents as my sources.[2] In what follows I will describe some characteristics of the *rescate* mobilizations with the aim of assessing their potential for turning into a long-range social movement. The criteria to be examined are: type of organization (local or regional), form of negotiation (institutional or non-institutional), the use of violence, and the role of external political organizations vis-à-vis the mobilization. I will also present some features of the responses of the State which will help explain why the mobilizations succeeded in satisfying the particular demand for housing but not the general demand of political autonomy by the communities.

Background

In 1940, the Popular Democratic Party, PDP, won the colonial elections in Puerto Rico. With the support of Rexford Tugwell, the appointed governor of Puerto Rico, the PDP-controlled Legislature launched a series of political and economic reforms. From 1940 to 1948 the reformers sought to deal with the immediate consequences of the sugar plantation system, especially the impoverishment of the agricultural proletariat. The axes of these reforms were the Agrarian Reforms of 1942 and several state-operated projects.[3] These programs were accompanied by a political-administrative reform of the State apparatus in order to create a modern bureaucratic body with the technocratic bases necessary for industrialization. The immediate consequence of these processes was the increase in internal migration to the urban areas, which accounted for the tremendous growth of the *arrabales* (shanty towns) in the decade. The basic pattern of Puerto Rico's best known *arrabales*—Caño de Martín Peña, Tokio, Trastalleres, El Fanguito, and Buenos Aires—was established. Their maximum physical extension was attained in 1950.[4] To prevent the development and proliferation of *arrabales,* the State forbade the repair of homes in the communities. A special body of vigilantes was created to enforce the law. In spite of all these measures, squatting by accretion continued in floodable lowlands, swamps, near the sea, and throughout the barrios that composed the urban municipality. They were characterized by spatial disorder and unhealthy conditions.

Squatters fought back and organized local committees for the defense and physical improvement of their communities. They demanded that the state provide services to urbanize the settlements. But, since the State's policy was one of eradication, the limited urban improvements were always temporary.

Using the federal housing programs that were available to the island as a U.S. territory, the colonial State developed a program of urban public housing projects. The groups of apartment buildings were known as *caseríos*. The reaction to public housing was another expression of resistance among some sectors. These sectors claimed that the *caseríos* took from the residents of the *arrabales* the right to own a home and turned them into government tenants.[5]

In the late 1940s, the government shifted to an industrialization strategy. The new strategy, known as "Operation Bootstrap," improved the living conditions of the population.[6] This period was characterized by a reduction in the growth of *arrabales* and in the consolidation of the existing ones. The reduction was the result of the massive public housing program which developed with the direct intervention of the metropolitan housing agency. The consolidation meant a liberalization of State norms, allowing permanent improvements to the homes and the reconstruction of the shacks with cement.

The political culture within which modernization occurred was sustained by an ideology that connected progress to industrialization and democracy to voting. This ideology was accompanied by a paternalistic political system based on social welfare and patron-client relations.

Economic growth increased the per capita income and the consumption capacity of some sectors of the population. Absolute wealth increased but remained unevenly distributed. Poverty and unemployment, although reduced, had not been eliminated either by industrialization or by emigration. Around 70 percent of the island's families remained under poverty level.[7] In the area of housing several factors neutralized the favorable effects of increases in income. Some of these were: the elimination of popular living areas by private industry so as to use the land commercially; the loss of housing units due to natural causes such as hurricanes; and the elimination, by the State, of *arrabales* and of workers' communities *(barrios obreros)* to obtain lands for the construction of roads and other public works.

By the mid-1960s, Operation Bootstrap had lost its effectiveness. As Puerto Rican workers demanded higher salaries and industrial incentives ended, U.S.-owned industries began to relocate to countries such as Taiwan and Singapore. The State turned to another option within the industrialization-by-invitation strategy: the invitation of capital-intensive industries such as petrochemicals, electronics, and pharmaceuticals.

In 1968, the elections were won by the newly created New Progressive Party (NPP). This party addressed the issues of political stability and social discontent with the promise of economic and social integration of Puerto Rico to the U.S. federation, that is statehood. Preserving the populist tone of the previous party in government, Luis Ferré, the NPP governor, promised to fulfill the unsatisfied expectations of the new urban population. It is within this context that the *rescate* mobilization of the late 1960s and the early 1970s took place.

The *Rescates*

The *rescate* mobilization began slowly in 1968, attained a peak in 1972, and began to recede in 1974. From 1968 to 1972, most activity was geared to the creation of new communities. From 1972 to 1976, activity was geared to the maintenance and legitimation of the existing *rescates*. From 1968 to 1976 approximately 16,821 structures were built, 186 communities were established, and a population of 84,104 people was mobilized.[8] By 1976, the "wave" of *rescates* had ended and with it, an attempt by a popular sector to redefine their relations with the State apparatus. In 1978, a national committee of *rescatadores* was formed. This committee, formed by representatives of *rescates* of different parts of the island, negotiated two important amendments to the law that ruled the legalization of the *rescates*.

The *rescates* of the late 1960s differed from earlier ones in several respects. They were well-organized and the community was physically well-planned. The land selected was not marginal land, but instead was of high potential value for either private or public use. After the *rescate*, the new community opened streets, organized lot distribution, and developed neighborhood organizations. Unlike previous squatters, the *rescatadores* had widespread support, including legal aid from government corporations (such as the Legal Services Corporation), religious groups, civic organizations, and political parties of the left. Even representatives of the political parties that alternated in the control of government sometimes came in support of the *rescatadores*.

The struggles coincided with a period of student mobilizations against the ROTC, compulsory military service, and the war in Vietnam, as well as a continuing struggle for university reform. There were also popular mobilizations against the presence of the navy in Culebra, against the proposed mining of copper and nickel deposits by U.S. corporations, and against the proposed establishment of a so-called superport on the island for the transshipment of petrochemical products. These years also witnessed an increase in the militancy of industrial workers and the emergence of the public workers' assertion of their right to unionize and strike.[9]

The relationship between the *rescates* and the State took the form of an urban struggle.[10] The *rescates* were mostly realized by an urban population moving from the overpopulated cities to lands on the periphery of the urban centers. The displaced urban population was economically excluded from the productive process. This population represented the lack of economic and urban space for the young, second generation of urban dwellers. Thus, the emergence of the *rescatadores* in Puerto Rico, as in many other developing countries, was the result of urban growth marked by poverty and inequality, and especially by a scarcity of housing among the popular classes.[11] This scarcity became a crisis when urban dwellers mobilized against the state to satisfy their collective need of shelter.

Types of organizations

The existence of local committees indicated the presence of an organized will of autonomous action by the *rescate* communities. Institutionalized practices such as writing letters or holding meetings with government officials or their representatives were mostly done by these elected committees. The objectives of the local committees between 1968 and 1972 included organizing for defense, discipline, and task assignment; planning and constructing houses and roads; solving the daily problems of community development; accepting new residents; administering a census in order to know the population better; and negotiating with the State for property titles and public services.[12] Other local committee objectives were to prevent evictions, eliminate those who used the *rescate* for speculation, connect into the public water systems, help organize new *rescates*, and develop strategies for avoiding clashes with the police.[13] But for a social struggle to become a movement with a long-range impact on society as a whole, it needs regional or national organizations.

The presence of regional committees, such as the Committee for the Rescue of Land (CRT) and the Movement of *Rescatadores* of the Western Zone (MURT), indicated the existence of organizational objectives that transcended the particular interest of each community.[14] MURT united Villa Hostos, Villa del Mar, Villa Lorencita in Mayaguez, and Villa Ruiz Belvis in Hormigueros. It promoted a better communication between the different *rescates* and proposed their collective protection against repression. For MURT the *rescates* were part of a wider struggle of the working class.

Following the triumph of the PPD in the elections of 1973, the Secretary of Housing announced the new policy towards *rescates*. This policy included a plan to legalize all *rescates* previous to January 18, 1973, and another to prevent the creation of new *rescate* communities. In view of the new context, the local and regional organizations centered their objectives on obtaining services and gaining assurance for property titles. They also carried out non-institutional actions to confront police brutality and to (illegally) install public services in the community.

During these years there was a greater thrust of regional organizations whose main objective was to demand and negotiate the survival of their respective *rescate* communities. Three were reported in the northern part of the island. One was the Federation of Land *Rescatadores (Federación de Rescatadores de Tierras)* created in 1973. This Federation was the result of a mobilization of five northern *rescates* (Villa Pangola I and II, Villa Clemente, Villa Hostos, and Villa Dávila). The Federation of Land *Rescatadores* had the specific objective of putting pressure on the municipal assembly of Toa Baja, in order to receive titles and services. They demonstrated in Toa Baja to support a resolution sponsored by the Puerto Rican Independence Party (PIP), calling on the municipality to give property titles to the *rescatadores*. This meant that the Federation would have legal right to inhabit that land. The approval of that resolution was the primary organizational objective of the Federation.[15] Unfortunately, it was not approved. Another regional organization formed in 1975, was the Committee for Property Titles. The third was Communal Union, Inc. *(Unión Comunal Incorporada)*. It was legally formed as a nonprofit corporation on March 31, 1975. The Communal Union had many long-range objectives, among which were the organization and social development of the poor and the creation of a civic conscience among them. The Union also proposed providing legal assistance to the poor and promoting their participation in the decision-making processes of government agencies. The communities comprising the Communal Union were capable of organizing the mobilization to oppose the approval of Law 132.[16]

This law, after all, sought their disappearance as communities: "You must take our lives before you take back our land, We will fight back" was their slogan. This mobilization included a picket against the governor held in Washington, D.C. in May 14, 1975, which condemned discrimination against poor homeless people, and a letter requesting the governor to drop the eviction orders that were pending. The letter stated, "We have found new confidence in ourselves as individuals and as groups...we have rescued our destiny...help us consolidate it."[17] The lively picket lasted 66 days and was filled with slogans and chanting. The demonstrators brought mattresses, cartons, blankets, and everything else needed to spend the night. The activity reflected the dynamics of a poor people's picket, as well as the organizational capacity to negotiate, administer a budget, systematize the cleaning of the area, and even protect the communities at home. The homes of these leaders were burned in reprisal for their activism in favor of the squatters.[18] By June 1975, the State attorneys were able to obtain a permanent injunction to limit the protest to quiet picketing during the day. Slogans and loudspeakers were forbidden.[19] On June 24, 1975, the First Circuit Court of Appeals in Boston ruled that squatters had no property right to the land they had invaded and were not necessarily entitled to a hearing prior to their eviction. This decision overturned previous rulings by Judges Toledo (*Amezquita vs. Hernández Colón,* 378 F. Supp. 737 [D.C.P.R., 1974]) and Cancio (*Caballero vs. Ferré,* Civ. No. 71-598, [D.C.P.R. 1971, unreported]). Both Puerto Rican federal district judges had recognized the right of a hearing before an eviction. On July 5, 1975, Law 132 was finally approved. The demonstration did not succeed; 11 days later (July 16) four leaders of the marathon picket, members of Communal Union, Inc., were found guilty of charges of disrupting the peace. "The decision apparently broke the spirit of the group...in front of the gates of *La Fortaleza* [the governor's home] for months. The demonstrators were all gone by Tuesday."

This was the extent of the Union's activities, the longer-lasting regional organization of *rescatadores,* in the eight-year process of mobilization. In 1976, there were five sporadic land invasions, but State officials, with all the legal apparatus on their side, prevented their development. As before, there was violence in some cases (Sector Bechara, Puerto Nuevo) and resistance and organization in others (Cañaboncito, Caguas). Squatters by invasion subsided until the 1980s. On July 15, 1977, the NPP administration prepared legislation to grant title deeds to 17,000 families who took over land from 1973 to mid-1975. In 1978, the national organization of some of the existing *rescates* negotiated two new amendments to Law 132.

Forms of negotiation

The use of non-institutional mass activities signals a loss of confidence by *rescatadores* in the conventional methods of participation legitimized by the State: petitions, applications, meetings, and committees. These popular sectors acknowledged that mass actions were the most effective form of political pressure outside electoral periods. The threatening potential of these mass demonstrations lay in their strength for carrying out direct action, thus alarming the regime and frightening possible investors. The State apparatus sought to repair the fissure in the system of legitimation by either satisfying the demands or repressing the demonstrators, or both.[20] In the case of the Puerto Rican colonial state, the NPP and the PDP administrations promised to do the former but enforced the latter.[21]

The *rescatadores* increasingly engaged in non-institutionalized forms of negotiations, such as pickets, vigils, caravans, mass mobilizations, and a whole variety of creative activities such as a *via crucis* (stations of the Cross), a picket with their mouths taped, and the use of folk percussion instruments.[22] Some of these non-institutionalized practices were intended to pressure government representatives by interrupting everyday activities, the flow of traffic, and the day-to-day functioning of government offices. Between 1968 and 1972, most mass activities were pickets to protest evictions by the State officials and the police. From 1973 to 1976, they were centered in the demands for property titles for the communities. They also mobilized to demand the end of police aggression and judicial eviction orders.[23]

One instance of non-institutional mass activity happened in 1971. Villa Kennedy, the first *rescate* to become a public issue, was evicted by the police in April 1971 and by the order of La Plata Development, Inc. The evicted families picketed *La Fortaleza*, carrying signs that read: "Now we know that the rich are the first," "The poor will be the last," and "Enough of abuse."[24] This mobilization dramatized the injustice done to the *rescatadores* in such a way that public opinion was outraged. The governor ordered an investigation to determine the legality of the eviction and introduced a bill to guarantee an alternative home to all eligible evictees.[25] This dialectic of popular protest and State response—followed, as in Villa Kennedy, by a combination of social welfare and repressive actions—characterized the relationships between the *rescatadores* and the State apparatus. In the case of Villa Kennedy, the families were moved to a government-owned tract. The community was isolated by armed members of the civil defense and the NPP so that not even representatives of the press were allowed to go in.[26]

The use of violence

Direct mass activities by the popular sectors are effective because of their threatening potential. But this potential is not based on the use of forceful violence. The Puerto Rican experience with land invasions confirmed the hypothesis that in an urban struggle, violence is mostly initiated by the State apparatus through its agencies or its police.[27] The *rescatadores* mobilizations were fundamentally non-violent. Most of the violence of the process was exercised by the State. This was evidenced by the systematic use of police force to stop a *rescate* or to prevent it from growing, thus violating the privacy rights of the residents. Violence was also used in arresting and imprisoning *rescatadores*.[28] In razing one community, a *rescatador* was killed. No policemen or any other State agents were killed. In the eight years of the mobilization only four instances of offensive violence by the *rescatadores* were recorded.[29]

Law 132 and the First Circuit Court of Appeals decision legalized the use of violence against the land invaders, thus contributing (along with other organizational factors peculiar to the communities) to the prevention of new *rescates* and the demobilization of the existing ones.

External political organizations

The *rescates* became a social struggle against the State. Every social struggle has to deal with the presence of external political organizations. Historically it has been important to clarify if the popular mobilization reproduces, with the external organization, the same relation of dependence created by the State apparatus, or if it establishes a relation of autonomy with respect to that group. A relation of dependence implies that the popular organizations are subordinated to the goals, leadership, and methods of the State or of the political organizations. An autonomous relation implies that mass organizations respond to their own needs and define their opposition to the State *without* submitting to the priorities of other parties or groups.

In the late 1960s and early 1970s the *Partido Independentista Puertorriqueño* (PIP) and the *Partido Socialista Puertorriqueño* (PSP) merged two political issues: the issue of colonialism and independence for Puerto Rico and the issue of economic inequality, that is, the unequal distribution of wealth. While the PIP, even in its most radical moment, presented a social democratic platform, the PSP, although influenced by nationalism, presented a marxist-oriented program.

Until 1972, the parties' support for the "underdog" explained the presence of their representatives in a considerable number of *rescates*. The interaction with the *rescates* was the result of initiatives of party members at the local level. The official intervention of the party followed these initiatives. In the case of the PSP this was expressed organizationally in the creation of a Community Affairs Secretariat. The PSP was especially active in the southern and western parts of the island.[30] The *rescates* in the northern part of the island were organized with the support of PIP members.[31] At the local level, the *rescatadores* managed their affairs with a degree of autonomy. But aside from the ideological content provided by their political supporters, their struggle was limited to their communities. This was somewhat overcome by the creation of regional organizations.[32] Support and influence from the pro-independence political parties began to dwindle in 1973. The PSP, on the one hand, decided for the first time to participate in national elections. All its organizational energies were then redirected towards the election process. The Community Affairs Secretariat was replaced by a Secretariat of Electoral Affairs. The PIP on the other hand, experienced an internal crisis in 1972. As a result, the most radical sectors, which promoted grassroots involvement by the party, were expelled from the organization. The party retained only those individuals who saw the election process as the most important objective of their political practice. Meanwhile, some *rescate* communities developed an autonomous leadership who, although *independentista*, organized the Communal Union independently from the PIP. Nonetheless, the *rescatadores* always had legal assistance or public support from the PIP, the PSP, civic and religious organizations, and their respective attorneys.

The relationship between the parties and the *rescatadores* showed that political parties have their own objectives which do not necessarily coincide with the collective needs that created the conditions for urban mobilizations in the first place. What the squatters needed was a new type of organization that would satisfy short-range needs with clear general political objectives. As the *rescate* process evolved, Legal Services became the only organization that helped the *rescatadores* consistently. Besides offering legal assistance, it gave communal and organizational help. The legal struggles eventually became so urgent that they tended to obliterate other organizational tasks. In other words, the increasing intervention of Legal Services transformed the social struggle into a battle fought by lawyers. This legalistic dimension had the advantage of incorporating the *rescate* struggle within the system, but it also limited the possibilities of using more non-institutional forms of community struggle. Consequently, the intervention of Legal Services had a demobilizing effect. This capacity of the State to demobilize a popular struggle has to do with Puerto Rico's colonial status. The Commonwealth was able to provide the protesting masses with the services of Legal Services, a corporation financed by the metropolitan State, despite the fact that these masses were challenging the authority of the State and were morally questioning the overall value of private property. These legal methods of co-optation, typical of state governments in the United States, distinguishes Puerto Rico from other sovereign Latin American dependent states in which mass illegal land occupations have been an important issue.

State responses

The State's answer to the issues raised by the *rescatadores* was to establish long-run social-welfare programs such as new land distribution, construction, and loan programs. In the short run, the State policy was based on the use of criminal charges, injunction procedures, police surveillance, and, as a last resort, violent razings. The pattern of State action towards the *rescatadores* was, first, tolerance of previously established *rescates*; second, the use of the police for surveillance, arrests, and razing to discourage new *rescates*; third, the use of judicial procedures; last, the creation of anti-*rescate* legislation. This pattern was followed by both the NPP (1968-1972) and the PDP (1973-1976).

The party administering the State adopted the strategy defined by the State's apparatus. Neither party changed the strategy or the State functions; rather, once in control of the State, they changed their own strategy and tactics. Since Puerto Rico lacks sovereignty, the local State had to respond to the organizational demands of a more inclusive State apparatus, that of the U.S. metropolitan state. The main policies on housing stemmed from the metropolitan federal policies.[33]

Another strategy utilized by the State, and specifically the politicians, was to discredit the *rescatadores* by blaming their actions on the influence that pro-independence political activists had on their movement. In terms of long-run strategies, both parties responded in a similar way: by promoting social-welfare housing programs and by approving a body of stricter laws and court decisions against any form of illegal land occupation.

Conclusion

The effects of the *rescate* mobilizations were contradictory. In terms of the immediate objective of obtaining shelter, the *rescatadores* won an urban struggle. The State legitimized most communities. Besides, the *rescates* developed a different form of "doing politics" which provided an avenue of political participation for the popular sectors. The conventional methods of participation on the political process were transcended by the use of non-institutionalized mass actions geared to put pressure on society and State. The basic organizations were local and regional committees; the fundamental means of mobilization were pickets, caravans, and other non-conventional practices. The methods chosen prove that there are alternative ways of obtaining political power outside the conventional political parties.

The committees showed the tensions of a colonial society. On the one hand, they asserted their autonomy vis-à-vis the state and other conventional parties. On the other hand, they reproduced dependency relations with their political allies, who were conventionally or unconventionally organized. The constant pressure of goverment agencies to re-establish a social-welfare relationship with the mobilized masses reduced the space for autonomous action on the part of the committees. Notwithstanding the tension, the traditional political organizations were pushed to redefine their tactics during the mobilizations in view of the new issues posed as a result of social struggle.

The *rescatadores* brought about another form of political change. The actions validated the need for primary relations, solidarity, self-help and mutual aid; the incorporation of rational planning; organizational techniques; and the recognition that knowledge is power. These processes became the basis for a collective action that defied both the capitalist logic of private property and the colonial logic of social-political dependency. In the colony, the process I have just described was also contradictory. New attempts at autonomy co-existed with old patterns of dependency within the committees. Nonetheless, during the mobilization, the conventional political organizations, even if anti-colonial, had to review and revise their hierarchies and tactical priorities.

In sum, a popular social struggle may become a social movement that realigns the political forces within the colony if their innovative forms of political and communal organization are stimulated and reproduced, not limited or co-opted. One thing is sure, the conventional anti-colonial organizations will have difficulty in attaining their political goals if they do not incorporate these struggles as the social basis of their strategies. It is too soon to assert that the only effect of the *rescate* mobilization was the satisfaction of the need of shelter. Many questions are yet to be answered by academic research and political practice.

Puerto Rican Feminism at a Crossroad:

Challenges at the Turn of the Century

Margarita Mergal

> Il y a un fascisme anti-intellectuel et anti-femme qui se déchaîne dans ces moments—là où justement une femme essaie d'exister, où elle avance sans parapluie, parce que quand vous faites un roman, vous n'avez pas ce parapluie de concepts. Vous avancez a découvert et tout les flèches sont bonnes contre vous, donc c'est un moment difficile.
>
> *Julia Kristeva*[1]

In this essay I will discuss the present situation of the women's movement in Puerto Rico, and some of its main dilemmas. At the turn of the next century, Puerto Rican feminism will have arrived at a crossroads in its history. It is important to carefully assess women's social conditions and the challenges these conditions represent. This process will help feminists to better their theoretical perspectives, to strengthen women's faith in their struggle, to take the necessary steps to develop a strong, democratic, and pluralistic organization, and to define a utopian project for attaining a truly egalitarian, just, and free society.

There are two main currents of feminist action and ideology. First is a reformist tendency, which proposes that women will achieve equality within the present structure of society and is mainly preoccupied with the specific question of women's rights. Second is revolutionary feminism, which predicates not only equality but also the need for a society organized on very different principles. Of course, there is much diversity within these main currents as well as continuous debate between them. There are also men and women who negate feminism as a legitimate and liberating movement. They either believe that women are not subordinated to men and exploited, or that this is women's natural condition.

The main currents within which feminists are organized or through which concern over women's issues manifests itself are political parties or organizations, feminist organizations, and the incipient social movements that are developing in Puerto Rico, for example, anti-militarist and ecologist groups. Liberal feminists, socialists, and revolutionary feminists of varying degrees of radicalism have learned to co-exist; there are petit-bourgeois, working-class, and Christian feminists. There are also feminist cultural and professional groups such as the Association of Women Artists and the Women's Commission of the Puerto Rican Bar Association.

Women's and feminist organizations are also representative of widely different views. On the one hand, women are organized into groups like the *Damas Cívicas* where they get together to show off their stylish clothes and hats and organize philanthropic activities for "poor women" on Christmas Day and Mother's Day. Women are also organized within the Christian churches—Catholic and mainline Protestant—mainly as support groups. Many of these women are also very active in the right-wing political parties and in the Protestant fundamentalist sects.[2] There is also a small but growing number of Christian groups that follow liberation theology. These have organized women's groups that have become a significant new voice within Puerto Rican feminism. All political parties have women's support groups, except for the Puerto Rican Independence Party. Some labor unions have women's secretariats or committees. Women are a fundamental part of all community organizations and political action groups and often hold leadership positions. And of course, there are the small, but very militant, autonomous feminist groups and women's groups in academic, community, and service organizations. Puerto Rican women living in the United States have always been very active in the organizations and struggles of their communities.

Today Puerto Rican feminism is at a critical historical juncture which should lead to a re-evaluation of strategies and goals. It is necessary to attain a clearer and more political view of Puerto Rican society and of the part women are to play in it. I use the term political to describe social relations pertaining to power—political, therefore, in terms of an assessment of the role power structures play in what has been called our *"estado criollo."*[3] In this essay I will assess the role I believe women and feminism should play in the macro-political process of Puerto Rico.

The crisis of feminism

To understand the new political role for women it is necessary to understand first the crisis of feminism. The problem of identity is the first aspect of this crisis. Women have become aware, and have raised their voices to make the rest of society take notice, of many of the basic problems women face: violence against women by husbands, lovers, and friends causes many deaths and injuries every year; working women are becoming sick and even dying due to occupational and environmental hazards; Puerto Rico is much flaunted as an economically developed country, but its women remain the "poorest of the poor;"[4] women have won some political victories, but their political participation has remained at the token level.[5] However, becoming aware of these facts is not enough. To gain a clear identity, feminists must also understand the socio-historical processes within which these conditions have developed, and to become aware of the intimate and multiple ways in which these processes impinge on women's lives. This analysis will lead to an understanding of how these problems are interwoven into the fabric of society as a whole, and that therefore women's issues must be linked to macro-politics. An all-encompassing political perspective is needed; otherwise small victories will be granted, but women's subordination to men and discrimination against women will not be overcome. Empowerment will remain out of reach.

On the other hand, feminists must decide questions of strategy. Should their organizations remain small, more often than not auxiliary groups with short-term goals? Should their political action be subordinated to other interests? Or should feminism develop into a strong and autonomous social movement with long-term goals, a movement capable of acting in concert with other social movements without losing its own identity?

Another aspect of this crisis, closely bound to the first, is the need to create a historical project: a flexible but clear set of goals and strategies that women of different political persuasions can identify with, but which nevertheless has a progressive ideological content. As long as pro-independence women keep identifying women's liberation with pro-independence politics, they are destined to have a very marginal political voice. On the other hand, a woman's movement centered within and controlled by regressive politics[6] would never be able to overcome the incapacitating ballast of party interest and conservative ideology, debilitating and stultifying women's struggles.

Political sectarianism is another problem that must be conquered for it only leads to tribalism, in-fighting, and stagnation. Women should rise above traditional authoritarianism, the kind that is dominant in party politics controlled by men. Women must develop a new praxis, one that is unequivocally democratic. It is important to be able to distinguish between those issues on which there must be agreement if effective political action is to result, and those which are of a secondary nature or are simply irrelevant to the movement's main pursuits. Dogmatism must be overcome.

The lack of identity, of a clear political project, and of unity have prevented Puerto Rican feminists from consolidating into an authentic social movement. A social movement must have a principle of identity and also of opposition, in other words, a clear definition of its adversary. It must also espouse a principle of totality, a project of universal alternatives for the transformation of society.[7] The women's movement in Puerto Rico has been able to achieve some important triumphs and to hold its own with quite a strong voice in the national public debate, bringing some of the problems of women to the forefront of public awareness. In fact, feminism's voice has been much stronger than the movement's size would seem to render possible. Still, the problems mentioned hold the movement back from becoming a major political force in Puerto Rican society capable of becoming an essential and indispensable element in the transformation of society.

Women's political participation

In Puerto Rico, women's political participation takes place through political parties, labor unions, community and political action groups, government and private service establishments, and academic feminist organizations. Still, there are many problems women must face. Women strive within party structures to win broader participation but their situation isn't very auspicious. For instance, Senator Victoria Muñoz Mendoza of the Popular Democratic Party was asked if she thought the Puerto Rican people were ready to accept a woman as governor, as she has been often mentioned as a candidate. She believes the Puerto Rican people would have no qualms in accepting a woman as governor; it is rather a question of party machines and top leadership preventing the advancement of women's leadership.[8] Congresswoman and militant feminist Zaida Hernández of the New Progressive Party is also very critical of the position of political parties, including her own, towards broadening the participation of women. She believes that parties use women for everyday crucial but menial tasks, rather than letting them attain leadership positions. She has said that "if women were aware of their real strength, parties would tremble."[9]

As for the independence parties, the Puerto Rican Socialist Party has a very small Women's Commission that engages in traditional activities. Women active in the Puerto Rican Socialist Party are limited by the party's organizational weakness, as well as its insistence on orthodox structures, practice, and outlook. The Puerto Rican Independence Party, the largest pro-independence organization, recognizes that it has not been able to promote feminist leadership in party structures. President Rubén Berríos and Vice-President and Senator Fernando Martín believe there is nothing that can be done to remedy this situation, mainly because women must take care of their homes, children, and husbands. The Independence Party's retrograde position has not advanced in the last 20 years.[10]

The situation of women in their unions is even worse, particularly those unions which have a predominantly female membership. In Puerto Rico, 75 percent of public elementary and high school teachers are women. The Puerto Rican Teachers Federation organizes most of these teachers, yet its bylaws do not provide for a women's commission and leadership at all organizational levels is predominantly male. In the University of Puerto Rico Non-Teaching Workers Union, the Health Services Workers Union, and the Legal Aid Services Union, all of which also organize a majority of unionized women, the situation is more or less the same. Leadership is of a token nature and, as in political parties, women must work twice as hard as men to gain recognition and decision-making positions. Union leaders, who are predominantly male and very traditional and authoritarian, are frightfully scared of having to share leadership with women.

Women are also very active participants in community and political action groups. In certain ways, these groups are becoming schools for feminists. The main causes addressed by these groups are environmentalism, anti-militarism, and programs for adequate housing, health, recreation, and education. Wilfredo López Montañez, an organizer for Industrial Mission of Puerto Rico, is convinced by his experience with community organization and environmental struggles that women are an essential element for the success of his organization. He believes women are more committed, work harder than men, and are better organizers.[11] Most people in Puerto Rico who have worked with women share this view. Even an organization like the Puerto Rican Independence Party benefits from women's activism. Thirty percent of the party's grassroots-level committees have women presidents and the leadership admits that these are the committees that get the most and more effective political work done.

The government has established women's commissions at both the state and municipal levels, and the leaders of the Senate and House have consulting bodies on women's issues. The Commission for Women's Affairs, is under the governor's office and was created in 1973.

The main feminist organizations in Puerto Rico are *Feministas en Marcha* (Feminists on the March) which defines itself as "an alternate organization for political feminism"; the *Organización Puertorriqueña de la Mujer Trabajadora* (Puerto Rican Organization of Working Women) whose principal objective is "the feminist education of the working-class woman" and "to better the situation of working women and the working class in general in Puerto Rico"; and the *Taller Salud* (Health Workshop), whose main interest is to "offer guidance to women and develop among them an awareness of the critical health situation...[in Puerto Rico] and of the need to make health a major issue of [political] struggle."[12] These are all groups with a small core of militants and a somewhat larger group of followers. Yet in spite of this, their public activities are usually well-attended and their voice in public debate is quite significant.

There are also a good number of small, independent groups. Usually they meet at women's own homes and focus on consciousness-raising, feminist education, and offering support networks to women. Though these groups are generally short-lived, their work, seen as a whole and from a long-run perspective, will probably prove to be a significant element in the development of a feminist movement in Puerto Rico.

The other two primary forms of women's organization are service entities and research centers. Of the first, the most important are the *Casa Protegida Julia de Burgos* (Julia de Burgos Shelter), a shelter for battered women, and the *Centro de Ayuda a Víctimas de Violación*, a rape crisis center. Casa Julia is a privately run institution, the rape crisis center is run by the government health department.

Puerto Rico has two research centers devoted to women's issues, both at the University of Puerto Rico. Project CERES, *Centro Coordinador de Estudios, Recursos y Servicios a la Mujer* (Coordinating Center for Research, Resources, and Services for Women), is part of the Social Sciences Research Center in the Río Piedras campus and serves students and personnel, as well as the community. The Center for Women's Studies is located in the Cayey campus. It offers a women's studies program to students and promotes research on women's issues. Recently, it has developed a vigorous program to encourage and assist in the inclusion of women's issues in curricula.[13]

Thus, at the beginning of the last decade of the twentieth century, the women's movement is centered in political parties, labor unions, autonomous feminist organizations, and service, research, and resources centers. Women are very active, and their voices are being heard. They have recently won important battles such as legislation on sexual harassment in the workplace and criminalizing domestic violence and prompted public awareness on these issues. A women's movement definitely exists in Puerto Rico. But does its existence alone guarantee the development of a *feminist* movement? Is feminism an ideology that binds women into a cohesive social movement? These questions pose difficult problems that women have begun to discuss and ponder in Puerto Rico, as well as elsewhere in Latin America.[14]

At the waning of the twentieth century status debates have again intensified in Puerto Rico. So far, the only acknowledgement that women are part of the political population and should participate in this debate, or at least be taken into account, has come from the pro-statehood movement, one of the most conservative political forces in Puerto Rican society. A statehood leader has argued that women are in charge of "programming, conserving, and protecting their progeny. This is the inexorable mandate of natural law."[15] Therefore, he argues, since Puerto Rican society is in total disorder and statehood will bring a "well structured system, disciplined, organized, powerful..."[16] women, especially mothers, will vote for statehood.

If this discourse is analyzed, some of the basic myths underlying the subjugation of women can clearly be seen. Lukács explained how classes whose interest lies in perpetuating the existing order also have a vested interest in perpetuating the myths that justify their domination.[17] Sexism constitutes an umbrella of myths (see opening quote from Julia Kristeva) and these myths are among the cornerstones of capitalist society. The women's movement has first-hand knowledge of this process. Therefore, feminist and women's movements should be seen as a fundamental part of the revolutionary process of demythification, of deconstruction, that lays bare structures of domination and subordination.

Jane Flax has pointed out that, "From the perspective of social relations, men and women are both prisoners of gender, although in highly differentiated ways."[18] Present-day social movements may hold the key to these prison doors, and it is up to us to meet the challenge of learning how to open them. In Latin America, the process has already begun. Housewives, farm laborers, workers, African-Americans, and indigenous peoples are becoming Gramsci's philosophers—human beings who change the world as they change themselves in the dialectics of social relations.[19]

Feminists have a very serious responsibility. As their praxis unravels a mythologized reality, the process leads them to develop a new and different understanding of social relations, and concordantly, of history. Thus, feminism can provide a major contribution to the human sciences. But, a better understanding of society must also engender commitment—commitment to struggle, to convince others that it is possible to change as one becomes a part of a theory and a science and at the same time, to develop the ideology of a cohesive movement for social change.

This can be a dangerous adventure. Strong forces will oppose such a project. Néstor Braunstein believes that "science will encounter the cruel violence of the power structures when its explanations have a direct or indirect effect...when its consequences have an effect on relations of production."[20] Yet there is no other way to change society. Women must confront this violence and overcome it. Women must continue to develop feminism as a part of the human sciences, thus helping to understand the social relations women are a part of and helping to lay the theoretical foundation of the women's movement.

The new challenges of feminism in Puerto Rico

I believe that the women's movement in Puerto Rico is growing, but it has yet to transcend immediate and concrete issues and gain a stronger voice in mainstream politics. Feminism should lead the march for emancipation from patriarchy and, therefore, to a profound transformation of society.[21] As part of women's effort to become an integral and cardinal participant in the building of a new society, feminists should analyze the other problems that characterize present-day Puerto Rico. For example, contrary to the postulates of orthodox feminism, the incorporation of women into professional and industrial work has not necessarily led them to break their dependence on men. The particular context of Puerto Rico's worsening economic crisis indicates the limits women face in a third-world setting. Inflation, wide unemployment, and low salaries—combined with the growth of the number of women who head households—have promoted what economists have called the feminization of poverty in Puerto Rico.

Dependence and discrimination characterize the massive growth of the State bureaucracy in Puerto Rico. The State has become the principal employer on the island—and labor unions are prohibited in most government agencies. The multiplication of national and federal welfare programs, widespread migration to the United States, along with the government's population control program that imposes massive sterilization on women, are also important aspects of the widening role of the State. Feminist organizations have addressed massive sterilization and migration but mostly from a nationalistic and very dogmatic perspective. Feminist theorists need to listen to women, to understand them not solely as victims of colonialism, sexism, or men, but as social actors who within the totality of social relations in which they live and according to their own perceived interests, have decided on a particular and reasonable course of action. It is in this context that new options for women can be put forward.

Women must also take advantage of the feminist perspective to try to understand the wide-ranging deterioration of civil society. Rising crime rates, widespread drug abuse, a galloping AIDS epidemic (the percentage of women with AIDS in Puerto Rico is double that of the United States), functional and absolute illiteracy coupled with an incompetent public education system (see Chapter 11), an acute housing problem, and environmental problems which pose serious health hazards are only some of its most salient characteristics. A feminist political program must offer women, and society as a whole, strategies to overcome some of these concrete problems of everyday life.

Women have proven to be very creative. For example the intensification of the use of the media in Puerto Rico, specifically TV and videos, as instruments for the transmission of ideology is being addressed by the women's movement.[22] Awareness and wide debate of feminist and women's issues has been achieved. These accomplishments should be analyzed, for valuable lessons can be learned from them.

The general socio-economic crisis on the island has reached a point at which it poses a threat to women's very survival and turns everyday problems into political ones. As a result, the government, along with right-wing parties and organizations, are co-opting traditional feminist goals and objectives and even reproducing feminist discourse, in a decontextualized, deformed, and manipulative effort. Thus, women are facing a process that might be called the nationalization of feminism—a process that tries to domesticate feminism and render it ineffectual. Small concessions are made to women, but feminism as a force that promotes a new society is abolished. This nationalization has transformed feminism into a mass culture farce.[23]

To successfully face such challenges, a main objective of feminism should be to achieve a diverse, autonomous movement, capable of bringing together women of different races, classes, and political persuasions. Women must understand that these distinctions are important to historical and politico-sociological analysis, as well as long-run strategies, but can be detrimental to immediate and effective political action leading to significant and advantageous changes in women's lives. Progressive Puerto Rican women must learn that they can struggle for socialism and independence through their political parties and organizations, but as feminists, they struggle in organizations in which they should not impose a particular political ideology. Of course, within these feminist organizations, as within labor unions and community action groups, they can exert a progressive influence. There is certainly a very fine line between imposing and persuading, and between pro-independence politics and progressive ideology. However, that line does exist, and if women aspire to build a strong feminist movement in Puerto Rico, women must find that balance. It is also important to understand that political action groups, social movements, and the feminist movement have distinct processes. Sometimes they come together, but at other times they follow different paths. Each has its own rhythms and diverse

diverse functions in women's struggles and in the transformation of society. Women have a role to play in all of them.

Another challenge Puerto Rican feminists face stems from the difficulties middle-class and working-class women have had in working together. Middle-class women, and especially socialists, have usually been arrogant and maternalistic in their approach to working-class women. Women from the popular segments of the population are the most grossly wounded by the problems of Puerto Rico, and their particular situation provides insights that more privileged women should take into consideration. Privileged, educated, and theoretical perspectives dialectically joined with the concrete experience of working-class women will engender a more fruitful movement. In the long run, as feminism advances we will sharpen our understanding and move towards more advanced positions. Women who feel their class interests threatened will on their own disengage themselves from these struggles.

Women cannot be successful if they reproduce the authoritarian, anti-democratic practices that have weakened progressive political organizations in Puerto Rico. Women in political parties, academia, unions, and feminist organizations have been adamant in their democratic demands. In patriarchal society, women have been subjected to authoritarianism. They are not willing to participate in yet another anti-democratic organization which, after all, can be quite ineffective. Ours is an authoritarian and undemocratic society. How can a truly democratic society be built through undemocratic organizations?

The exercise of power is mediated by gender as well as class and race. Within our gender definitions, the exercise of power is a masculine prerogative. This, of course, makes power politics an improper sphere for women. Senator Velda González of the Popular Democratic Party in a recent interview faced this fact when she first arrived at the Legislature.[24] She was uncomfortable and felt that her inexperience in the exercise of power was a disadvantage. She was unfamiliar with the work styles common to legislative politics and it was very hard for her to participate. González was pointing to a problem all women who have become involved in politics have had to face: they must either be silent, or adopt problematic approaches to power and decision-making that men usually use, such as authoritarianism, shouting down your opponent, submission to the "leader," back-room deliberations and decisions, and locker-room language. But women can also create a feminine approach to new work styles.

Ideally, in their daily lives, women are flexible, democratic, prefer to debate over concrete and not about abstract issues, and make decisions in open forums and not in locker rooms. Too often, men exercise power as an instrument of domination, from a patriarchal perspective. They love to hear themselves talk, even if they have nothing to say. In contrast, women's personal life practices provide a better basis for the participation and creativity so badly needed in politics.

Women in Puerto Rico continue to face many problems in their daily lives. Rapidly developing technology offers women efficient options for reproductive control and yet, they must still fight the same old battles against the Church and the State, which insist on exercising control over women's bodies. Women still bear unwanted children and often confront domestic violence. Some women now have access to education and jobs their grandmothers wouldn't have dreamt of, yet most women are still slaves to the drudgery of domestic work.[25] Women who have found a place of their own in the job market work for lower salaries than what men earn. Women fight for their rights as workers and citizens, but still unions and political parties preclude women's full participation.

Feminists have many different answers to these problems, answers which are sometimes also contradictory. If they are to truly change their world, women must build the road towards a coherent, unified movement, yet one that is also pluralistic. Women must keep fighting for concrete, immediate vindications, but at the same time create their own place in the macro-political world. After all, women's issues are in a true sense *human* issues. As long as feminists continue to place themselves only in the micropolitical arena (or let themselves be kept there), they can only force the patriarchal political system to grant them "rewards" every so often. Nevertheless, feminists will never become a part of the new social movements which, within a framework of a new political action that questions traditional power politics, are struggling to change power relations.

If feminism grows into a vigorous social movement, if we struggle to produce new concepts, a new understanding of the human situation, the arrows Julia Kristeva speaks of will also be felt by the men and women who become social actors in this struggle. Feminists must believe, though, that these wounds will heal, that survival in a new world is possible. Because, as we are learning across Latin America, this process can finally lead towards humanizing society, towards a re-evaluation of human potential towards recapturing subjectivity and understanding the importance of personal change in the construction of the social subject.[26] As feminists, we will lead to the creation of a society in which art, knowledge, science, wealth, and technology will be resources with which we may liberate human feelings and creativity. This goal must become part and parcel of our present-day feminist utopia.

The Puerto Rican Labor Movement in the 1990s

Carlos Alá Santiago-Rivera

For many years now, labor leaders in Puerto Rico have supported the independence movement, while the workers themselves have belonged to the traditional colonial parties. Very often, the absence of consensus on controversial issues relating to the status of the island within the union membership has prevented its leadership from expressing any particular position. This long-standing political divide might not change in the near future. During the recent plebiscite debates, the labor movement revealed its inability to take a position. This essay will discuss some of the most pressing issues facing the Puerto Rican labor movement during the 1990s, with particular emphasis on the effect of industrial restructuring on unions' organizing ability.

Industrial restructuring, as I discuss it, describes the process of radical technological innovation that has taken place in leading productive sectors, transforming the organization of work, the way labor power is used, and the production process itself. Although these changes have not been felt in most of the traditional industries, they clearly have affected high-technology industries such as electronics and pharmaceuticals. Industrial restructuring is spreading rapidly throughout the financial sector and has begun to take root in public corporations such as the Electric Energy Authority, the Public Television Station, and the Communications Authority.

In Puerto Rico, industrial restructuring involves automation, computerization, satellite telecommunications between parent companies and their subsidiaries, and the introduction of microelectronics, robotics, and other technologies on the shop floor. These innovations take place in the context of a new system of labor control that I term the qualitative rationalization of work. Managers use "the development of workers' potential" as a strategy

143

Table 1: Employment Growth in Some Economic Sectors, 1980-90

Employment	1980 (thousands)	1990 (thousands)	Increase (percent)
Finance, insurance and real estate	21	33	57.0
Manufacturing	143	153	7.0
Services (including hotels)	135	156	15.0
Transportation and other public utilities	47	45	-.5
Trade (wholesale and retail)	138	128	-.8
Construction	44	42	-.5
Public Administration	202	211	.5

to co-opt workers, making it harder for them to identify with organized labor.

At the same time, this corporate rhetoric is being echoed by the State, deepening the ideological reach of the so-called "industrial modernization." The government presents this process as a universal remedy for improving productivity, one that will make the island more competitive on the international market and create more and better jobs, as well as producing a myriad of other socio-economic benefits. In this view, unions are outmoded structures that oppose progress, block development, create rigidly adversarial labor relations, fail to organize part-time workers, and do not offer concrete benefits to the new worker elites.

The reluctance of many labor leaders to share decision-making power in their unions contributes to the political stagnation of island unions and to lost opportunities for organizing new shops. As a result, the legitimacy of organized labor is now in question by liberals, who at one time were known for their solidarity with unions.

Labor movement activists face many problems, all grounded in present-day realities: first, whether to defend marginal and unproductive industries, given the potential impact of new models of economic development on the production base of the island (see Chapters 6 and 7); second, whether to challenge the traditional political parties by organizing their own; third, whether to agree to more flexible forms of work organization, giving in to management's accusation that unions lower productivity and create economic stagnation; fourth, how to respond to technological change, in light

Table 2: Percentage Organized Workers in Trade Unions by Industry (1970-90)			
Industrial Group	1970	1980	1990
All industries	20	11	6
Agriculture	29	10	a
Construction	17	6	a
Manufacture	30	19	9
Trade	6	3	1
Transportation, Communication and Public Utilities	61	50	95
Services	20	9	4
Public Administration	7	5	2

a. Too few cases for a certain estimate.

SOURCE: Labor Department, Bureau of Statistics, Division of Group Workers.

of its impact on relations of production and the organization of work. These dilemmas and realities are by no means all the elements in the picture, but they are useful as a conceptual framework for analyzing the situation in Puerto Rico.

The labor movement must develop some concrete strategies to counteract the capitalist offensive that is clearly underway. On the one hand, subcontracting, privatization, "teamwork," and part-time employment undermine union organizing; on the other hand, demands for "flexibilization," merging job classifications, and other tactics aimed at protecting individual employees threaten union power. Unions need to re-evaluate and democratize their internal structures in order to respond effectively to the challenge. "Democratic centralism" and "efficiency" without real grassroots participation are no longer successful strategies.

Economic restructuring and the labor movement

The situation faced by organized labor in Puerto Rico began to change with the stagnation of the populist economic development model of the 1950s and 1960s. Since the 1950s, government promoted industrialization and North American investment by offering tax exemptions, low wages, and a cooperative and highly productive labor force. The program, called Operation

Table 3: Strike Activity
1971-1989

Period	Number of strikes per year	Average workers in strike per year	Average person-days lost in strikes per year
1986-1989	7.7	574	15,541
1981-1985	11.4	2,988	108,122
1976-1980	32.6	9,011	268,284
1971-1975	85.6	19,688	313,810

SOURCE: Department of Labor, Bureau of Arbitration.

Bootstrap, encouraged labor-intensive manufacturing and resulted in a rapid change in Puerto Rico's productive base. Undoubtedly, this transformation, along with the taylorist or fordistic organization of work that these industries instituted, stimulated the development of the Puerto Rican labor movement.

Unemployment remained a stumbling block, and the government proved unable to reduce it without increasing the public-sector labor force. Its efforts to industrialize generated only 102,000 manufacturing jobs in the 1970s, while 179,000 jobs were lost in agriculture alone. More than 20 percent of the labor force remained unemployed despite the "elephantiasis" of the public sector, which hired almost 100,000 new employees between 1970 and 1988. Meanwhile, despite the doubling of the island's GNP, real salaries of Puerto Ricans stagnated.

As one way of dealing with the unemployment crisis, the government began transforming the island's industrial structure, shifting its support to capital-intensive manufacturing industries such as pharmaceutical plants and electronics firms. Also during this period, service, and financial sectors enjoyed substantial growth: 15 percent, and 57 percent respectively (see Table 1).

Within the capital-intensive manufacturing sector the above-mentioned industries generally have a participatory organization of work, with wage scales far above the local norm and close linkages to the international market. These characteristics have helped these industries thwart almost every single union organizing effort. Clearly, the expansion of these industries induced the steady decline in union membership and the neutralization of the labor movement's political influence. During the 1970s, the labor movement achieved some autonomy from the Popular Democratic Party

Table 4: Employment by Industrial Sector and Sex, Fiscal Years 1970 and 1988

Industry	1970	1988	Percent Change 1970-88
Total Employment	685,270	873,400	1.4
Men	471,520	533,000	0.7
Women	213,750	340,400	2.6
Women as % of total	31.19	39.00	1.2
Agric., Forestry, and Fishing	68,250	31,000	-4.3
Men	65,750	29,700	-4.3
Women	2,500	1,300	-3.6
Women as % of total	3.66	4.19	0.7
Miners and Construction	77,030	48,800	-2.5
Men	76,047	47,780	-2.5
Women	983	1,020	0.2
Women as % of total	1.28	2.10	2.8
Manufacture	132,490	157,000	0.9
Men	68,940	83,400	1.1
Women	63,550	73,600	0.8
Women as % of total	48.00	46.90	-0.1
Not durable goods	96,520	98,000	0.1
Men	43,500	49,400	0.7
Women	53,020	48,600	-0.5
Women as % of total	54.93	49.60	-0.6
Durable goods	35,970	59,000	2.8
Men	25,440	34,000	1.6
Women	10,530	25,000	4.9
Women as % of total	35.42	42.37	1
Trans., Communications, & Public Utilities	45,180	50,800	0.6
Men	40,850	43,100	0.3
Women	4,330	7,700	3.2
Women as % of total	958	15.16	2.6
Trade	128,120	173,000	1.7
Men	93,840	119,900	1.4
Women	34,280	53,100	2.5
Women as % of total	26.76	30.69	0.8
Finance, Insurance & Real Estate	13,070	30,000	4.7
Men	8,180	14,760	3.3
Women	4,890	15,240	6.5
Women as % of total	37.41	50.8	1.7

continued on next page

Domestic Services	41,838	31,700	-1.5
Men	16,432	15,350	-0.4
Women	25,406	16,350	-2.4
Women as % of total	60.72	51.58	-0.9
Entertainment	8,060	8,740	0.4
Men	6,320	7,200	0.7
Women	1,740	1,540	-0.7
Women as % of total	21.59	17.62	-1.1
Professional Services	46,050	98,800	4.3
Men	19,430	35,455	3.4
Women	26,620	63,345	4.9
Women as % of total	57.81	64.11	0.6
Government	105,680	200,800	3.6
Men	57,130	97,450	3
Women	48,550	103,350	4.3
Women as % of total	45.94	51.47	0.6

SOURCE: Housing Sample. Angel L. Ruíz, "Changes in pattern of feminine employment". Unidad de Investigaciones Económicas, november 1989. p.13

(*Partido Popular Democrático,* or PPD). Independent Puerto Rican unions competed with U.S. internationals to represent workers. Between 1965 and 1969, 51 percent of the unions which won NLRB-supervised elections were AFL-CIO locals. A decade later, independent unions won 45.6 percent, while the share of AFL-CIO affiliates had dropped to 38.6 percent.

The Puerto Rican labor movement took an important step towards overcoming its historic fragmentation in the 1980s. The formation of the Committee of Union Organizations (*Comité de Organizaciones Sindicales,* or COS) is the strongest expression of trade-union unity since the 1940s (see Table # 6 at the end of this essay). The COS is made up of three labor confederations, with three different ideological leanings. The leftist confederation is the General Workers' Council (*Concilio General de Trabajadores,* or CGT), with nine member unions. The second is the Puerto Rican Workers' Central (*Central Puertorriqueña de Trabajadores,* or CPT), a social-democratic, "anticommunist and anticapitalist" international labor confederation. It is affiliated with the CLAT (*Central Latinoamericana de Trabajadores*), and has 16 member unions. The last confederation is the Labor Federation of Puerto Rico (*Federación del Trabajo de Puerto Rico,* or FTPR), formerly the AFL-CIO's Central Labor Council on the island. The CGT is independent, and the CPT has been regarded as the labor wing of the Puerto Rican Independence Party, while the FTPR follows the standard AFL-CIO practice of "backing our friends and punishing our enemies" in the Legislature. The

COS also includes some seven independent public-sector unions (generally led by UTIER, the Electrical and Irrigation Employees Union), eight independent private-sector unions, and four government employee associations which are not recognized as unions and cannot legally go on strike, but do negotiate "understandings" *(cartas contractuales)* with the government.

In spite of these gains in labor unity, the membership and militancy of the labor movement as a whole has not recovered from the industrial restructuring of the 1970s or the rivalry between the independents and the internationals. The proportion of unionized workers dropped from 20 percent in 1970 to 6 percent in 1990, and shows no signs of levelling off (see Table 2). This drop is most evident in agriculture, manufacturing, and construction, where the battle between independents and internationals took place, and the percentage of organized workers dropped. Labor militancy also fell dramatically, even in the public sector which showed some signs of vitality in the early 1970s (see Table 3). Of the 591 strikes held during that decade, 428 took place between 1971 and 1975, with the number falling off sharply from then on.

Puerto Rican labor unions, finding themselves unable to effectively organize private firms, have concentrated their efforts on the public sector. Transportation, communications, and public utilities have a significant percentage of organized workers, with 45 percent union membership at last count (see Table 2). However, considering the substantial growth of the public sector (nearly 100,000 new employees, as several public corporations were created and others expanded), organizing has stagnated. Union membership in that industry dropped from 61 percent in 1970 to 45 percent in 1990.

At the same time, although services, commerce, and manufacturing accounted for some 61 percent of the island's total employment, unionization rates have dropped steadily since the 1970s. Only 1 percent of the 128,000 commercial workers and 4 percent of the 156,000 service employees were union members in 1988. Of the three sectors, manufacturing shows the sharpest drop in percentage of union members: from 30 percent in 1970 to just 9 percent in 1990.

Challenges to the labor movement

The labor movement faces a two-fold challenge in organizing the manufacturing sector. On the one hand, new strategies must be developed to organize capital-intensive industries. On the other, the labor movement needs to generate new structures to organize small manufacturing workplaces. As argued before, capital-intensive industries represent the fastest growing industrial sector and there is a growing awareness among labor leaders

Table 5: Arbitration in Puerto Rico
1979 - 1989

Fiscal Year	Number Of Cases			Workers Involved		
	Public	Private	Total	Public	Private	Total
1989	882	642	1,524	93,261	9,307	102,568
1979	685	843	1,528	8,372	16,569	24,941
Difference	+127	-201	-4	+84,889	-7,262	+77,627

SOURCE: Department of Labor, Bureau of Arbitration. Fiscal years 1979-80 to 1988-89.

of the need to organize this sector. However, small firms traditionally have been regarded as not worth the effort and expense needed to organize them. By 1988, 49.5 percent of manufacturing shops employed fewer than 20 people. It is common knowledge that these firms are grossly unfair to their workers and that receptivity to union organizing is high. It is crucial that the labor movement study capital-intensive industries and small firms by promoting and/or sponsoring related labor research both in-house and outside the union structures.

Labor organizations need to overcome their traditional sexism to organize women (see Chapter 6). Women accounted for 48 percent of all manufacturing employment in 1988, and represent a high percentage of total employment in both traditional and capital-intensive manufacturing firms. In this regard, Angel L. Ruíz concludes that "Between 1970 and 1988, total employment rose by 188,130. Sixty-seven percent of this increase (126,650) was accounted for by women.... In 1970, female employment was 31.2 percent of total employment on the island. By 1988 this percentage increased to 39 percent." Table 4 reflects that the average rate of growth in women's employment is considerably higher than the same figure for the employment of men. If this trend continues, by 1992 the percentage of women employed will have grown to 41.2 percent of the total. Women have a strong presence in those sectors that constitute the greatest organizing challenge for the labor movement: 42.3 percent in manufacturing, 30.6 percent in commerce, and 50.8 percent in banking. Thus the need for labor to create a strategy oriented toward women workers is clear.

Challenges to the public sector

In the public sector, unions have dedicated themselves to winning the right of union membership for all employees. Permitting all public employees to join unions could add more than 200,000 workers to union ranks, which would significantly strengthen the labor movement. Despite being a campaign promise of the colonial PPD and its rival the New Progressive Party (*Partido Nuevo Progresista,* PNP) in every election from 1972 to 1984, the political consequences of building public-sector unions have made it impossible to carry out. In the face of the government's refusal to allow public-sector unions, the labor movement has founded alternative organizations like bona fide associations, brotherhoods, and so on. In 1990, 14 percent of the labor force was organized in such organizations. If these associations are added to the percentage of formal union membership, 20 percent of the labor force is organized. (see Table 2).

Finally, most union efforts are taken up not by organizing, but through arbitration. The number of cases in arbitration remained steady from 1979 to 1989, with 1,528 and 1,524 cases respectively, submitted in each of those years. The importance of those cases increased considerably, however, because the total number of workers involved was 24,941 in 1979 as compared with 102,568 in 1989. As Table 5 shows, arbitration came to be more widely used in the public sector, while both the number of cases and the number of workers involved in arbitration in the private sector dropped. The increasing importance of arbitration in the public sector is indicative of new management strategies. If the government succeeds in generalizing them, profound changes in the organization of work would result at the expense of union power. Some labor leaders have expressed privately that the greatest conflicts are related to "flexibilization" (either restructuring of the appropriate unit or revision of job classifications), introduction of new technology (retraining, replacement, or relocation of workers), new union demands for health and safety standards (meaning multimillion-dollar investments by the government), and indiscriminate subcontracting. The Electric Power Authority employees have been in conflict with management over subcontracting and job-classification issues arising from asbestos removal in electric power plants. Their struggle exemplifies the challenges to the labor movement in the present context.

The electrical workers' dilemma: flexibilization or subcontracting

The Electrical and Irrigation Employees' Union (*Unión de Trabajadores de la Industria Eléctrica y de Riego,* or UTIER) faces a terrible organizational dilemma. Its most recent contract—signed for the period July 1, 1985-June 30, 1989 and in effect until a new contract is negotiated—includes ambiguous wording on subcontracting that has allowed the Electric Power Authority to subcontract much of its work. UTIER has submitted several amendments to the contract that would more closely regulate subcontracting. If the Authority wants to subcontract work that would normally be assigned to a particular unit, it would have to: 1) state which specialized equipment the work requires, and why the acquisition of such equipment would not be justified; 2) state what skilled personnel would be required; and 3) show that the work is in fact non-recurring. A further amendment stipulates that if a subcontracting issue were brought before a third party and deemed unjustifiable, the Authority would have to compensate the union for 100 percent of the subcontractor's labor costs.

The Electric Power Authority wants subcontracting provisions to remain unchanged. Management presented two alternatives for the development of a "plan to totally revise the current evaluation system" included in the contract's article on job reclassification. The first involves a classification study by outside consultants, whose recommendations would be final and cannot be appealed; the second would involve the creation of a job reclassification committee made up of two members each from both management and labor. Either way, it is clear that the Authority intends to negotiate a "flexibilization" of job classifications. UTIER's dilemma is clear: Should the union try to stem the subcontracting tide by agreeing to the likely broadening and merging of job classifications that would result from the Authority's new proposals?

The subcontracting dispute is aggravated by the discovery of asbestos in the Authority's generating plants. Asbestos removal generated a controversy in 1989, involving issues of occupational safety and security, subcontracting, and job security. The Authority and the union signed an agreement in July 1989, defining the areas of asbestos exposure and setting forth procedures for operation, preventive maintenance, asbestos removal, and emergency work procedures. The agreement stated that UTIER members' work schedules would be respected in all cases.

Asbestos removal was temporarily overshadowed by the emergency caused by Hurricane Hugo in September 1989 (which cost the lives of five UTIER members who were clearing and reinstalling power lines). In January

1990, the Authority violated the July agreement, laying off 170 temporary workers in the San Juan and Caguas metropolitan areas, and reassigning others from the Palo Seco thermoelectric generating plant—one of UTIER's strongest and most militant bases of support—to other parts of the island. Asbestos removal was subcontracted to private companies.

The lessons from the UTIER case are straightforward. The use of subcontracting to undermine unions is becoming widespread in public corporations and several other public-sector unions are facing similar situations. Many public sector unions, like UTIER, while still negotiating subcontracting clauses have succeeded in "protecting" job classifications and assignments. They have not, however, limited the number of subcontracted employees. The end result is that organized job classifications do not increase, while other non-union and managerial positions do. Public sector unions have learned that with subcontracting, union influence wanes.

Economic restructuring and union organizing

Puerto Rico's economy experienced a massive restructuring process over the past 20 years. Some labor-intensive or light manufacturing industries have disappeared, and so have most oil refineries. These traditional manufacturing sectors have been replaced by high-technology industries like pharmaceutical and electronics firms. Workers in these industries enjoy better salaries and working conditions than in the traditional manufacturing sector, which makes them difficult to organize. The past two decades have also seen the decline of construction and agriculture, where union support had been strong, and the expansion of the service, banking, and commercial sectors, which have historically been removed from union activity.

The labor movement must expand its agenda in order to be attractive to women workers and other professional employees who form a substantial part of the labor force. Unions should finance studies of the new rationalization of work in order to develop alternative union organization techniques in step with the times. In the capital-intensive industries, unions must develop a new discourse, one geared toward the issues raised by the changed work organization. Research must be done to prove that these industries pollute the environment, disrupt the island's ecological balance, and represent significant health risks for workers. Labor organizing must become professionalized to serve the interests of workers in small firms and to effectively organize the new production workers. If unions don't develop a new discourse, they will systematically be reduced to maintenance, competing for already organized shops, and will play a progressively less important role throughout the island.

Because of these changes, the focus of union organizing has shifted to the public sector. Yet, organizing possibilities in the public sector seem to have been exhausted. The public sector's growth potential, from the labor movement's point of view, depends on new legislation, which seems very unlikely in the near future. Mobilizing popular support for workers' right to organize unions in the public sector should become a high priority for the labor movement.

The political consensus of the 1950s, with its populist ideology, has not carried through to the 1990s. The traditional political parties no longer see the labor movement as a necessary ally for maintaining electoral power. The growing Puerto Rican state apparatus has expanded political control at the expense of social responsibility, using mechanisms such as subcontracting and privatization of public corporations to undermine union influence. As we have seen in the case of the UTIER, through subcontracting, the government is undermining the development of unions in the public sector. The end result is that organized job classifications stagnate while other non-union and managerial positions are expanding. Currently, workers organized in the two public telephone companies (Puerto Rican Telephone Company and Communications Authority) are facing job insecurity because the government is in the process of selling these companies to the private sector. Although this action took the labor movement by surprise, unions reacted promptly with a national strike to stop the selling of the agencies. However, it is not clear to what extent labor can change the government privatization policy. Unions need to study the transformation of the managerial strategy and technological innovations taking place in the public sector corporations. They also need to organize "political" networks and action committees with other constituencies to have a real impact.

In the private sector, management has intensified its campaign against trade unionism. For instance, the hotel industry, a traditional labor stronghold and one of the most solvent and best able to absorb the costs of improving working conditions, has unleashed multimillion-dollar campaigns against unions. Unions' ability to pressure management in the hotel industry has declined significantly.

Knowledge of the new industries and their internal contradictions has become absolutely necessary to organizing workers. A new organizing "pitch" will have to be developed for the banking, commerce, and service sectors. The new labor discourse should take into account the great technological changes now taking place and their effect on workers' lives and feelings. Finally, unions must begin to develop links to workers in unorganized sectors as diverse as the "underground economy" of street-corner vendors and the self-employed, and to non-union associations such as the

Policemen's Association, the professional medical interns groups, and the supervisors associations that are growing rapidly throughout the island.

Table 6: Labor Bodies Affiliated to Trade Union Organizations Committee (COS)

Comite De Organizaciones Sindicales (COS)

Concilio General de Trabajadores (CGT)
Unión General de Trabajadores
Federación de Maestros de P.R.
Unión Independiente de Trabajadores de Servicios Legales
Hermandad de Empleados Exentos No Docentes de la UPR
Unión Nacional de Trabajadores de la Salud
Unión Independiente de Empleados de la Autoridad de
    Comunicaciones
Asociación Puertorriqueña de Profesores Universitarios
Union Independiente de Empleados del Departamento del Trabajo

Central Puertorriqueña de Trabajadores (CPT)

Unión Empleados Profesionales de la AEE
Unión Independiente Auténtica de la AAA
Unión Independiente Empleados Autoridad de Edificios Públicos
Unión Empleados Compañía de Fomento Industrial
Unión Empleados Comisión Industrial
Hermandad Empleados Junta de Retiro para Maestros
Confederación Laborista de Puerto Rico
Hermandad Independiente de Empleados
Profesionales de la AAA
Unión Trabajadores Banco de la Vivienda
Unión de Trabajadores de la Construcción de la AAA
Sindicato de Trabajadores de la UPR
Unión de Trabajadores Industriales
Unión Independiente Empleados Banco Gubernamental de Fomento
Unión de Auditores de la AAA
Confederación Unida de Trabajadores Estatales

Organizaciones Bonafide

UTIER
Unión del Fondo del Seguro del Estado
Unión de Empleados de la Corporación de Credito Agrícola
Asociación de Inspectores de Juegos de Azar
Unión Independiente Empleados de la ACAA
Unión Independiente Empleados Telefónicos
Unión de Empleados Profesionales y Clericales de la Autoridad de
    Edificios Públicos

A Community-Based Approach to Educational Reform in Puerto Rico

Ana María García Blanco
José Javier Colón Morera

Impoverished Puerto Rican communities cannot wait any longer for top-down educational reform. The mediocre conditions of the public schools that serve the barrios, the *caseríos* (public-housing projects), and poor rural areas keep the children of these communities from benefiting from educational advancement, marginalized from any kind of meaningful socio-economic progress.

While the Puerto Rican government spent eight years and millions of dollars working on the legislative definition of educational reform, communities of the island have been dealing pragmatically and creatively with a mediocre public educational system. This essay is about these emerging community-based efforts to restructure the learning process at the school level with the collaboration and active support of students and parents, those individuals who are going to be the main beneficiaries of school reform.

Puerto Rican society as a whole manifests extremely high levels of dissatisfaction with the present conditions of our public educational system. The roots of discontent are simple: a drop-out rate of about 50 percent, alarmingly low levels of academic achievement and motivation, excessive bureaucratization and centralization at the administrative level, endless infighting among political parties, and so on.[1] The educational system is failing to prepare the majority of Puerto Rican youth to assume the future direction of the island and, by default, is fomenting anti-social, criminal, and drug-related activities. It is almost impossible to visualize a productive Puerto Rican society in the future without, among other reforms, a radical transformation of its educational system.

In this article we present a reformist agenda for the school system that is rooted in community service, and closely tied to the need of expanding the political, social, and cultural empowerment of those communities. We propose a process that visualizes school change as a constructing, decolonizing, and liberating experience. We will discuss the emergence of this community-based agenda in contrast to, and within the larger context of, the current attempts by the Puerto Rican government to revamp the educational system. Recently enacted, the Educational Reform Law defines the policy of the Commonwealth of Puerto Rico regarding public education.[2] The law establishes new layers of bureaucratic accountability, declares Spanish as the primary language of instruction,[3] and creates school councils composed of parents, teachers, and students intended to foment school autonomy, among other things.

In this essay we will briefly mention some aspects of the new school reform law, contrasting it with the community-based model we propose. Although the new legislation has been praised for its humanistic approach to the learning dynamic and for presenting a more participatory structure, we will underscore that some of its contradictory features still make participation and humanistic education difficult to achieve. For example, even though parents and teachers will be represented in the new school councils, it is important to highlight that, in general, there was a notorious lack of parental participation in the negotiations that led to this legislation. Also, the voices of the young students who are leaving schools were left out. It is ironic that the so-called reform movement alienates those who are supposed to be its main beneficiaries, thus "inheriting" the harmful practices that govern the Department of Education. Until the approval of this new Department of Education's Organic Act, this office was called the Department of Instruction, implying that the system was mostly interested in promoting the acquisition of basic skills and not education, broadly defined.

The law is also intended to foment so-called "critical thinking" learning skills and curriculum revisions. However, we have serious doubts that change will come from its top-down enforcement,[4] when powerful school administrators do not agree and do not promote change through their day-to-day practice.

The case of the New School in Barrio Juan Domingo of Guaynabo is a community-based model of educational reform. In our view, the consolidation of a community empowerment process intended to encourage the active involvement of parents and community organizations in the policy-making and implementation roles at the school level is the only long-term guarantee of a meaningful school reform. In this sense, a significant part of the revamping effort has to occur outside of the formal schooling structures.

We believe the best avenue for generating structural transformation is the "clients" of the system, who see their children fail year after year in the hands of ill-prepared and ill-motivated teachers. In other words, parents should help to define an educational program that is relevant and useful to their communities. The system is presently failing the majority of poor and working-class families at disproportionate rates.

The New School in Juan Domingo

Juan Domingo, an urban barrio in the San Juan metropolitan area, is an example of the critical and chaotic conditions of schooling, and the feasibility as well as the impediments of renovating community-based initiatives.[5] In Juan Domingo, about 18 years ago, a movement started to promote academic achievement to create a better atmosphere in which to conduct academic and extracurricular activities. Parents, students, and teachers, with the support of the nearby more affluent neighborhoods, have established a public library, tutoring programs, youth groups, drug-prevention programs through direct contact with the barrio, a preschool program, street theater, and positions for social workers and music groups.

This initiative started in the 1960s as a project of socially conscious Catholics who were troubled by the lack of educational and cultural institutions and incentives in Juan Domingo. In conducting *catecismos* (catechism circles) they recognized the need for a continued socially responsive commitment to education.

While the Juan Domingo project was flourishing, the public schools in the area degenerated, dropping programs in the sciences, physical education, music, and art. One of the public schools that served the barrio was closed because of poor physical conditions, a shortage of teachers and curriculum offerings, high dropout rates, and low enrollment. The community fought for three years for its reopening. Ultimately, the community opened the Juan Ponce de León public school under the direction of a school council in which parents, teachers, students, and the principal are members.

The experience of the people of Juan Domingo illustrates how community-based activism is responding to mediocre schooling. Theirs is a concrete and effective local response to the well-recognized educational crisis throughout the island.

In the next section we will present some important aspects of that broader crisis. We want to create greater consciousness of the depth of the problems we now face, and the shallowness of governmental alternatives, the top-down approach. In contrast, the proposals that community-based groups are putting forth are not only more far-reaching, but also real, in motion and in harmony with the people who feel alienated from the current educational structure.

The educational crisis

Parents are concerned and dissatisfied with the less-than-adequate conditions of island schools. Parents are specifically dissatisfied with crowded classrooms (often 30 students in a section) and the resulting inability of teachers to establish meaningful relationships; the pervasive presence of a bureaucracy that prevents the implementation of urgently needed services; inadequate special-needs programs; scarcity of books and other teaching materials; deteriorating physical conditions, and so forth.[6]

The island's fiscal crisis is affecting not only the conditions of existing school facilities, but is also provoking potentially more damaging consequences: the permanent closing of many schools all around the island. In 1990, just before the beginning of the new academic year, the Department of Education announced that it was contemplating closing 100 schools as a budget-saving device. The schools that would be most affected by those decisions were in poor, marginal barrios, where people have been uninformed of the government's strategy.[7] As far as we know, the Department of Education did not make any meaningful attempt to integrate the affected communities or parent organizations in a dialogue to seek alternate ways to face the budget crunch or, at least, to decrease the impact of those harsh decisions.

Additionally, there has been a lack of public information as to which and how many schools were finally closed. In the midst of legislative-reform declarations on the need to decentralize the decision-making process and to encourage school autonomy, the realities of bureaucratic centralization and paternalism proved to be alive and kicking.

The centralized and authoritarian decision-making process that characterizes the Department of Education is generally kept out of the public spotlight. Only the powerful and very conservative *Asociación de Maestros* (Teachers Association), a highly centralized and bureaucratic association that is itself a major financial contributor to the *Partido Popular Democrático* (PPD), is able to influence the internal decision-making process of the Department of Education. In Puerto Rico, as in many other places, the political structure of organizations has been a major impediment for radical transformation.[8]

Puerto Ricans have always been eager to show how much they value education. Government reports emphasize how almost one-third of the island's local budget is spent on education, around one billion dollars of joint federal and Commonwealth funds. We realize, however, that money alone —insufficient as it is to cover current needs— is not creating even minimally satisfactory levels of education. The limited financial resources are misplaced, far away from the nerve center of the educational experience, far from the school (the basic unit of the education system under the terms of the new legislation). Worse, school officials have have few options for allocating resources in order to strengthen direct services to students.

In 1976, the Commission on Educational Reform released a report showing that only 52 percent out of every 100 students registered in the first grade reached high school. Less than half of the population that enters school finishes a high-school degree and moves on to college. The message is clear: school is failing the students. Another study carried out by *La Junta Rectora de Educación* (Higher Education Board) interviewed 73,400[9] high-school students to learn why they were abandoning schools. According to them, the main reasons were: a boring curriculum, deficient academic orientation and counseling, problems with teachers and school personnel, a lack of meaningful relationships between teachers and students, their own economic and health problems, lack of transportation, and low academic achievement.[10] Students are frustrated because they are not acquiring very basic language skills, another element that contributes to the dropout rate. The official illiteracy rate for the island was 11 percent in contrast to 1 percent in the United States.[11] According to a study conducted by the Government Planning Board, only 9.5 percent of public elementary and intermediate students mastered basic skills in Spanish. In general, students see a lack of correlation between what they study and their day-to-day lives, between school and their future earning capacity and labor-market potential. In short, the present school system is not doing its share to prepare youth for the demands caused by the rapid social transformation that is clearly manifesting itself on the island.

At the same time, teachers express a clear and profound dissatisfaction about the role presently assigned to them. Everyone agrees the teacher should be "at the center of the educational process." Educators also agree about the need to significantly improve the salary and working conditions, as they are vital components of the school community.

In the midst of this educational crisis, there is a growing consciousness of the need to radically alter our educational philosophy, and practices. This reality predominantly affects the poor and working-class communities, essentially confined to the public system because of their inability to afford the more expensive, religiously oriented, English-speaking private schools.[12] It is important to note that there are good public schools on the island that serve certain sectors of the Puerto Rican society relatively well. In fact, in the

1980s, a relatively high percentage of the University of Puerto Rico's students came from the public schools. It is useful to remember, however, that those "effective" schools are mainly those which serve the middle-class neighborhoods. This reality is explained in the following terms by a group of scholars that have researched this problem.

The schools that are effective, which mainly serve middle-class neighborhoods, are in harmony with the mentality of students. The orientation of the curriculum and the way the school functions are familiar to them. In addition, this population's employment expectations are positive. Finally, the financial support their families provide helps them finish school.[13]

In this sense we should highlight that it is almost impossible to discuss the educational crisis without considering the students who are served by the school, their social and economic backgrounds. These factors are key since the cultural dynamics at school and its social context are extraordinarily important variables in explaining school failure or success. It is precisely the Department of Education's bureaucratic tendency toward further uniformity in a very diverse social context that creates alienating social settings and practices in schools.

Educational Reform Law: The official response

Even though the legislature approved the Educational Reform Law, discontent and skepticism abounds as to the real consequences of reform. In this sense, we see a window of opportunity to discuss and involve large sectors of the population in real reform, especially the working-class and poor communities.

Those who take a more positive view of the law highlight the higher levels of school autonomy created by the school councils, the law's recognition of the school as the basic unit of the educational system with the students as its center, and the prioritization of special-needs education for children with learning disabilities.

The new legislation does open certain space for democratic participation: the school council is composed mostly of teachers, some parents, interested citizens, and students, together with the principal of the school. Councils can approve curriculum changes formulated by the teachers or the principal. Councils also have the authority to elaborate on the school disciplinary guidelines and to put forth plans to create better relationships between school and community.

Those positive elements of the law, however, have to be considered in the context of the fact that, in general, the new Department of Education's legislation still gives too much authority to the superintendent and other higher-ups in the system, mainly the Secretary of Education. Specifically, superintendents still hire teachers and allocate budget resources throughout their districts. More importantly, the final decision on whether or not a school is accredited and will remain open will be made by the Council of Education, a newly created supervisory organ.

Under the terms of the new legislation, the Secretary of Education remains in charge of establishing the basic curriculum and materials, defining the basic skills that students must have accomplished at each grade level, and controlling the administration and upkeep of buildings, to cite only some examples. Although the law declares the need to restructure the system, it still maintains highly problematic hierarchical structures that depend on the Secretary of Education and the school superintendents.

The Reform Law does not respond concretely to the main concerns of students and parents. It does not provide space for teachers and students to establish strong and deep relationships that will give more meaning to school for both. Additionally, the law does not provide for more participatory mechanisms for distributing funds across the system. It does not give local schools autonomy at that level. Finally, the government completely failed to review the issue of resource allocation based on the particular socio-economic needs of its diverse student body. In a system accustomed to centralization, authoritarianism, and bureaucratization, it is naive to believe that the mere creation of these new school councils will significantly alter the present decision-making process. As we have underlined earlier, in the absence of a community-based effort supporting school-based initiatives, the present realities of stifling uniformity and alienating regulations will remain. Almost completely absent from the current legislation is the need to re-articulate school-community relations in order to allow these communities to have more control of the schooling process. The new community-based approach advances concrete alternatives and some solutions to the crisis.

A community-based approach to educational reform

As early as the 1960s Puerto Rican educators, like Dr. Angel Quintero Alfaro, have argued that one of the problems of the educational system is the growing gap between the schools and the communities they serve, the gap between their cultures, between their characters. Leaders of large, community-based movements have argued the same: we need a change in structure where school and community become one.

More recently, Dr. James Comer, a U.S.-based educator, argued that successful schooling depends on closing the school-community cultural gap. Although many of his studies have concentrated on poor, urban, African-

American communities, some of the theoretical implications of his work are relevant to our school reform effort. Comer's model promotes "[children's] development and learning by building supportive bonds that draw together children, parents, and school."[14] Comer emphasizes the fact that children do not enter the classroom ready to benefit from school. There are basic elements related to the disintegration of the traditional community bonds (family, church, disruption of social interaction due to criminal activity, etc.) which helped to create the previous social cohesion of those urban communities and contributed to the healthy development of students and their mastering of what he defines as "mainstream social skills."[15] Comer's approach is very helpful to understand some of the ramifications of the educational crisis face by Puerto Rican students.

Although mired in poverty, the barrio Juan Domingo has many of the strengths that Comer is looking for in his model school. The community serves an important function in cushioning its members from the harsh realities of the external world. Children receive support and encouragement from family members and neighborhood networks, and get a sense of control over their lives.[16] According to one resident, "Living in the barrio is like living in a huge house, where your neighbors are like family members that live in different rooms. [The barrio] is a big family."[17] The barrio, an essential element of the educational process, should be part of the reform. According to Comer, these resources should be brought *into* the school and not left out, as they now frequently are.

The educational reform should go far beyond the mere acquisition of basic skills. The community-based approach starts by opening the gates of school so that people of the community can come in and teach, thus creating a secure environment and a sense of continuity for the students—the people they live with are part of their education. School is transformed from an alien place where knowledge is imposed from far away, to a place where knowledge is given in communion with the community, its strengths, its culture, its history and its characters.

The New School in Juan Domingo is an example of how community-based reform can bring the content of school closer to the students. The school incorporates into its curriculum and its program both the strengths and the needs of the community. For example, children who come from broken homes where domestic violence and unemployment or sub-employment is prevalent, require a multifaceted educational approach that has to include, along with a re-creation of the concept of community, the decisive participation of social workers, psychologists, psychiatrists, and other specialists, working hand-in-hand with those communities. In this context, participation from parents and community becomes a critical factor in successful schooling.

Until now, parental participation in island schools has been generally seen as a fundraising mechanism, a way for organizations to overcome the very real material shortcomings they face on a daily basis. At the New School parental participation is seen as a way for parents to become better teachers of their children, for teachers to become better facilitators of knowledge and growth of children, and as a concrete way to democratize the decision-making process at the school level. Parents participate in policy decisions, curriculum design, and the development of better methods of teaching that are in harmony with the culture of the children.

School children soon realize that their learning process is important to the family and to the community as a whole. In the particular instance of Juan Domingo, where parents participated in the rebuilding of the Juan Ponce de León facility (the school's present location) those children show genuine pride over the fact that their parents repaired the classrooms, installed the windows, and constructed their tables. In the community as a whole, the reconstruction initiative generated a sense of dignity and self-sufficiency. Parents were able to overcome bureaucratic hurdles and students began the school year in a "good" school. Today the children see their parents "constructing" the school yet in other ways. Parents work in the classrooms as teachers' aids; in the office as administrators; in the school council where decisions about policy, budget, and curriculum are made; in the school store; and on the funding and disciplinary committees.

More and more people understand how the community can play an important role in the educational process. Fernando Picó, a Puerto Rican contemporary historian, found in his oral history research that the barrios represent an important part of the island's history: "In their daily life we find many values and characteristics that today we call Puerto Rican [as well as a] concentration of the problems that are Number One on our agenda; [for example,] unemployment, drop-outs, drug abuse, among others."[18] Picó also found "survival mechanisms, developed outside official institutions, [that are] used by the community to deal with these problems; collective structures, cooperative in nature, that reduced the sense of the rootlessness inherent in the industrialization process of Puerto Rico."[19] It is in this effort to create alternatives outside of the "institutions and official solutions" that the strength of community-based reform lies. Community work and questions about the nature of schooling that arise from this process should be incorporated into the efforts in school reform; we will go even further, and say that these should be the *starting* points for change.

Within this setting of marginal communities and their struggles emerges a concept of education: to base the school on the culture of the communities it serves. A new communal model of schooling characteristic of decolonizing projects is coming to life in Puerto Rico—a pedagogy of participation, of action, of possibilities. This is an educational philosophy that starts from the people, their culture and their aims, and not against them, and not in spite of them—a school with them, from them.

The New School of Juan Domingo emerges from a poor barrio of Puerto Rico in which people have been searching for alternatives, a belief that things could be and have to be better for their children. The work done in and by the barrio is in response *and in resistance to* a mediocre educational system that squanders human potential, promotes anti-democratic structures, and alienates poor people from the educational process. The New School's main traits are born from a practice of democratization and resistance. Barrio Juan Domingo's quest is for humanization, a quest that is to be historical even as it deals with the present relevant issues, a quest that is to be participatory, to address and respect the people involved in the situation. Thus, the New School aims to prepare students for the future by having them constructively deal with the present. The school intends to become a workplace for the new generation to take control of their lives.

The New School is made up of a variety of programs and projects. Classroom work is done in groups of no more than 20 to 23 students, usually with two adults in the class (a teacher and a parent or a practice teacher). Cooperative learning methods are promoted to generate a collective search for knowledge among the students and their teachers. A concept called "alive curriculum" is emerging from this work—the curriculum required by the school department is transformed into "alive" exercises, activities, research projects that make learning a more interesting and relevant process for the students.

Issues such as illiteracy within the classroom and low academic achievement are addressed through media that have been in use in the barrio: theater, music, radio, and the newspaper. A "Group of Young Writers" was born, in which students read and write poems, stories, and essays. They edit these in collective sessions, illustrate them, and choose the best drawings to include in books. Both group and individual publications are produced throughout the school year.

A group of parents and young people of the barrio have been working on a tutoring program that has been in existence for more than 20 years. This project encourages parents to help their children academically, studying with them in the community library every afternoon after school. A summer program has been created when the staff prepares the children for the next school term, and exposes them to areas school never offered before: arts, health courses, physical education, cultural visits to historic places—now seen as essential aspects of education.

Parents and young people have come to look critically at the educational process. Parents participate in curriculum committees where decisions are made in terms of what and how things will be taught. They are part of the evaluation committee that supervises the school staff, from the principal down to teachers, volunteers, and other workers. Parents comprise the majority on the New School's school council, the body that "rules" the New School, that is, decides on policy, discipline, calendar, curriculum, and staff selection. There is also a growing sense in the community that if we were able to rebuild the school over 20 years we can reconstruct the entire barrio.

In a highly bureaucratic context that constantly says "No" is embedded a feeling of impossibility. The New School challenges structures that promote dependency and a sense of helplessness. Reform in Juan Domingo occurs from the "bottom." People learn about schooling by doing, by teaching, by learning, and by evaluating what they do. Parents learn what a school should be by observing, participating, and thinking critically about the experience their children are having. This approach was made into a proposal of reform, and now is part of the practice of reform.

The people in the barrio do not wait for the next attractive theory or piece of legislation to pass. The barrio is too far removed from these anyway. Instead, they come in and construct classrooms, put up windows, make round tables (instead of individual desks), taking a hands-on approach, the same way they develop literacy and health projects, to give an example, within the curriculum, concretely addressing the urgent issues students are confronting. School children cannot wait. Community reform is closer to their rhythm than the top-down reform.

We can further talk about four pillars of this school reform born in the barrio. The search for a vocation founded on ideals as a way of taking control of our lives—discovering our talents, our wants, finding meaning in life, developing our life-projects and ideals are essential parts of our education. One often finds people of the barrio telling stories of how school "killed" their vocation, how many people tell the children of the barrio what they cannot aspire to be. The New School resists this type of education—it aims to open doors with the tools that lie within children and young students: the capacity to project themselves into the future, to dream, to think; and look critically at a reality that limits them. The New School carries within its walls the hospitality, the human warmth, and the familial feeling present in the barrio, recognizing these as central values in its work. Discipline and the quest for academic excellence is carried out with dignity. Discipline, love, and care go hand-in-hand.

The school depends on structures of *participation* and *dialogue*. The students participate in the teaching and learning process through the cooperative learning, dialogue with their teachers, and the "alive curriculum" (based on their questions and interests). The children participate also in the construction of the school through the daily evaluation, when they reflect and speak critically about their day together with their teachers. Based on this conversation, teachers design future classes. At the same time this dynamic contributes to the students' change of behavior, becoming better "co-workers" to their teachers and classmates. The teachers and parents also participate on the construction of the school through constant meetings and workshops where they develop their own tools of work.

There is an overall feeling of creative *resistance* to a system that limits the possibilities for a meaningful educational program. Students, teachers and parents feel they are coming out of a school where the possibilities are limited and decided by forces far away from them. People in the New School are beginning to own their work, and they are flourishing, they are resisting efforts to kill their energy, their ideas, their capacity to create and change.

The New School is as much a process as an end result. At this point in its history—when it has just become the public school of the community—people are concretely working on five main objectives that takes us closer to an ideal school. First, we are looking for (and practicing) effective and real ways of parent and community participation on the children's education. Second, we are providing for the continuing education of teachers geared to an improvement of their pedagogy and to greater unity and harmony with the needs of the students. Third, we are strengthening the curriculum so that it can lead to the utmost development of the students and faculty. Fourth, we are addressing the issue of dropouts through community-building strategies that start from the first grades, and with the recruitment of those students who have left school already. And fifth, our priority is to strengthen the dialogue between students and teachers through the restructuring of the school and classroom.

The community of Juan Domingo brings reform from the base by changing the rules of the game; by changing an authoritarian, highly hierarchical structure into a collective, democratic one where parents and teachers, administrators and children participate in the articulation of their setting. That is why the New School is the first on the island to operate with a school council.

The New School brings to the school-reform debate concepts that emerge from an experience of inclusion and activation. The community-building experience that the people of Juan Domingo have carried out to re-open their school is one of decentralization and local control, concepts generally alien to the transformation process.

The New School has already been visited by other island parent's groups which are also searching for alternative ways of educating their children. This is a good momentum to "gather" these quests and energies of other communities and incorporate them in the formulation of a New School that will serve the people of Puerto Rico.

The community struggle to reform schools is also part of a new emerging political movement and discourse. Although somewhat peripheral to the larger struggle against colonialism at the present time, creating avenues for democratic participation in the schools could be a significant social and political development.

There is a very broad consensus on the need to improve the quality of life on the island. The high rates of criminal activity, anti-social conduct, drug abuse and alcoholism are central civic concerns. There is more and more popular awareness of the relationship between the increase in these rates and a failing school system. An alternate vision of school reform has, in this sense, the possibilities to generate broad citizen support that could "overflow" the traditional disputes of political parties.

Up to now the crisis of the public educational system has not been faced in a collective manner. Most professional and upper-class families have circumvented these issues by sending their children to private and costly schools. On the other hand, the main victims of the public system had not then devised or articulated common strategies to face the failure of schools. This seems to be changing. A new plight for participatory democracy inside the schools and a preoccupation with academic excellence and responsiveness of the educational system seems to be creating a new political space. As Carl Boggs argues, the main challenge of these new social movements is to generate "generalized (and effective) political impact."[20] Only the future can tell us whether these emerging tendencies will fully blossom, but the mere existence of these "new voices" is a source of hope.

PART IV: VIEWS FROM THE UNITED STATES

A Divided Nation

The Puerto Rican Diaspora in the United States and the Proposed Referendum

Angelo Falcón*

In 1990, when the proposed referendum on the political status of Puerto Rico came before the U.S. Congress, the role of the 2.5 million Puerto Ricans living in the United States in this issue became surprisingly salient. As with most things colonial, the referendum revealed a paradox. While Puerto Ricans in the diaspora assumed a surprisingly high profile in the initial phase of this debate, it turned out ultimately to be a debate of little concrete consequence to them. The referendum also revealed that the assertion of the "divided nation" thesis put forth by Puerto Rico's political leaders, whether from the right, middle, or left, was no more than rhetoric. As such, the view that we are one nation, divided only by geography did not cover up a deeply seated suspicion that those in Puerto Rico didn't mind if their darker skinned and poorer relatives from the North visited, but they surely did not want them to stay for dinner!

A major problem in analyzing this complex relationship and its implications for the status question has been the lack of information on the attitudes of Puerto Ricans in the United States. In order to remedy this, the Institute for Puerto Rican Policy (IPR) conducted an opinion poll, the National Puerto Rican Opinion Survey (NPROS), in the summer of 1989, surveying the views of Puerto Rican activists throughout the United States and on the island on the referendum and other issues.

---

*A version of this essay originally appeared in the Spring 1990 issue of *Diálogo,* the newsletter of the National Puerto Rican Policy Network.

The survey was mailed in July 1989 to members of the IPR-sponsored National Puerto Rican Policy Network. Out of 1,493 contacted, 615 responded (a 41 percent response rate). They included persons residing in 18 states, Washington, D.C. and Puerto Rico. The findings of this poll focus on four issues: 1) Whether U.S.-resident Puerto Ricans should participate in the referendum; 2) How U.S.-resident Puerto Ricans would vote in the referendum; 3) Levels of support for the Puerto Rican government's newly established Department of Puerto Rican Community Affairs based in the U.S.; and, 4) The activists' views on the "national question."

Background

Until now, U.S.-based Puerto Ricans have expressed only in limited ways their opinion on whether or not they should vote in the projected status referendum. Their participation was barely touched upon in the series of public hearings on the proposed referendum held in Washington, D.C. and Puerto Rico in the summer of 1989, and in early 1990 by the U.S. Senate Committee on Energy and Natural Resources, the House Subcommittee on Insular and International Affairs, or other congressional committees.

Even when Governor Rafael Hernández Colón came to discuss this matter with Puerto Ricans in the United States in 1989, he held only three meetings with small, handpicked delegations in three cities—New York, Chicago, and Hartford. There he assured attendees that he definitely supported their participation in the proposed status referendum. But, once back in Puerto Rico, he qualified this support. Elsewhere, unfortunately, the only organized effort to advocate for the participation of U.S.-Puerto Ricans, the *Comité Pro Voto Ausente,* was spearheaded in the South Bronx by political operatives who had questionable motivations and a strong statehood bias. Later another more politically balanced group, the Pro-Puerto Rican Participation Committee, was established that largely represented the views of Puerto Rican elected officials in the United States. As a result, the role of U.S.-Puerto Ricans in the referendum process remained uncertain.

In Puerto Rico, commentators perceive U.S.-resident Puerto Ricans as either overwhelmingly in favor of independence, even socialism, for Puerto Rico, or overwhelmingly in favor of statehood. Even the efforts of pro-Commonwealth Hernández Colón to court U.S.-Puerto Ricans can be interpreted as his Administration's belief that they could easily be persuaded to vote for Commonwealth status. Prominent examples of his efforts include his: 1) general, but highly qualified, support for their participation in the referendum; 2) the over $1 million that his government spent in the *Atrévete* voter registration project in New York City and other U.S. cities; and 3) his recent creation of a cabinet-level Department of Puerto Rican Community Affairs headquartered in New York City. In short, many Puerto Ricans on the island believe U.S.-Puerto Ricans have political status preferences markedly different from their own.

At the end of 1990, Congress ended its session without taking action on the proposed status referendum and remained with two very different bills in the House and Senate. The House eventually left the issue of U.S.-resident Puerto Rican participation in the hands of the three dominant political parties in Puerto Rico. At that point in the process (November 1990) the Commonwealth party, the *Partido Popular Democrático* (PPD), publicly supported stateside Puerto Rican participation, but only in what became a maneuver to kill the legislation. It appears that since Hernández Colón's initiation of the referendum idea, public opinion in Puerto Rico had shifted away from Commonwealth, and he changed his strategy to one of stalling or sabotaging the referendum that his party would likely now lose.

The pro-independence, democratic socialist party *Partido Independentista Puertorriqueño* (PIP) and the pro-statehood party *Partido Nuevo Progresista* (PNP), historically the most antagonistic of the island's parties, wound up by the end of 1990 as political allies on the referendum. The PNP was the main beneficiary of the shift in public opinion in Puerto Rico and felt its position would be victorious. The PIP also saw this shift in positive terms, based on their belief that the U.S. Congress would never grant statehood to Puerto Rico. Thus, they saw a strong statehood vote in Puerto Rico turning into a broad independence sentiment once the statehood preference was rebuffed by the United States, as they felt was inevitable. Both of these parties came to see the introduction of the U.S.-Puerto Rican vote in the referendum as an unwelcomed "wild card" in their neatly laid-out political plans and became the least supportive of any party. With two of the island parties taking such a negative stance, and with the governing party attempting to use U.S.-resident Puerto Ricans for its own ends. The stateside Puerto Rican vote in the proposed referendum remained in their hands and stateside Puerto Rican participation (and, interestingly enough, the status referendum itself) became a dead issue.

When the status referendum proposal came up again in 1991, Congress turned the issue of U.S.-resident Puerto Rican participation over to the island's political leaders. The participation of the Puerto Rican diaspora was only supported in this sense by the sole Puerto Rican Congressman, José Serrano from New York. However, their position on the status issue remained open to much speculation.

Should U.S.-Puerto Ricans participate?

The Puerto Rican activists surveyed in the IPR poll were asked whether they felt Puerto Ricans in the United States should be allowed to vote in the proposed referendum on the political status of Puerto Rico. A majority (59 percent) felt that U.S.-resident Puerto Ricans should be allowed to participate, while a significant 38 percent felt they should not, and 3 percent stated they did not know. Significantly, among those surveyed from Puerto Rico (only 3 percent of total respondents), 60 percent opposed their participation.

Since this was a survey of activists and not of the general community, the question legitimately arises of how representative of the total Puerto Rican community their views are on this question. While to my knowledge no other U.S.-wide surveys of stateside Puerto Rican opinion on this question have been conducted, Local 1199 of the Health and Hospital Workers Union did explore this issue in a telephone survey they sponsored of Latinos in New York City in April 1989 on the upcoming mayoral election. The Puerto Rican respondents were then asked their position on U.S.-resident Puerto Rican participation in the referendum. The result was that 60 percent supported participation, 23 percent opposed it, and 17 percent either stated they did not know or that "it depends." These results are remarkably similar to those of the IPR's poll of Puerto Rican activists. The evidence, therefore, shows a strong desire by Puerto Ricans in the United States to vote in the referendum.

In the IPR survey, those activists who supported participation were also asked which U.S.-Puerto Ricans should be eligible to vote in the proposed referendum—all Puerto Ricans or only those born in Puerto Rico? A majority (61 percent) felt that *all* Puerto Ricans in the United States should be eligible to vote, while 36 percent felt eligibility should be limited to those "born on the island." The rest, only 3 percent, stated they did not know.

Despite the desire of U.S.-based Puerto Ricans to participate in the referendum, the greatest opposition to their participation came not from Washington, D.C. but from Puerto Rico. Part of this had to do with pure political calculation by the island's major political parties both on the right and on the left.

At a deeper level, however, the rejection of U.S.-resident Puerto Rican participation by most people on the island seemed more socio-psychological in nature. The island's news media projected the image of a country having to deal reluctantly with a part of its past it would sooner forget. The hundreds of thousands of Puerto Ricans who were propelled by socio-economic and political forces to the United States, particularly following the Second World War, were being treated like a bad memory and told that they could never really go home again. The possibility of U.S.-resident Puerto Rican participation in the future of the island triggered associations from the 1970s, when "Nuyoricans," as islanders derisively referred to stateside Puerto Ricans, were all charged with bringing drugs and crime (and low-class "salsa" music) to Puerto Rico during the major return migration of that decade.

How would they vote?

The IPR poll asked Puerto Rican activists how they thought U.S.-resident Puerto Ricans would vote on the political status of the island. The largest percentage (45 percent) projected that the majority of U.S.-Puerto Ricans would support continued Commonwealth. Statehood came in second (30 percent), followed by independence (14 percent), with 12 percent stating they did not know. Interestingly enough, when the Puerto Rican activists were asked their own personal status preferences in an October 1988 IPR poll, the largest percentage (44 percent) chose independence, followed by 14 percent each for Commonwealth and statehood. A significant 24 percent felt this was a decision for those on the island.

The activists' preferences, therefore, clearly diverge from their views of preferences of the U.S.-Puerto Rican community. Again, in comparison with the community-wide telephone survey by Local 1199 in April 1989, the IPR results were similar. According to Local 1199's poll, 40 percent of Puerto Ricans preferred Commonwealth status, 36 percent statehood, 11 percent independence, and 13 percent indicated they did not know or that the island's status did not matter to them.

Both sets of findings challenge the notion that U.S.-Puerto Rican status preferences are overwhelmingly in one camp or the other. In early 1989, *El Nuevo Día* newspaper sponsored a telephone poll in Puerto Rico among 500 registered voters. According to the poll, 45 percent of islanders preferred Commonwealth, 35 percent statehood, and 5 percent independence.

The status preferences of Puerto Ricans in the United States are, therefore, not all that different from those on the island. This may be an indication that Puerto Rican political culture is more continuous between island and metropolis than most commentators assume.

Turning to another survey conducted in 1989-90, the Latino National Political Survey (LNPS), preliminary findings show much stronger support for the Commonwealth position than previous surveys. Commonwealth was preferred by an overwhelming 67 percent of the Puerto Rican LNPS respondents, with statehood being supported by 26 percent, independence by a minuscule 3 percent, and 4 percent having no opinion. This could reflect the shifts away from Commonwealth that occurred in Puerto Rico in 1989-90. The Latino National Political Survey (LNPS) is the largest survey of political attitudes conducted to date of Latinos in the United States, specifically comparing Mexican-Americans, Puerto Ricans and Cuban-Americans. Initial analyses of the survey results appeared in mid-1991 and should help clarify many of the issues raised here.

Looking at the relationship of the place of birth of U.S.-resident Puerto Ricans and their status preferences, the LNPS data further indicate greater support for Commonwealth among those U.S.-based Puerto Ricans born in Puerto Rico than those born in the United States. Among the island-born, 71 percent preferred Commonwealth, 25 percent statehood, 1 percent independence, and 3 percent had no opinion. Among the U.S.-born, 59 percent supported Commonwealth, 30 percent statehood, 7 percent independence, and 4 percent had no opinion.

Puerto Rico's new Department of Puerto Rican Affairs

In his inaugural address in January 1989, newly re-elected Governor Rafael Hernández Colón formally expressed his intention to establish a new cabinet-level Department of Puerto Rican Community Affairs in the United States as part of his Administration. In so doing, he expressed the view that Puerto Ricans in the United States and Puerto Rico are part of "one nation."

In the summer of 1989, Puerto Rico's Legislature replaced the existing Migration Division of their Department of Labor and Human Resources with this new department. Once implemented by law, this new unit met with much skepticism among many U.S.-resident Puerto Ricans, whose objections were formally presented at the June 1989 hearing held by the Legislature at the Commonwealth office in New York City. In 1990, the *Partido Nuevo Progresista* (PNP) challenged the constitutionality of the new department, calling it part of the political maneuvering by Hernández-Colón around the status referendum. This constitutional challenge was upheld by the courts in Puerto Rico, a decision currently under appeal, and putting a cloud over the future of the agency.

In July 1989, the IPR poll asked Puerto Rican activists whether or not they supported the creation of the new department. Their reaction was mixed: although the largest percentage expressed support (41 percent), an almost equally large percentage stated they either never heard of the proposal, or did not know what to think of it (40 percent). A small percentage was opposed (19 percent). Therefore, this new department was created by the government of Puerto Rico without very much support from Puerto Rican activists. The question remains: what is the role of this department in relation to the Puerto Ricans on the island—and those in the United States—especially in light of the proposed referendum?

Divided nation or national minority?

Is Puerto Rico, in fact, a "divided nation"? Or are stateside Puerto Ricans a "national minority" of the United States, with a distinct culture from island *boricuas*? The Puerto Rican activists were asked their views on this "national question." The majority (58 percent) felt they could not decide between the two perspectives, that the Puerto Rican reality reflected elements of both. Close to a quarter (23 percent) supported the divided nation thesis, and 20 percent supported the national minority position. In New York City, 27 percent of the Puerto Rican activists felt that U.S.-Puerto Ricans are a national minority, while 21 percent felt that they are part of the divided nation of Puerto Rico. In the rest of the United States, 24 percent of the Puerto Rican activists supported the divided nation thesis, while in contrast only 13 percent supported the national minority position. This difference could be explained as the result of large second and third generation communities in New York City, which might tend to view themselves more as distinct from island Puerto Ricans, and more similar to other racial-ethnic minorities in the United States.

The relationship between U.S.-Puerto Ricans and those in Puerto Rico is clearly complex. It is obvious, however, that the forces of assimilation and racial-ethnic oppression have not weakened the sense of belonging that a large majority of Puerto Ricans in the United States still feel with the island. Island activists should recognize this feeling of connection and the potential political leverage it can give them given the right that Puerto Ricans in the United States have to vote for congressional representatives in some key states, a right that residents of Puerto Rico do not enjoy. This is a situation that, for example, Israel has been able to creatively use by encouraging a strong Jewish pro-Israeli lobby in the United States. This neglect by Puerto Rican activists was not always the case. In the recent past, for example, the Puerto Rican Socialist Party (PSP) had a significant presence in what they once called the "U.S. Zone," and even published a U.S. edition of their newspaper, *Claridad*. Today, except for the politically dubious Department of Puerto Rican Community Affairs in the United States, nothing like this exists on the left. If the referendum debate taught us anything, it is that progressives in Puerto Rico need to re-evaluate their approach to their counterparts in the "belly of the beast."

The desire of a large majority of Puerto Ricans in the United States to participate in the proposed referendum represents the strong ties they have to the island, because of both a significant circular migration and family connections. They also recognize that a change in the island's political status would have important implications for them, culturally, legally, economically, and politically. For example, statehood may mean drastic cuts in federal spending in Puerto Rico, in response to the growing federal budget deficit. This would spell serious short-term economic problems for the island that would affect both migration to the United States and, as a consequence, the socio-economic status of U.S.-resident Puerto Ricans. In addition, Puerto Rican cultural institutions (including the Spanish language) on both the island and in the United States could be undermined by statehood, by an "enhanced" Commonwealth and, in the United States, by independence. Even the U.S. citizenship of island-born Puerto Ricans, regardless of their length of residence in the United States or their age when they left Puerto Rico, could be threatened under independence, since this citizenship was granted directly by Congress in 1917 and is not constitutionally provided for unincorporated territories like Puerto Rico. The impact of all three status options on Puerto Ricans in the United States would be felt in many other spheres. The status referendum would, therefore, be difficult for them to ignore.

Over the last decade and a half, the terms upon which the relationship between Puerto Ricans on the island and those in the United States were once discussed—under the rubric of the "national question"—have been, unfortunately, reformulated along narrow pragmatic lines. Nonetheless, the broader implications of the Puerto Rican national question remain relevant. These include Puerto Rico's colonial dilemma, the role of international law and organizations in its resolution, the definition of national identity, the involuntary or voluntary nature of Puerto Rican "(im)migration" to the United States, and so on. That these more substantive, if controversial, questions have not been incorporated into the referendum discussion, however, is most telling.

The referendum, in addition, raises important questions about the viability of an electoral strategy for achieving sovereignty in Puerto Rico, given the colonial context within which it has been unfolding. If the status debate has engendered cynicism, it should push Puerto Rican progressives to avoid putting all their eggs in the electoral basket. Finally, this debate highlighted the major, though problematic, political resource that Puerto Ricans in the United States, as well as in Puerto Rico, must draw on for strength—their nationalism as a people.

An important lesson of this recent referendum debate is that the ultimate resolution of Puerto Rico's political status is not possible without the involvement of Puerto Ricans in the United States. The evidence, after all, indicates that the political divide between Puerto Ricans in the United States and on the island is not very great.

Migrants, Citizenship, and Social Pacts

Frank Bonilla

A striking representation of capital on the move in the new global economy has surfaced recently. Robert Heilbroner, economist and philosopher, evokes the image of a world-straddling, elevated superhighway with its pillars anchored in great cities, regional growth poles, and small nations. The political apparatus linked to each point of entry and exit, now more than ever, lacks the power to independently control this soaring traffic. Along these circuits move not just capital but trade goods, workers and, increasingly, information. Each of these commodities poses its own set of challenges to political control.[1]

Heilbroner dramatizes the decoupling of the economy from its traditional political and spatial moorings. At issue is not only the nature of political economy itself but especially the continued use of the Nation as the central unit of economic analysis and point of reference in the mobilization of human resources. Capitalists with no enduring commitments to localities or sets of workers operate through and around political spaces in which State power is both maximally permissive, especially toward transnational investments, and shies away from guaranteeing social infrastructures for the whole population except as these may hinder or discourage the movement of capital.

The new ascendancy of the business class as the universal or undisputed legitimate ruling elite, especially in the United States, constitutes, in Heilbroner's view, the key ideological underpinning of a new regime of accumulation that has taken form on the heels of the collapse of an earlier "Fordist" class arrangement. The "accumulation regime" construct thus seeks to capture not just changes in the technological and managerial ordering of production but also the accompanying shifts in value and ideology, especially in class relations, that are implicit in the ongoing restructuring.

The present "triumph" of capitalism has allegedly been built on failures now entirely imputed to a breakdown of the earlier Fordist, nation-centered equilibrium—productivity decline, deployment abroad of manufacturing, investment inertia, the glutting of local markets, international debt and sluggish markets abroad, and increased international competition. Implicitly labor unions are guilty parties, for pushing wage demands in excess of productive performance, but also for acquiescing to values that shore up the primacy of the entrepreneur. These same working-class sectors have opted in present circumstances to protect their status and pass along the downward pressures on wages and reductions in the social wage to their less secure comrades—that is, young workers, women, minorities, and immigrants. The victory of capitalism, however, may be short lived, for the social crisis visibly in the making foreshadows, according to Heilbroner, "a coming meltdown" of the new regime, that is, an eventual and perhaps imminent reassertion of State controls and new demands for a more convincing social justification for capitalism as we know it.[2]

Latinos are emerging as a living link between the socio-economic crisis in the United States and in their home countries. In both locales they confront massive shortfalls in the capacity of market and State to provide employment and adequate income. The UN Secretary General's 1988 report on the socio-economic outlook for the world in the year 2000 provides a somber perspective on North-South relations. Slow growth, stagnation, and further economic polarization are the dominant features of the UN's reading of the future. Falling per capita incomes and standards of living are tied directly to the dynamic of an oppressive debt, the volatility of money markets, growing protectionism, and creditor-imposed austerity in public spending. The movements of capital and attendant migration flows augur a further intensification of a crisis of urban growth, housing, and environmental change. The long neglect and waste of human resources and social infrastructures means that the situation has built-in, long-term effects that will take decades to overcome. Thus the combined $1.2 trillion international debt of the developing nations symbolizes capitalism at its most brutal and irrational phase.[3] International cooperation and internal democratization and class collaboration are named in the UN report as the chief ways out of this quandary, but trade imbalances and internal conflicts present formidable barriers.[4]

Varying dynamics generate inequality and absolute poverty within and across Latino and other social sectors in the United States. Impoverished barrios seem a long way from "the strategic interactions of classes and states" that are said to be at work on a global level. But it is precisely an intelligible and practical bridging of these conceptual and political distances, however modest, that is attempted in the sketch that follows.

The Puerto Rican experience

The achievements and shortfalls of post-war industrialization in Puerto Rico guided by the 1947 Industrial Incentive Act and successive legislation have been extensively catalogued.[5] The key anomalies of that process are, first, that reliance on external investment has meant not just growing dependence but absorption into the U.S. economy, part of the "silent integration" others have observed to be under way on a broader scale in the hemisphere.[6] "The Puerto Ricans have lost the ownership of their economy and the control of its course."[7]

Questions of separatist sentiment or national identity aside, external ownership and control of island resources have steadily undermined local capabilities to meet urgent island needs. Post-war industrialization in Puerto Rico followed a design widely heralded as a peaceful path to self-sustained growth but which has proved instead a means of eroding the material and political base for attaining these goals. The plebiscite being discussed in Congress clearly reflects the smug conviction in Washington that hegemonic interests and controls, economic and military, can be adapted to almost any political formula.

The second anomaly is that a plan intended to capitalize on the island's most abundant resource, its labor power, instead has cast a majority of the population into forced idleness, underemployment, and a restless circulation between colony and metropolis. Two and one-half million Puerto Ricans now in the United States probably represent about half the work force of Puerto Rican descent. Soaring investment and steady accumulation on the island have brought *more* not less unemployment, a shrinkage rather than an expansion in the proportion of the working-age population that is economically active. As the decade closes probably not much more than a third of working-age Puerto Ricans on the island actually have jobs. The average income of Puerto Ricans there is no closer to that of residents in the poorest mainland state than it was in 1940.

All this has occurred against a background not only of unprecedented investment and profit-taking but with the labor market stretched to its outer limits.[8] Wholesale emigration, a sharp reduction in family size, enormously expanded public payrolls, early retirements, runaway numbers of withdrawals from the workforce on the grounds of disability—all have proven unavailing as means of opening up spaces in the labor market for all who need jobs. Yet the same forces fueling migration toward the United States also propel people toward Puerto Rico in ways that have begun to internationalize the island workforce. As in the United States, policy-makers fear that further efforts at job generation by the government may attract more of the idle into the ranks of active job seekers.[9] The corollary of this failure is a demoralizing dependence on federal transfers and a swelling public and private debt, all leading to further consumption of imports and outward flows of capital rather than to locally productive investment.

Puerto Ricans in the United States

The first results of ongoing research by a working group of the Interuniversity Program for Latino Research (IUP) confirm the operation of parallel processes on the social condition of Puerto Ricans in the United States. Between 1970 and 1988, while the proportions of Cubans and Mexicans and Mexican-Americans in the U.S. workforce held fairly steady, the Puerto Rican presence in those ranks fell from 20 to 10 percent. In those same years, the participation of "other" Latinos rose from 7 to more than 20 percent. Most studies of the impact of new immigrants on labor markets insist that these effects are small and that the displacement of native workers should be of slight concern.[10] Among Latinos, Puerto Ricans generally have the lowest rates of participation in the U.S. workforce, the lowest earnings, the highest proportions of unemployed and families living in poverty, most of these with a woman as head. In most regards this situation is now worse than it was at the beginning of the decade.

Puerto Rican communities in the United States thus extend and reproduce the effects of a development strategy in which mass migration figures as an integral component. Though there is some evidence that the dispersal from the long-time core concentration in New York City has been selective, Puerto Ricans have made no clear socio-economic gains by assimilating to the mainstream. Ironically, the reverse is also true. While Mexican-Americans have won substantial political gains by legally challenging redistricting designs, Puerto Rican settlement patterns have not enabled a parallel strategy.[11] The states in which congressional representation is likely to grow after the 1990 census (by an estimated 13 to 17 seats) are states of heavy Latino but not Puerto Rican concentration. Puerto Ricans face the worst conditions precisely in those locales where they have been represented for the longest periods and in the greatest numbers.[12] In sum, Puerto Ricans have been playing the same role in the metropolis that was assigned to them within the restructured island economy.[13]

Migrants and the politics of interdependence

What kind of response will workers and migrants be able to muster in reply to the conjoint actions of capitalists and the State, as they become increasingly a part of multi-ethnic workforces for an internationalized production system whose true nature they may only dimly perceive? Political responses by organized labor to global restructuring have been clearly fragmented and set at cross purposes by the unevenness of the internationalization processes. Labor resistance, according to observers in strategic settings, has been individualistic, conservative, and reactionary rather than unified, collective, or progressive. The new interdependence has in fact meant a serious erosion of the two main anchors of workers' power—labor unions and citizenship. Unions may eventually become principal arenas and instruments for trans-ethnic and international worker action, but they are starting from a low ebb on both fronts. The shifting bases of state sovereignties, permeable borders, and mass migrations throw into question two traditional grounds of citizenship; citizen rights (especially economic rights) and active participation in political rule.[14] With the slippage of both class bonds and ethno-national unity, individualistic mobility striving and survival strategies prevail as adaptations to shortfalls in the performance of market and state. Where do Latinos, especially Puerto Ricans, fit into this dynamic?

In Puerto Rico, union membership has dropped to less than 10 percent of the workforce. There were 100 strikes in 1972; only 10 in 1988. The successful union-busting strategies in major industries, such as pharmaceuticals, have been well documented.[15] Latinos in the United States are in fact astir on the union front. Fragments of good news surface here and there.[16] The proportion of Latinos in unions, notable among Latinas where it reaches about 30 percent, is approaching twice that of the U.S. workforce as a whole. Nevertheless, entrenched leadership, rigidities, and organizational disarray, along with interlocking structures of workplace and union hierarchies resulting in practices of discrimination and exclusion, keep Latinos very much on the margin of power in major unions. The troubled international record of U.S. labor organizations, their subservience to U.S. foreign policy and intelligence objectives, and their projection abroad of anti-communist phobias from both the political left and right, fetter the transnational labor response.[17] Counterpart unions in many Latin American countries are equally implicated in this past record of political servility, corruption, and manipulation of members.

Again, fragments of promising news also surface on this front. For example, U.S. unions have been organizing undocumented immigrant workers in Los Angeles, and Brazilian and British auto workers coordinated a strike against Ford plants in their respective countries via a computer linkage. Still, these events only hint at what may be possible rather than give evidence of growing union leverage due to multi-ethnic and international collaboration.[18]

Dualities in citizenship

The citizenship issue is, if anything, more complex than the migration issue, being tied up with deep-seated attachments, loyalties, and identities that are neither casually shed nor assumed. Puerto Ricans, endowed with U.S. citizenship by congressional fiat in 1917, have generally been seen as privileged in this regard. Their *Puerto Rican* citizenship was, however, recognized by U.S. law only in 1927, the unanglicized name of the island in 1932.[19] Puerto Ricans have been asked to explain why the formidable advantage of dual citizenship has not served to thrust them ahead of other newcomers in the U.S. ethnic queue or at least helped them to maintain their position on the escalator to full assimilation.

Interestingly, about 60 percent of Puerto Ricans in the United States are still island-born, and with migration from the island newly picking up, that proportion is probably being replenished. Though fresh arrivals from Mexico have been slow to naturalize in recent years, Mexicans and Mexican Americans are in almost exactly the reverse situation—nearly two-thirds are U.S. citizens by birth. Cubans are now naturalizing faster then any other immigrant group except Asians. These three Latino groups are simultaneously engaged in a struggle for inclusion and ethnic affirmation within the United States while they seek to maintain some voice in affairs "back home." The current mix in each community of citizens, native or foreign-born, will weigh considerably in political actions and outcomes for the foreseeable future.

Thus, global restructuring has drawn millions of Latinos into ever widening circuits of labor migration. Many Latinos, not just Puerto Ricans, commonly alternate periods of work and unemployment in their home countries and in the United States or other foreign countries. Recent studies of Mexican undocumented workers, for example, suggest that most are not interested in U.S. citizenship but desire legal residence for determinate periods. Despite the growing number of migrants who see themselves as transients, many do become permanent U.S. residents and have offspring who assimilate into the mainstream. More importantly, these new conditions create objective and practical grounds for the preservation and renewal of national traditions and language, however these may be marked by the U.S. experience. Constant circulation, the ever present prospect of repatriation, the self-containment and isolation of many communities, the uncertainties and pressures of U.S. life and demands for unconditional assimilation—all require adjustments that satisfy neither the demands of U.S. assimilationists nor the strictures of traditional nationalists in the home countries.[20]

The pull of home-country politics

The contradictions posed by dual-citizen rights are dramatized among Puerto Ricans by two recent events: first, the creation by the Commonwealth government of a cabinet-level agency responsible for the affairs of Puerto Ricans in the United States (the Department of Puerto Rican Community Affairs) and second, the omission of any provision for participation by U.S.-Puerto Ricans in the referendum on Puerto Rico's political status originally projected for 1991. In both instances the responses of community leaders and organizations bring into the open long-standing tensions around questions of the citizenship and rights of migrants in the United States and in their home countries. Parallel constellations of issues arise in the case of initiatives by the Mexican and Cuban governments to establish more structured relationships with their communities as they, and Latinos as a whole, acquire greater visibility and weight in U.S. public affairs.

A change in the island's juridical status, community leaders in the United States argue, will have important legal, political, and economic implications for the U.S.-Puerto Rican community. The referendum bill proclaims that negotiations and consultations are to be held with "the people of Puerto Rico." The only equitable way to include the views of Puerto Ricans in the United States is to permit their vote in the referendum. International law defines a people as a human group bound by common language, tradition, culture, and institutions. A people is not defined by territoriality. There are irrevocable bonds between Puerto Ricans wherever they may live. The government of Puerto Rico, in close association with the interest of U.S. policy-makers, has actively encouraged the massive relocation of Puerto Ricans. Their joint policies continue to generate conditions on the island that are impelling new thousands to leave. How can Puerto Rican politicians and political parties complacently exclude nearly half of the people from the most important political choice to be made in their lifetime? Are we one people or not?

Though coupled to political strategies just as direct as those applied in the legislative hearings mentioned above, these rationales expose the painful tensions arising from the prolonged transience of migration in the modern mode of capitalist expansion. These repeated dislocations of attachments to place, identities, and rights in decisions will no doubt remain a part of contemporary realities for a long time. The idea of interdependence holds no mysteries for the migrant. The devastation wrought by Hurricane Hugo on the heels of the events just noted has served to intensify awareness of the emotional and practical dilemmas faced by a people uprooted and dispersed by forces that seem to work in equally destructive and uncontrollable ways both in their homelands and host countries. It is, nevertheless, at least clear that Puerto Ricans and other Latinos in the United States will not easily become either passive tools of U.S. policy or willing, uncritical agents of home governments eager to capitalize on their presence in the metropolis. It may yet be that in the long run, Puerto Ricans and other Latinos will help change the Americas—by changing the U.S. from the inside.[21]

U.S. Solidarity with Puerto Rico:

Rockwell Kent, 1937

Carlos Rodríguez Fraticelli

Puerto Ricmiunun ilapticnum! Ke Ha Chimmeulakut Engayscaacut, Amna Ketchimmi Attunim Chuyl Waptictum itt/icleoraatigut.

"All that is worthwhile is propaganda even if it is nothing more than propaganda for the beauty of life."

—*Rockwell Kent*

The U.S. solidarity movement with Puerto Rico dates back to the mid-1930s. Between 1936—the year the Puerto Rican Nationalist leader Pedro Albizu Campos was sentenced to 10 years in prison for sedition and conspiracy to overthrow the U.S. government—and 1947, the year of his return to the island, U.S. progressive forces launched an intense campaign in support of Puerto Rico's independence. In this movement, many well-known U.S. intellectuals and artists, including Pearl S. Buck and Paul Robeson, raised their voices to call for an end to U.S. colonialism in Puerto Rico. One, however, stood out in this effort. His name: Rockwell Kent.

By the mid-1930s, a devastating crisis had seriously undermined the colonial arrangement that had governed Puerto Rico since 1898. Expounding an anti-imperialist program, the militant Nationalist Party refused to recognize U.S. rule over the Island. They demanded an immediate transfer of power to the Puerto Rican people, proclaiming their right to use any means at their disposal, including armed rebellion, to recover national sovereignty. Nationalism, until the beginning of that decade a marginal political movement, became a force to be reckoned with.

To quell the unrest, President Franklin D. Roosevelt appointed a career officer, General Blanton Winship, governor of the island. With an iron fist, Winship pursued a policy of force. With the support of the unconditionally pro-U.S. *Coalición Socialista-Republicana*, a two-party coalition that controlled the insular Legislature, the colonial state launched an all out offensive to neutralize the pro-independence elements by any means necessary, especially the Nationalists and their charismatic leader, Pedro Albizu Campos. Political repression became the order of the day.

Meanwhile, in the United States, the public remained unaware of the crisis that was developing on the island. Indeed, the vast majority ignored the fact that the United States had a colonial possession called Puerto Rico—and cared much less that Puerto Ricans had been U.S. citizens since 1917. The media did little to rectify this state of affairs. Who cared about one and one-half million ungrateful, colored, tropical natives? Puerto Rico was not marketable news.

In this context of anti-imperialist struggle, colonial political repression, and generalized ignorance and apathy in the imperial nation, Kent launched, in November 1937, a one-man media campaign to inform the U.S. public about the plight of Puerto Rico. For several weeks, the U.S. press closely followed a heated controversy among Kent, federal, and Puerto Rican officials. The bone of contention: a barely noticeable inscription, written in an obscure Eskimo dialect, which Kent had included in a mural painted for the federal Post Office headquarters.

A mural for Puerto Rico

In 1935, as part of a Works Progress Administration's project for beautifying federal buildings, the Procurement Division of the United States Treasury Department commissioned the painting of two murals for the newly built Post Office in Washington, D.C. The murals were to illustrate the wide range of the United States mail service—from the Arctic to the Tropics.[1] To carry out the assignment, the Procurement Division hired Kent.

At age 53, Kent was a successful and highly regarded artist. He had travelled in the Arctic region and through South America. The artistic product of these voyages—several paintings on Arctic themes and two books on his experiences in the Alaskan wilderness and the Southern Cone—had won him critical acclaim. His radical politics and outspokenness earned him a reputation as "America's fighting artist."[2]

To collect material for the Arctic scene, Kent travelled to Alaska in 1935. Then he returned to New York to work on several projects, including the Post Office murals. But by the summer of 1936, the concept for the "tropical mural" had not yet taken shape. Finally, in July 1936, Kent decided to go to

Puerto Rico for a week to gather the "atmosphere and data" needed to finish that sketch.

Kent's short stay on the island proved to be an awakening experience. He had never been there before and, like the average U.S. resident, knew practically nothing about the land or its people. The stark contrast between the luxuriant beauty of the landscape and the widespread misery and poverty of the majority of Puerto Ricans, especially blacks, shocked his moral sensibility.[3]

The colonial government's response to the Nationalist challenge distressed Kent even more. By then, the Winship Administration had already declared an open war against the Nationalists. The first of two political trials against Albizu Campos and seven other Nationalist leaders accused of conspiring to overthrow the U.S. government was underway. To the chagrin of colonial administrators and federal officials in Washington, the jury could not produce a guilty verdict. A new trial was necessary.

The day after the end of the first trial, Kent attended a cocktail party at the governor's mansion. Among those present was Cecil Snyder, the federal prosecutor. When some of the guests expressed disappointment with the outcome of the Albizu Campos trial, Snyder produced a list containing the names of prospective jurors for the second trial. A guilty verdict, he boasted, was guaranteed. The Justice Department had instructed him to proceed with the case until Albizu Campos was convicted. Disturbed, Kent prepared an affidavit stating what he had witnessed and sent it to Washington.[4] Shortly afterwards, he returned to New York.

Puerto Rico remained alive in Kent's mind, however. He had to finish the mural. Besides, political developments on the island continued to trouble him. Several weeks after returning home, a second jury, composed mostly of U.S. natives residing on the island, found Albizu Campos and the others guilty as charged. Several of the individuals on Snyder's list were among the jurors. The federal judge sentenced the Nationalists to 10 years in prison, six of which were to be served in the Atlanta, Georgia, federal penitentiary.

During the following months, the Winship administration intensified its offensive against the pro-independence forces. The *Coalición* unconditionally supported Winship's reign of terror. Anyone who dared to question or even criticize any aspect of U.S. control over the island was suspected of harboring anti-U.S. ideas. Suspected government workers, including public school teachers and university professors, were harassed; many were fired. Rallies, demonstrations, and other activities in support of the Nationalist prisoners were banned.

On March 21, 1937, Palm Sunday, the insular police opened fire on a peaceful Nationalist parade in the city of Ponce. Twenty-one persons were killed and over 200 wounded. Two policemen died in the cross-fire. The Winship Administration blamed the Nationalists for the incident, and ordered the arrest of six Nationalists, who were accused of killing the two policemen.

The American Civil Liberties Unions (ACLU), of which Kent was a member, appointed a commission to investigate the matter. The commission concluded that responsibility for the massacre rested exclusively on the Winship Administration. The representatives of the federal government in Puerto Rico, concluded the ACLU, were guilty of a gross violation of civil rights and of incredible police brutality.[5]

Yet, with the exception of the small radical press, the U.S. media paid no attention to Puerto Rico. There was practically no coverage of the Albizu Campos trial, the Ponce Massacre, or the ACLU report. In the best of cases, there was a short note buried in an inconspicuous placed in the newspaper; no follow-up, no editorials or investigative reports were published.

Outraged at this situation, Kent decided to do something to direct the eye of the media and through it, the attention of the public, to Puerto Rico. An idea began to take shape: he would deliver a message to the U.S. people via the mural commissioned by the Treasury Department's Procurement Division. What could be more effective and at the same time more symbolic than to deliver a message in support of Puerto Rico's struggle for political freedom from the federal Post Office building itself? One major obstacle had to be overcome: the mural had to be formally approved by the Treasury Department. Clearly, official sanction for a painting containing a message critical of federal government policies towards Puerto Rico was out of the question. How then could he send his message?

Kent's answer was simply brilliant. There was to be no major deviation from the preliminary designs approved by Procurement Division's officials. The Arctic mural depicted sleds laden with mail and several hearty Eskimos attending the departure of the mail plane. The central scene of the tropical mural showed a man on horseback delivering mail to a group of women; happiness fills the air as the women begin opening their correspondence. Kent's idea was to include a cryptic message in an unfolded letter held by one of the women. When unwary officials of the Painting and Sculpture Section of the Procurement Division inspected the mural, they approved it. On September 4, the paintings, placed in the corridors near the Postmaster General's office, were unveiled. The next day, the publicity about the new murals was distributed to the press.[6]

To carry out the next stage of his plan, Kent had secured the support of a Washington-based journalist, Ruby Black. An expert on Puerto Rican affairs, who was actively involved in the struggle to get Winship off the island, Black was more than willing to cooperate in the ploy—which would involve deciphering his message.[7] Shortly after the mural was publicly displayed, Black dropped the bombshell to the media. The painting in the Post Office building, she informed, bore a mysterious inscription, which included the words "Puerto Rico." Could it be a hidden message? Black prompted the public. Kent was nowhere to answer the question. Undeterred by this minor complication, she began an intense search, which included visits to language experts in the Post Office Department, the Smithsonian Institute, the Department of State, the Bureau of Indian Affairs, and the Division of Territories and Island Possessions. Eventually, she contacted the famous Arctic explorer Vilhjamur Steffanson, a close friend of Kent's and an expert on Eskimo languages. Steffanson had the answer: The inscription was a message written in Kuskokwin, an obscure Eskimo dialect. Translated into English, it read:

> To the people of Puerto Rico, our friends. Go ahead, let us change chiefs. That alone can make us equal and free.[8]

As Kent had foreseen, the "discovery" became instant news. Newspapers across the nation covered Kent's daring stunt. "Revolt Plea Seen in Kent's Mural" reported the *New York Times;* "Eskimo Inscription Urging Free Puerto Rico Intrigues Capital" read another New York daily; "Shocking! Eskimo Urges Puerto Rico to Toss Off the Yoke of Uncle Sam," flashed a Washington newspaper.

They asked a barrage of questions: Who was Rockwell Kent? What was the true meaning of the Eskimo message? Was the message really written in Kuskokwin or was it simply a nonsense scribble? Were government officials involved in the ploy? What was the federal government going to do with the mural and, for that matter, with Kent?

During the following weeks, Kent exploited the publicity around the mural to present Puerto Rico's case directly to the U.S. public. The message, he explained, was not a call for an armed revolution; it simply suggested a change of chiefs. In fact, Kent noted, Eskimos had no formal government and the Kuskokwin word translated as chief also meant "guide" or "leader." Therefore, the message could have meant many things: it could be understood as a call for changing colonial administrators, or a call for an end to Puerto Rico's colonial status. Indeed, the message did not favor a definite political formula, although Kent personally supported independence for Puerto Rico. But regardless of the specific meaning, Kent contended, it was a profoundly U.S. message, inspired by and in complete harmony with the U.S. Constitution and the U.S. democratic spirit. As to what the United States should do with Puerto Rico, according to Kent, there was only one answer: It should remain true to its political tradition and allow Puerto Ricans to decide by themselves in a democratic way whether they wanted to become an independent nation or not. A plebiscite, Kent insisted was in order.[9]

The controversy over the mural went far beyond Kent's original expectations. He miscalculated the potential effects of his action and the federal officials' reaction to it. The mural became the object of a heated debate not only among federal bureaucrats and U.S. politicians but among the principal leaders of the *Coalición*—the socialist Santiago Iglesias Pantín and the republican Rafael Martínez Nadal—who were in Washington when the news hit the press.

Martínez Nadal, the president of the Puerto Rican Senate, visited the Post Office as soon as he heard about the "Puerto Rican mural." But the political message did not offend him as much as the way Kent had depicted Puerto Ricans. In Martínez Nadal's opinion, the mural was a "calumny and an insult" to Puerto Rico because it represented Puerto Ricans as "a bunch of half-naked African bushmen."[10] The Puerto Rican government's representative in Washington, Resident Commissioner Santiago Iglesias, was equally outraged. He immediately sent a press release informing the U.S. public that they had been deceived. The painting, Iglesias insisted, did not represent Puerto Rico at all. Therefore he wanted to "disabuse the minds of people who may have been misled to thinking it symbolizes our culture." The mural, according to Iglesias, was "nothing but perverse propaganda against our country."[11]

Iglesias took the case directly to members of the presidential Cabinet. He accused Ruby Black and United Press International of fabricating the story for the purpose of selling news, and Kent for siding with the reactionaries and anti-labor forces in Puerto Rico. Finally he indicated the willingness of the Puerto Rican Legislature to defray the cost of replacing the mural with another truly representative of Puerto Rico and its people.[12]

Kent had not counted on Martínez Nadal's and Iglesias's angry reaction and the accusations of racism they leveled against him. What was important to him was the anti-colonial message—an open message that implicitly recognized statehood as an acceptable political option. But for the *Coalición* leaders, Kent's portrayal of Puerto Ricans as Eskimos—or "bushmen" in Martínez Nadal's words—had probably more damaging political implications than the message. In those days they were diligently lobbying in Congress for a bill supporting statehood for Puerto Rico. There was a lot of resistance to overcome, since prejudice against Puerto Ricans had been on the rise as a result of the Nationalist actions. Now Kent was supplying more ammunition to those who opposed the annexation of the island. A black state? Never!

To the Puerto Rican community in New York, the biggest and most politicized Puerto Rican community in the United States, Kent had become a hero. In Spanish Harlem, a Nationalist and communist stronghold, an assembly of over 2,000 Puerto Ricans voted overwhelmingly to condemn Martínez Nadal's declarations. The *Junta Nacionalista* invited Kent, along with Vito Marcantonio—the champion of Puerto Rican independence in Congress—to be the main speakers at an important political event scheduled for the celebration of the Lares Revolt, the most important Nationalist holiday.[13]

Kent was unable to attend the celebration. Instead he sent a solidarity message, explaining that he had used blacks to represent Puerto Ricans because he wanted to portray the poorest element of the population. Besides, his message was one that poor people all over the world needed to hear. He was confident that it would inspire the Puerto Rican masses to fight for freedom.[14]

Kent's outspokenness exacerbated Iglesias's wrath. Once again, he accused Kent of complete ignorance of the insular reality. The socialists—not the Nationalists—were the defenders of the Puerto Rican masses. Kent, Iglesias declared, was making common cause with "the fascists and Nazis, who were trying to destroy the freedoms of the productive masses and the democratic institutions of the Island."[15]

The controversy continued making headlines in the press. Kent declared that the hostile reaction against the mural was a warning that fascism was making headway in U.S. society. Still he was willing to compromise with some of his critics. If the Treasury Department was agreeable he would include free of charge several members of the Puerto Rican House of Representatives in the mural. He was afraid, however, that such a change might then truly offend the Puerto Rican people.[16]

Through the debate, Kent continued offering possible "alternative messages" and alterations to the mural. To the Procurement Division, he submitted the following message:

> To the people of Puerto Rico. Have you read the wonderful words of the Great Emancipator Abraham Lincoln? "If by the mere force of numbers a majority should deprive a minority of any clearly written constitutional right, it might, from a moral point of view justify revolution—and certainly would if such a right were a vital one.

On another occasion, he proposed to include the preamble of the U.S. Constitution—either in English or Eskimo, or the words of President Wilson concerning the self-determination of small nations. He even offered, supposedly to appease Iglesias's anger, to include the portraits of Iglesias's three daughters—America, Libertad, and Fraternidad—in the mural.[17]

In the meantime, the Secretary of the Treasury demanded an investigation. The Procurement Division reported that the approved design had not included any message. The Division, therefore, proposed that the message constituted a deviation from the original intention. An investigation of the translation and the real purpose of the message was undertaken.[18] Other public officials and politicians entered the controversy. Following Iglesias's steps, the Alaskan delegate to Congress, Anthony Diamond, presented a formal protest to the Treasury Department demanding drastic action. By portraying Eskimos urging the people of Puerto Rico to change chiefs, Kent was implying that the Alaskan natives desired to take the same action. The natives of Kuskowin, he insisted, were loyal and devoted U.S. citizens. Two former chiefs of the Procurement Division also lashed out at Kent and the "Puerto Rican mural."[19]

As pressure mounted, federal officials sought to expedite the solution to the increasingly irksome problem. The Postmaster General's Office contacted Kent and requested several acceptable alternatives, this time in English, from which the directors of the Procurement Division would choose to replace the controversial message.[20] On November 26, Kent responded, this time seriously, to the official request for alternative inscriptions with four equally politically charged options:

1. To the people of Puerto Rico, our brethren: Let us, in the spirit of America, fight for life, liberty and the pursuit of happiness.

2. To the people of Puerto Rico, our friends: We are told that you want equality and freedom. We, people of the Far North, wish you success.

3. To the people of Puerto Rico, our friends: Success to you in your fight for freedom, for freedom is a tradition of our country.

4. To the people of Puerto Rico, our friends: May our people win the freedom and equality, in which lies the promise of happiness.

Along with the alternative messages, he notified the Postmaster General of his willingness to go immediately to Washington to make the agreed change.[21] The Procurement Division called him in.

On November 1, Kent conferred for two hours with several representatives of the Procurement Division. Finally they compromised on a revised version of the fourth alternative, which was directed to address the concern of the Alaskan delegate. "May you persevere and win the freedom and equality in which lies the promise of happiness." The prospective agreement, however, was rejected by the Procurement Chief.[22]

That very same day, Kent stunned the press with another sensational declaration. In a meeting of the National Women's Press Club, he made public what happened at Winship's cocktail party in July 1936. He also stated that he had evidence that proved that the Justice Department had ordered the prosecutor to produce a guilty verdict in the Albizu Campos case.[23]

Kent's last declarations were too much. The next day, the press reported that Kent's intransigent position had left the Treasury Department no choice but to commission another painter to blot out the controversial message. Kent would be paid the agreed fee minus a deduction to cover the cost of the alteration by the new artist.[24]

Kent fought back. He accused the Treasury officials of censorship. Since he had not been paid in full, he warned them, the painting remained his property. If they dared to tamper with it "even were it but to change a comma in the decoration message," he would take them to court. Furthermore, any less than the original payment agreed in the contract was unacceptable.[25]

The Treasury Department responded with another threat. They were weighing the return of the mural since the work was "unsatisfactory." But after considering all the legal and political aspects of the case, the officials opted for fulfilling the original contract. On November 6, the press was informed that Kent had been paid in full.[26]

Kent's revelation concerning the trial of Albizu Campos involved him in one last controversy over Puerto Rico. At the time of the disclosure, the colonial government was prosecuting the Nationalists accused of killing the two policemen during the Ponce Massacre. When the attorneys for the defense heard the news, they immediately contacted Kent. His testimony was needed to support their contention that the trial was part of the federal government's conspiracy to repress the Nationalist Party.[27]

By then Kent had been elected vice-president of the National Committee for People's Rights. As part of his organizational work, he was scheduled to travel to Brazil for a first-hand report on political repression under the Getulio Vargas regime. After meeting with Puerto Rican leaders in New York, Kent agreed to stop briefly on the island to serve as a defense witness.

On November 18th, Kent arrived in Puerto Rico. Over 500 people, representing progressive, civil rights, and cultural and political organizations greeted him at the airport. On the 20th, he travelled to Ponce to participate in the trial. The judge, however, ruled that his testimony had no direct bearing on the case under prosecution and he was not allowed to testify.[28]

The next day, Kent left for Brazil. Before boarding the plane he read an anti-colonial message to the Puerto Rican people. The United States, he declared, should as soon as possible, do everything in its power to assure that Puerto Ricans were absolutely equal to the U.S. people—either by allowing Puerto Rico to become a state, or a free nation.[29]

Conclusion

Upon his return to the United States, Kent continued his tireless involvement in progressive causes, including solidarity with Puerto Rican independence. During the 1939 congressional backlash against communism, he was accused of un-Americanism before the Dies Committee: the "Puerto Rican mural" was used to support those charges.[30] During the McCarthy era, he was again persecuted: a subpoena to appear before the House Un-American Activities Committee; later, denial of a passport because of his political activities. Still, until his death in 1971, he remained true to his beliefs.

In the meantime, the painting remained on display in the federal Post Office building. Although the original inscription was no longer there, the "Puerto Rican mural" fulfilled Kent's original objective. In Kent's own words:

> In forty-eight hours, a nation ignorant of Puerto Rico, of the desperate plight of its crowded inhabitants and of the long series of usurpations practiced against them by ourselves [the United States], was alive to it all. The message had struck home.[31]

PART V: LOOKING TOWARD THE FUTURE

The Struggle for Independence: The Long March to the Twenty-first Century

Wilfredo Mattos Cintrón

The independence movement in Puerto Rico has always been beset by grave difficulties. While it probably enjoyed an unstable majority in the 1930s, previous to that decade and afterwards it has been a minority. The reasons for it being so prevail even today, to a large degree, and must be examined before attempting any sort of projection for the next century.

Even under Spanish dominion, independence as a political solution did not enjoy a large following as it did, for example, in Cuba. Reasons for that are to be found in the slow differentiation process of the indigenous social forces: dependence of the *hacendados* on the colonial power for the exploitation of workers, late development of an intellectual strata, and small agricultural holdings as a cushion against slave and tributary labor.[1] As a consequence, self-government under Spanish rule became the most radical demand of the principal Puerto Rican political leadership. Independence as an ideology—and a mass movement—is mainly a product of twentieth-century politics in Puerto Rico, notwithstanding its presence during the previous century.[2]

Why is independence not a stronger movement today? The reasons are to be found in the early days of the U.S. intervention in the island and the fact that there was not, as in Cuba, a social class clearly committed to define and defend a national project; such a class had not developed under Spanish rule, and U.S. colonialists were not interested in furthering its development once the island was wrested from Spain. U.S. rulers strove to differentiate themselves from the authoritarian Spanish governors: they guaranteed labor union rights, they weakened the hold of the Catholic Church on civilian life, they put into place a massive education program—albeit used also as an "americanization" project—and they sponsored a public health program.[3] All these efforts in illustrated colonialism were met with almost unanimous petition for statehood, by all principal political parties. By 1905, though, that near unanimity had died away.

U.S. intervention in Puerto Rico unleashed a powerful popular movement against the remnants of Spanish influence that can only be termed as a partial bourgeois-democratic revolution. Though not sponsored by the United States, that revolution clearly stemmed from the new political and social conditions created by the U.S. presence.[4] Unlike the sort of passive revolution that theorist Antonio Gramsci analyzes,[5] this powerful social movement was led principally by the working class, and demanded that the freedoms enjoyed in the United States, unknown under Spanish rule, be extended to Puerto Rico. After all, we should not forget that a span of only 25 years stood between the abolition of slavery and U.S. colonization of the island; 12 years since the massive repressions of 1886; and that at the moment that U.S. ships were cannonading San Juan, the most important labor leader on the island was in jail. The propertied groups in Puerto Rico, unleashed from centuries of oppression, had no other recourse but to act as they did under Spain: they relied on their new masters to protect them against the upsurge of popular demands for democracy and equality. Weak calls for independence in this context were viewed by the popular movement as a means for the propertied classes to reject the more democratic elements of U.S. rule.

One of the important consequences of that popular movement was the rift that developed between the Puerto Rican intelligentsia and the popular classes. The first group, with its Spanish overtones, represented the culture of the dominant class. Thus the emergent popular culture of the working class—with its own intellectual cadres—was confronted with that of the propertied class, and a wedge was driven into the process by which a national culture on the island developed.[6] While the "official" culture was dominated by elites, popular leaders cast a suspicious glance on the intelligentsia, who drifted steadily towards independence. The fast development, under U.S. rule, of the public educational system prevented the emergent popular culture from developing itself as an alternative to the "official" culture.

The popular forces behind the partial democratic revolution failed also to see the need for a nation-state. In part, that failure was the outcome of their immaturity and, to a certain extent, of the prevalence of anarco-syndicalism, which toned down nationalist fervor. A curious alliance evolved in which both sides of Puerto Rican society looked to U.S. colonialists for their development and survival: in the words of A.G. Quintero, it was "a triangular struggle."[7] The popular movement fought not so much against independence as for the movement's survival against an enemy they identified, properly or not, as the remnants of Spanish rule. The fact that this enemy, the propertied class, had also sought refuge in U.S. intervention became a blind spot that hid the fact that U.S. corporations were the main beneficiaries in the island's biggest industries, sugar and tobacco. Since neither the propertied nor the popular classes raised the banner of the nation-state, it was the radical sector of the petty bourgeoisie who filled that void up to this date.

The contemporary independence movement has failed to gauge properly the significance of that period. The fact that the popular movement helped thwart the establishment of a Puerto Rican nation-state has garnered it much ill feeling from independence activists. Traditional *independentistas* have been more focused on the freedom of the nation than on social inequities.

The U.S. regime criminalized the independence movement.[8] It is a measure of the prevailing situation that the invading nation could legitimize its actions, and at the same time paint as criminals those individuals who dared denounce military intervention and the imperial transaction that converted Puerto Rico into a U.S. war booty. The merging of the partial democratic revolution with the crystallization of U.S. hegemony served to dampen the development of the island's pro-independence forces.[9]

Nationalism in the 1930s

During the colony's first 30 years, independence survived essentially as a cultural aspiration. Not until Pedro Albizu Campos became the leader of the Nationalist Party (PN, from *Partido Nacionalista*) did this situation change. The emergence of Albizu's leadership must be seen against the background of the worsening economic conditions leading up to the Great Depression and the collaboration of the Socialist Party with its former enemies in the Republican Party.[10]

Albizu ushered in a new doctrine for independence. Under his leadership independence became the exclusive status solution of a party that had considerable influence.[11] For the first time, a Puerto Rican party made a clear statement challenging U.S. hegemony, and denounced U.S. intervention as an act of violence and expropriation. Albizu's points of view, however, were affected by a petty bourgeois notion of the State and a rosy view of Spanish rule, something that did much to detract from his influence in the popular classes.[12]

Overall, the PN did little to enhance its position among the working class. Although the PN was called to lead the strike of the sugar cane workers in 1934, and though it heeded that call to a certain extent, PN leaders failed to see the importance of developing ties to workers. Simply stated, class struggle was a concept alien to Nationalism.[13] And the PN was not to have any time to pursue such roads. The U.S. regime on the island acted swiftly to stamp out the Nationalist threat. The principal leadership was imprisoned under false charges and a veritable war was waged to crush Nationalist militants. As Nationalist influence waned, the Popular Democratic Party (PPD, from *Partido Popular Democrático*) founded by Luis Muñoz Marín was the main beneficiary of its struggle.

Independence and socialism

Although the PPD presented itself, at first, as an *independentista* party, the project was abandoned very early. Fearful that the non-partisan Congress for Independence (CPI) would drain its resources and establish a base for independence activists within PPD, the leadership declared that it was incompatible for PPD members to belong to CPI. The rift between the two organizations led to the formation of the *Partido Independentista Puertorriqueño* (Puerto Rican Independence Party, PIP) in 1946. The PIP renounced violence as a means for achieving independence, in contrast to the Nationalist doctrine, and espoused the electoral process as the way to ascend to power.

The post-war period, however, brought new conditions to Puerto Rican society that undermined both the PN and the PIP campaigns. A new industrial development program based on luring foreign capital by low wages, tax exemptions, and government subsidies, created favorable conditions for new U.S. investments and employment, encouraged by the PPD, just when the island was being bled by massive emigration to the United States[14] The combination of new investments and more jobs, along with a decreased workforce, was attributed to PPD. Neither the October insurrection of the Nationalists in 1950, nor the voting efforts of the PIP were able to turn the tide. The PN disappeared and the PIP took a distant third place in the elections after 1956.

Against that background the Cuban Revolution ushered into Puerto Rican politics a marxist-leninist influence. Although there were marxist-leninist forces already in the island—the Puerto Rican Communist Party was founded in 1934—they had never had a large impact on the political scenario. The Cuban Revolution breathed new life into waning efforts to organize pro-independence activists frustrated with the electoral process or Nationalist failures. About this time many *independentistas* finally realized the need to actively incorporate social demands, going beyond the national question.[15] The first stage was the formation of the *Movimiento Pro Independencia*

(MPI), which embarked on a series of efforts avoiding both electoral politics and direct confrontation with the regime. During the 1964 elections, the MPI campaigned for abstention from the polls. While abstention as such was not clearly significant, the MPI did increase its visibility. But the most important MPI-led activities during the 1960s were the internationalization of the Puerto Rican colonial problems by means of a bold thrust into the United Nations, aided by the Cuban government—the PIP joined these efforts but kept from any identification with the Cubans—and the scuttling of the government plans to exploit copper deposits on the island. The latter was important because early in the 1960s the PPD realized that its strategy for economic development was floundering, and discovered an alternative that rested in the establishment of oil refineries and the massive mining by U.S. companies of the copper deposits that had been discovered in the center of the island. The MPI, under the slogan "Puerto Rican mines or no mines" stopped such a plan. It must be noted that later on, increased ecological awareness during the 1970s has been a deterrent against the revival of similar plans.

The early 1970s were the high point of independence and socialism. The MPI became the *Partido Socialista Puertorriqueño* (Puerto Rican Socialist Party, PSP) in 1971, openly embracing marxism-leninism. This radicalization process also affected the PIP, which already had embraced the European social-democratic variant of socialism. The 1968 elections resulted in the PPD's first defeat at the hands of the newly formed *Partido Nuevo Progresista* (New Progressive Party, PNP), a party that advocated statehood. The defense of Puerto Rican identity vis-à-vis annexation became a rallying point for both the PIP and the PSP. Both parties enjoyed a surge that set into motion diverse cultural and social groups. In the late 1960s, while still known as the MPI, the PSP had discovered the labor movement and had begun a systematic effort of participation in strikes and diverse worker's actions. Not to be left behind, the PIP also competed with the PSP for the soul of the labor movement. Thus the range of action and influence of the independence movement as a whole was dramatically enhanced and ideologically radicalized.

In 1976 the PSP decided to intervene for the first time in the electoral process, fielding several candidates for a number of offices. Those elections, however, revealed the frailties behind the uneasy alliance between nationalist and socialist ideologies. The electoral outcome did not measure up to PSP expectations. A bitter struggle ensued over the proper strategy for Puerto Rican independence: armed revolution or elections? Military strength or massive civil force? The fact that these questions were being discussed showed the enormous resilience of the old Nationalist anti-electoral ideology, and the resulting inability of the PSP to properly analyze the extent of the U.S. hegemony in the island at that time. Puerto Rico was not El Salvador,

Somoza's Nicaragua, or Batista's Cuba. Nor was the U.S. presence on the island defended merely by the existence of several military bases. The PSP needed to make a deep and profound appraisal of U.S. hegemony and, for a time, it seemed that it would.

But the PSP quest for a strategy tailored to the prevailing Puerto Rican conditions was a short-lived effort. In 1981, the PSP embarked on a still-born project to become once again a national liberation movement, as it had been previous to its advocacy of marxism-leninism. Behind that new goal lurked several hidden objectives: to avoid the situation developing in Poland, to water down the commitment to marxism, and to maintain good relations with the official socialist world by not indulging in a critique of its travesties. The PSP also hoped to compete against the PIP after the realization that the candidacies of the PSP's secretary general, Juan Mari Brás, and the president of the party, Carlos Gallisá, in the 1980 elections met with strong support from different quarters of the political spectrum, particularly the PIP.[16] The struggle within the PSP led to the paralysis of its projects, and its activities. It has sailed through the 1980s and into the 1990s without any goals but independence, in a moment such a banner rallies little support.

The reasons for the PSP's failure—and the PIP's also—stem out of the new situation that was created in Puerto Rico after the 1974 economic crisis, triggered by the international oil crisis of the previous year. The PPD, with its development program faltering in the 1960s, tried to redirect the economy through the exploitation of copper deposits, the construction of a superport for the storage of oil, and other projects that would menace the environment.[17] When these plans failed to materialize, strong anti-crisis measures were needed to avoid the collapse of the economy and any political reverberations. These were forthcoming. The United States poured into the island massive amounts of direct economic aid while organized labor was unable to counter the closing of shops and the emigration of island-based industries. By 1975, the food stamp program had exploded: $282.2 million were transferred to Puerto Ricans, almost 20 percent of the budget for the year. In FY 1977, the net benefit from food stamps was $610.1 million.[18] Therefore the formation of U.S. hegemony, understood as dominion by non-coercive means—with military might in the background—acquired new momentum by means of these new programs of direct economic aid. All groups within the left, besides the PSP and the PIP, failed to address that new situation.

The impact of political repression on weakening the left has to be examined carefully. First of all, the rise of the PSP in the early 1970s took place in the wake of the fierce activities of the state security forces during the 1950s and the 1960s. The Party was never cowed into inaction, though *Claridad,* the PSP newspaper, was bombed, several members of the party were shot at, a bomb killed two people during a rally in Mayagüez, and even the son of the Secretary General, Juan Mari Brás, was murdered under circumstances that have not been fully explained. In this case political repression served not so much as a demobilizing force but as a powerful source of cohesion. On the other hand, legal and "extra-legal" measures taken by the government and private enterprise against that part of the labor movement influenced by the PSP, may have taken their toll on labor especially after the Ponce Cement strike and the closing of firms linked to the oil industry. The effect of those measures were magnified by the PSP strategy of relying chiefly on the organized labor movement for its growth within the working class. After several years of close involvement in strikes throughout all the island, in 1976-77, when labor activity dwindled, the PSP had almost no organized support in the workplace.

Socialist, pro-independence, and labor groups were all subject to covert actions by the government. During the 1992 public hearings concerning the 1978 murders of two young *independentistas* in Cerro Maravilla, Colonel José Nolla of the National Guard admitted that with the compliance of the Electric Power Agency, some obsolescent electric towers slated for removal could have been blown so as to discredit the radical movement on the island.

During the 1970s, the PIP also met with internal difficulties. The radicalization process of the 1960s had led to the formation of a marxist faction that eventually split off into the *Movimiento Socialista Popular* (Popular Socialist Movement, MSP).[19] Freed from its radical left, the PIP returned to its traditional project centered on independence and the promise of a clean and efficient government. Social projects of wider aspirations were quietly phased out. Even so, the PIP, which has always been the largest of the pro-independence organizations on the island, has fared better than the others. The PIP monopolizes the electoral representation of independence. Its legislative group provided an efficient and provocative fiscalization of the ruling party during the 1980s, garnering wide support for its legislative delegation, not for its program for independence.

Two other organizations must be mentioned. The MST claimed the marxist ideological space in the island since the PSP slid back to its origins.[20] The MST, ever since its foundation, has maintained a publicly critical attitude towards the so-called socialist bloc, and has also stressed the need for a social program that goes beyond independence. Nevertheless the MST has had no appreciable influence outside the labor movement, with its political practice poorly attuned to the character of contemporary Puerto Rican society. Political struggle in Puerto Rico must take into account several factors: the importance of the electoral process; the influence of the mass media, the emergence of new social actors; the diversified workforce with its many and complex interests in education, public health, housing, urban development, national rights, women's rights, and ecology. Therefore, to draw a strategy based principally on the organized labor movement and focused narrowly on economic demands whittles down the impact of any political organization that still has to establish itself as a rallying point of effective opposition.

Besides, the MST and similar marxist organizations in other countries face a similar situation: once in the shadow of organizations recognized by the Eastern Bloc countries, since the Bloc collapsed, even though they opposed it, they have been caught in the ensuing anti-marxist wave.

The other important organization has been the *Partido Revolucionario de los Trabajadores* (Revolutionary Workers party, PRTP), popularly known as the *Macheteros*. Their strategic option has been the armed struggle against U.S. domination: they have claimed several important operations such as an attack on U.S. personnel at the military base in Sabana Seca, and the blowing up of several national guard airplanes. The PRTP stresses its particular conception of Puerto Rican society as based on coercive means. There is no doubt that ultimately continuing U.S. presence on the island rests on its capacity for violent coercion. To prove this point it is sufficient to watch how Congress blatantly imposed on the PIP representatives the presence of military bases even if independence were to be the choice of the Puerto Rican people in a plebiscite.[21] The *Macheteros*' strategy relying principally on armed actions, however, underestimates the bourgeois-democratic development of the country, and the particular formation of the U.S. hegemony in the island.

Independence in the 1990s

History has not been kind to the independence movement. The 1990s brought a new crisis: the collapse of real socialism. Since, as I have shown, socialism became a means to renew *independentista* thought and action, the collapse of real socialism has been a setback to marxist organizations in Puerto Rico. The ideology and practice of parties such as the PSP were already under siege. Many of the elements that defined the crisis suffered by the communist organizations in the world were also at play in the PSP: anti-democratic party structures, a stalinist political culture, and reluctance to criticize openly the official socialist countries.

The fact is, though, that the political upheaval in Eastern Europe spread its potent waves across the world to reach even the shores of Puerto Rican politics and to deprive the pro-independence forces of a program that was dear to many as the sole way to challenge U.S. dominion on the island and the parties that represented it, the PPD and the PNP.

But at the same time, the collapse of real socialism may revitalize the independence movement. The re-emergence of nationalism and ethnic awareness, as in those countries that once formed the Soviet Union—the Baltics, Ukraine, Georgia—or those that formed Yugoslavia, such as Croatia and Slovenia, has given Puerto Rican nationalism a shot in the arm. It is ironic that at the same time that the 12 most important European nations are striving to put aside their national interests to form a larger union, the dismemberment of the Soviet Union and Yugoslavia has put new life in the coffers of nationalism. In fact, this phenomenon probably instilled some sobriety in Congress during discussion of a plebiscite concerning the island's political status. Even though nationalism in Lithuania cannot be compared to its extent in Puerto Rico, some congresspersons were impressed by the admonition of several pro-independence leaders about the possibility of Puerto Rico becoming the "Lithuania of the United States " in the next century if admitted as a federated state within the Union.

The collapse of real socialism has weakened anti-communism, once one of the most important ideological weapons in the annexationist forces' arsenal. Ever since the Cuban Revolution provided radical independence forces with a new political paradigm, pro-annexation forces, fueled by a rabid anti-communism reacted in such a way that the ever present tradition of criminalization of *independentistas* acquired a new belligerence. The PNP, especially under the leadership of former governor Carlos Romero-Barceló, became the most blaring expression of such tendency, but the PPD also housed its own faction of visceral anti-communists. An equation was therefore drawn that translated independence into communism. But the collapse of *real socialism* has deprived, or at the very least weakened, such an approach. I should mention, however, the opposite phenomenon: the marriage of independence and socialism did much to enhance marxism in the island. Contrary to the United States, during the 1970s, marxism, though berated in some quarters, became a respectable ideology among many people, even among non-marxists. Now, as the Red Danger recedes, the use of Cold War rhetoric as a means of coalescing the anti-independence forces is also receding.

We must consider, within this context the recent admission of the Puerto Rican government that pro-independence activists have been unlawfully persecuted by the State. After years of denunciations by the independence movements, the State has finally accepted the existence of thousands of dossiers involving people whose only crime was to advocate independence.[22] The existence of these dossiers clearly demonstrate the criminalization to which the struggle for independence has been subjected. The scope of that program can be compared only to the similar STASI effort in the now defunct East Germany.

Therefore, the fact that the Puerto Rican government has dismantled this effort—it's yet to be seen whether the federal government, the FBI and the CIA, will follow suit—points to a new acceptance of *independentistas*. Whether this perception will imply a new legitimacy for independence is also yet to be seen. But, at least the political climate in that particular aspect is different from the one prevailing in previous years.

Possibly the most important development that Puerto Rico will face in the 1990s is the integration of the Mexican economy into the United States as a result of the North American Free Trade Agreement (NAFTA). The presence of cheap Mexican labor, plus the proximity of the Mexican industrial base will undoubtedly undermine the strategy of development on which Puerto Rico has relied for more than 40 years. It has yet to be seen what the impact will be on 936 industries, enterprises that benefit from cheap labor, easy access to U.S. markets, and tax exemptions.[23] Evidently, Mexico will provide much of the same attractions as Puerto Rico, and in many cases, even more. The economic implications of NAFTA may also point to the need for flexibilizing the political powers of the Commonwealth to cushion the impact of the Mexican economy on Puerto Rico. That by itself will provide new scenarios in which several alliances between pro-independence forces and groups within the PPD seeking additional political powers may emerge.

Though pro-independence struggle may be rekindled by these new parameters, its political forces still have to come to terms with its long standing crisis, and the fact that events may override them. For example, the fact that the PSP was unable to put forward a substantive critique of socialism in the Eastern Bloc during the 1980s deprived the party of the opportunity to acquire the moral strength needed to seek a new project for a democratic and popular socialism. Instead the PSP sought refuge in a silence that has been understood as complicity by people in other leftist organizations.[24] After the collapse of the Eastern regimes, the PSP has come forward with criticism, but this after-the-fact conversion does not extend to Cuba, where some of the problems that affected the Eastern Bloc also manifest themselves. The return of PSP to its non-partisan, pro-independence origins, and its new openness to a wide diversity of ideologies, may finally end the vexing problems of its long association with the so-called socialist bloc. But twenty years have not passed in vain, and that political space is either closed or occupied by the PIP.

Most of the other marxist organizations have not fared much better than the PSP. In a sense, they should stand to gain for their open criticisms of official socialism. These are, however, groups that have so far acquired little presence in national life. Though some of them are influential in several important labor unions, they lack a comprehensive view of national politics and fail to question the multiple roles of the State in the wide diversity of instances that modern society provides. The PIP is the only group that maintains a national presence mainly through the work of its legislators. Its influence, however, is limited by its inability to trascend electoral politics.

Puerto Rican marxist groups have yet to analyze the impact of U.S. hegemony in Puerto Rico, or the fact that the island has been through a bourgeois-democratic phase, distinct from other Latin American nations. The acquiescence of society to U.S supremacy—that is, the problem of the formation of U.S. hegemony—is still *the most essential problem* that socialist and pro-independence forces must tackle both practically and theoretically. The enormous emphasis that *independentista* thought has put on political repression as a rationale for the movement's shortcomings has detracted attention from this fact.

On the other hand, the proponents of armed struggle, represented by the PRTP, received a blow during the 1980s. Their avowed leader Filiberto Ojeda was once imprisoned, along with other alleged members of the organization. At this date, Ojeda has gone back to the clandestine life and vows to continue the PRTP project. But the reconstruction of a dismantled clandestine network is not an easy task under any circumstances, much less easy without an active base of support. The survival, though, of the *Macheteros'* mystique is another thing. The U.S. government's attempt (aided by some of its Puerto Rican advocates) to label the *Macheteros* as terrorists has consistently failed due to the latent Puerto Rican nationalism that survives even in the annexationist party, the PNP.

The present weakness of the whole of the *independentista* forces can be assessed more clearly in light of the 1990-91 proposed plebiscite. That debate centered on Congress's intentions of letting Puerto Ricans choose from among independence, statehood, or enhanced Commonwealth. The PIP was forced to accept the permanence of U.S. citizenship, the military bases, and the continuation of a program similar to the 936 program, even after independence. Even the PIP's important new idea of demanding Puerto Rico's right to self-determination under statehood—that is, the right to secede from the Union after becoming a state—represented the realization that total annexation, as the plebiscite outcome, was more feasible than independence. Save for a large demonstration organized for the opening of the public hearings on the plebiscite bill held by the U.S. Senate in San Juan, the presence of pro-independence forces as an active focus of political activity during the 1980s was scant.

After the plebiscite debate, statehood forces were set back as a result of the refusal of several Republican congressmen to pave the way for statehood. Such a refusal, coming from people who were perceived as allies by the Puerto Rican pro-annexation forces, has weakened statehood and enhanced the Commonwealth movement as the meeting place of lukewarm nationalism and pro-U.S. feelings. The expression of that particular development is the growing hegemony of the PPD over the pro-independence forces, as it assumes the discourse of *Puertoricanism*. History forces on us a new irony as political *autonomists* and *independentistas* join forces, as they had done in the 1930s. The open question now is whether the *independentistas's* program as such has already become an ahistorical goal for the Puerto Rican people, faced with the new waves of integration prevalent in the continent.

The popular social movements, particularly the ecological movement, were the most important focus of radical activity during the 1980s. During the 1960s and the 1970s the radical left monopolized most of the program and activities of the popular social movement. While that hindered their independence from the strictly political organizations, at the same time it raised social awareness concerning the environment, the need for an alternative industrial strategy, feminism, the rights of gay men and lesbians, urban needs, anti-militarism and the struggle for peace, and Caribbean solidarity. As the political organizations lost their stronghold, all these movements gathered momentum as an autonomous social movement. Many activists from the radical left, disillusioned with their organizations, have flocked to the popular social movements, lending them their social awareness and organizational expertise. In spite of some efforts, these diverse movements—loosely referred to as "the Popular Social Movement"—have been reluctant to form a wide umbrella organization that could produce joint actions as has happened in other countries. But the possibility is still there, and it is one we should work towards.

The near future

There is little discussion that Puerto Rico, despite its extreme dependency on the United States, is culturally a *nation*. As Mexico and other Latin American societies rush to integrate themselves into the world market, they will assert their own particular national and cultural characteristics. In accommodating that diversity, global business people will need to respect or at least recognize important elements of Latin American culture, such as language, ethnicity, and history. Within the United States, more and more capital sectors are targeting the Latino population with market strategies that take into account distinctive cultural elements. While previously the development of the market required uniformity of cultures, new techniques today counsel just the opposite. In that way, globalization may eventually come to terms with nationalism, and even require it as an added asset.

The coming integration of markets may be a boost for cultural nationalism, and in that way aid the independence movement. This is especially important because what lies at the core of the survival of the struggle for Puerto Rico's independence throughout this century is the latent nationalism of the Puerto Rican people. Though it is customary to point out the poor showing of independence supporters in the elections, the fact is that after almost a century of U.S. hegemony, its mere presence and command of respect in the Puerto Rican society points to the importance of cultural nationalism as the underlying support of political nationalism. This cultural nationalism is wider in its appeal to the Puerto Rican people than pro-independence ideology, and is crossed with many contradictions stemming from the very chaotic development of the Puerto Rican classes in this century. Nevertheless cultural nationalism was one of the motivations behind the recent 1991 decision of the PPD to enact a law establishing clearly the Spanish language as the government's official language.[25]

The pro-independence movement, however, needs a long vacation from status politics if it wants to overcome its present limitations. If it continues to indulge in a strategy that puts independence in the forefront, and not the myriad social problems confronting society, it will not gain more support. The only way it will be able to cross the historical barriers posed by status politics is to devise a program of social revindications and practices that can be sponsored by people from the diverse spectrum of status options. As for status itself, it suffices merely to adopt the defense of national rights such as language, popular culture, and the right to secede from the United States if the country ever becomes a State of the Union.

Independence activists must recognize the need for the joint action of the Puerto Rican, the U.S., the Canadian, and the Mexican working classes. The establishment of a North American common market will produce important upheavals in all those countries. Puerto Rican and U.S. workers have experience with the sort of things that may happen. The example of the runaway plants leaving the U.S. to establish themselves in Puerto Rico under the benefits of the 936 statute will be greatly increased as even cheaper Mexican labor joins the market.[26] It is in the interest of all workers to develop a joint position that also demands higher wages for the Mexican workers and better labor conditions. This strategy developed also in the Caribbean will point to a new dimension of internationalism.

The social program of the independence movement must take into account the need to revamp socialism if it is to present an alternative to the current—and indeed overwhelming—belief that only capitalism holds an answer for humankind.[27] It is a belief sponsored by people that have decided to turn their eyes away not only from the status of capitalism in the third world but also from the appalling social conditions of the major urban centers in the United States.

Revamping socialism must include political pluralism, and the recognition of diverse forms of collective ownership besides democratic central planning. It must recognize also the popular social movements that have emerged in Puerto Rico during the 1980s and the importance of their autonomous efforts to develop an alternative society vis-à-vis the State.

It should be said that some of the pro-independence parties that advocated socialism during the 1970s tried a strategy that stressed social conditions instead of status politics. But those efforts were short-lived and fatally tinged with a tendency to indulge in the decades-old discussion on status as soon as the issue was pushed by any other political force.[28]

The growth of statehood forces during the 1980s led many *independentistas* to an apocalyptic thinking with regards to Puerto Rico's destiny as a nation. For them, statehood is the death toll for a Puerto Rican nation. Yet the fact is that Puerto Rico is a *nation,* although, lacking formal independence, it is not a nation-state. Few people in Puerto Rico—and even in the United States—are convinced that statehood will eliminate Puerto Rico's quest for national independence. Notwithstanding current political beliefs in the United States that once inside the Union there is no way out, political realities dramatized in what once was the Soviet Union clearly point out otherwise. In the future, even after statehood, if the Puerto Rican people militantly opt for independence, there will be little sympathy in the world for an imposition of statehood. Too much has happened in this planet since the U.S. Civil War ended. On the other hand, especially for Puerto Rican socialists, statehood opens up wide and diverse opportunities of cooperation with Latinos, blacks, Native Americans, poor whites, the disenfranchised aging population, and the feminist movement: this describes a very ample political arena in which to form new alliances, to conduct new struggles, and also to gain wider recognition for Puerto Rican national rights.

History shows that Puerto Rican independence as an ideology and as a social struggle is very resilient. But to survive through the 1990s activists must learn to fight in a wider and more complex arena than they have experienced so far. Above all, they must finally learn that it is not independence per se that the masses are after, but a political status that will clearly fulfill their aspirations to a better life. These aspects must be addressed before the island can make a commitment to break away with U.S. hegemony. If not, pro-independence forces will continue to survive merely as the watchdogs of Puerto Rican nationality, while the other parties, the PPD or the PNP, carry on the responsibilities of governing.

Notes

Chapter 1

1. Among the most salient issues are the federal budget deficits, the electoral defeat of the Sandinistas, the collapse of dictatorial regimes in Eastern Europe, the anticipated isolation of Cuba, and the declining threat of communist-inspired insurgencies in Central and Latin America.

2. See Congressional Budget Office, "Potential Economic Impacts of Changes in Puerto Rico's Status Under 712."

3. Cited in José Trias Monge, *Historia constitucional de Puerto Rico,* 4 vols. (Río Piedras, Puerto Rico: Editorial Universitaria, 1981), 3:53.

4. Trias Monge, 3:54. Congressman Vito Marcantonio, an outspoken advocate for independence who scorned Muñoz Marín and the PPD, expressed the same view, although in an unequivocal and flamboyant manner. In opposing the measure he argued:

> This bill is merely a snare and a delusion and a fraud perpetrated on the people of Puerto Rico to make them believe we are giving them something. We are giving them nothing...We are misleading them, and we are aiding the present ruling clique of Puerto Rico to dodge the responsibility they assumed at the time they won their election to bring an end to the colonial status. (Trias Monge, 3:56).

5. David Helfeld, "Congressional Intent and Attitude Toward Public Law 600 and the Constitution of the Commonwealth of Puerto Rico" *Revista Jurídica de la Universidad de Puerto Rico* 21, No.4 (May-June 1952): 307.

6. Emilio Pantojas-García, "Puerto Rican Populism Revisited: The PPD during the 1940s," *Journal of Latin American Studies* 21, No. 3 (January 1989): 521-557.

7. This is the title of Gordon K. Lewis' well-known study *Puerto Rico: Freedom and Power in the Caribbean* (New York: Monthly Review Press, 1963).

8. Robert Pastor notes, "Few domestic issues have consistently generated as much international debate as that of Puerto Rico. It has been on the UN agenda since representatives of the Puerto Rican Nationalist Party went to San Francisco for the signing of the UN Charter in 1945. Although the U.S. Government may have convinced itself that it removed Puerto Rico from the international agenda in 1953, few others are convinced," in "Puerto Rico as an International Issue: A Motive for Movement?" in *Puerto Rico: The Search for a National Policy,* ed. Richard J. Bloomfield (Boulder, Colo.: Westview Press, 1985), p. 114. He further observes, "The

United States invests a great deal of energy, prestige and resources—mostly diplomatic, but occasionally economic and political each year to try to keep from being condemned as a colonial power," p. 120. For a generously documented and exhaustive analysis of Puerto Rico before the United Nations, see Humberto García Muñiz, "Puerto Rico and the United States: The United Nations Role, 1953-1975," *Revista Jurídica de la Universidad de Puerto Rico* 53, No. 1 (1984): 1-265. For development since 1973, see Carlos Rivera Lugo, "Puerto Rico ante la ONU (1976-1983): Autodeterminación y transferencia de Poderes," in *Revista Jurídica de la Universidad de Puerto Rico* 53, No. 1 (1984): 267-299.

9. Arthur Borg, "The Problem of Puerto Rico's Political Status," United States Department of State, p. 7.

10. Ibid.

11. "Public Law 600 primarily recognized the right of self-government by the people of Puerto Rico and established the process by which their representatives, freely and specifically elected for that purpose, drafted a constitution which the people of Puerto Rico adopted." *Compact of Permanent Union Between Puerto Rico and the United States,* Report of the Ad Hoc Advisory Group on Puerto Rico (October 1975), p. 5.

12. The plebiscite was the outgrowth of the report submitted by the United States-Puerto Rico Commission on the Status of Puerto Rico. José Trías Monge, who was a member of the Commission and a high-level PPD official, observed that the U.S. government would not be obligated in any way to accept the plebiscite results. *Historia Constitucional de Puerto Rico,* 3:244.

13. Ibid., p. 245.

14. *La nueva tesis* (Río Piedras, Puerto Rico: Editorial Edil, 1986), p. 55.

15. Ibid., p. 53.

16. Fernando Byron Toro, *Elecciones y partidos políticos de Puerto Rico* (Mayaguez, Puerto Rico: Editorial Isla, 1989), p. 276.

17. According to Byron Toro's calculations, Barceló's votes surpassed Hernández Colón's by only 0.1875 percent, p. 291.

18. This period is covered by Edwin Meléndez, "Accumulation and Crisis in the Postwar Puerto Rican Economy," PhD thesis, University of Massachusetts, Amherst, 1985, and by Edgardo Meléndez, *Puerto Rico's Statehood Movement* (New York: Greenwood Press, 1988).

19. Committee to Study Puerto Rico's Finances, *Report to the Governor,* December 11, 1975.

20. Pedro A. Cabán, "The Colonial State and Capitalist Expansion in Puerto Rico," *Centro* 2, No. 6 (1989): 87.

21. Fernando Zalacaín, "La importancia económica de Puerto Rico para Estados Unidos," *El Nuevo Día,* 15 June 1989. Cited in *Pensamiento Crítico* 2, No. 2 (November 1989):1-2. Antonio Colorado, Puerto Rico's Secretary of State, was quoted in the 29 November 1990 issue of *Caribbean Business* as saying:

> The U.S. companies (936 and non-936) received $45 billion in net income from return on investment worldwide, a sizeable figure, but Puerto Rico alone produced $10 billion return on investment for

U.S. companies. There is no single country in the world that produces as much net income for U.S. companies as Puerto Rico. The $10 billion is not included in the $45 billion of foreign income because it is considered internal trade. When you add that $10 billion to the $45 billion, Puerto Rico produces more than 18 percent of the worldwide net income on investments outside of the mainland that U.S. companies receive.

22. John R. Stewart, *An Analysis of the President Tax Proposal to Repeal the Possessions Tax Credit in Section 936 of the U.S. Internal Revenue Code* (San Juan, Puerto Rico: Puerto Rican Development Corporation, 1985): iii. According to *Caribbean Business,* 30 March 1989, this amounts to approximately $9.5 billion.

23. Emilio Pantojas-García, *Development Strategies as Ideology: Puerto Rico's Export-Led Industrialization Experience* (Boulder, Colo.: Lynne Reinner, 1990), p. 155. Employment in manufacturing increased from 132,000 to 155,000 from 1970 to 1990 (17.4%), whereas employment in services industries registered an increase of 66% (from 117,000 to 195,000 workers during the same twenty-year period). See *Caribbean Business,* 1 November 1990.

24. Testimony of Kenneth W. Gideon, Assistant Secretary, Department of the Treasury, U.S. Congress, Senate Committee on Energy and Natural Resources, *Hearings on S. 710, S. 711, and S. 712 to Provide for a Referendum on the Political Status of Puerto Rico,* 3 parts, First Session, 101st Congress (Washington, DC: Government Printing Office, 1989):3, p. 205.

25. This is the Washington-based organization with an affiliation of seventy multinational corporations and financial institutions that support retention of Section 936.

26. U.S. Government Accounting Office (GAO), *Puerto Rico: Update of Selected Information Contained in a 1981 GAO Report* (Washington, DC: GAO, August 1989).

27. Minority views were included in Senate Committee on Energy and Natural Resources, *Report 101-120 to Accompany S. 712: Puerto Rico Status Referendum Act,* 6 September 1989, First Session, 101st Congress.

28. The political parties and their presidents are Rafael Hernández Colón, *Partido Popular Democrático* (Commonwealth); former Governor Carlos Romero-Barceló, *Partido Nuevo Progresista* (statehood); Rubén Berríos, *Partido Independentista Puertorriqueño* (independence).

29. The testimony and statements have been published: Senate Committee on Energy and Natural Resources, *Hearings on S710, S711, and S712.*

30. Ibid., pt. 3, p. 153.

31. Ibid., pt. 3, p. 202.

32. Ibid., pt. 3, pp. 142-143.

33. Ibid., pt. 3, p. 153.

34. Congressional Budget Office, "Potential Economic Impacts," p. 27.

35. Ibid.

36. Senate Committe on Energy and Natural Resources, *Hearings on S710, S711, and S712,* pt. 2, p. 132.

37. Ibid., pt. 2, pp. 441-442.

38. *El Nuevo Día*, 7 November 1990.

Chapter 2

1. Lyman J. Gould, *La ley Foraker: Raíces de la política colonial de los Estados Unidos* (Río Piedras: Editorial Universitaria, 1975); Truman R. Clark, *Puerto Rico and the United States, 1917-1933* (Pittsburgh: University of Pittsburgh Press, 1975); Surendra Bhana, *The United States and the Development of the Puerto Rican Status Question, 1936-1968* (Wichita: UP of Arkansas, 1975); and José A. Cabranes, "Puerto Rico: Out of the Colonial Closet," *Foreign Policy*: Winter 1978-79:66-91.

2. Gould, *La ley Foraker*.

3. Carmen Ramos de Santiago, *El gobierno de Puerto Rico* (Río Piedras: Editorial Universitaria, 1970) 107-114.

4. José A. Cabranes, *Citizenship and the American Empire: Notes on the Legislative History of the United States Citizenship of Puerto Ricans* (New Haven: Yale University Press, 1979) 6; and Clark, 5.

5. Lyman D. Bothwell, "Capital Formation in Puerto Rico, 1950-1960," George Washington University, 1964.

6. United States, Department of Commerce, *Economic Study of Puerto Rico* Vol. 1 (Washington: GPO, 1979) 14-15.

7. United States, Cong., House Committee on Insular Affairs, *Investigation of Political, Economic, and Social Conditions in Puerto Rico,* 79th Cong., 1st sess., H. Rept. 497, (Washington: GPO, 1945) 25. See also the 1945 report by the U.S. Tariff Commission in Reece B. Bothwell, ed., *Puerto Rico; Cien años de lucha política* Vol. 3 (Río Piedras: Editorial Universitaria, 1979) 477-94.

8. "From Our Editor to Eisenhower," *El Estado* Jan-Feb 1954:5.

9. United States, United States-Puerto Rico Commission on the Status of Puerto Rico, *Commission Report* (Washington: GPO, 1966) 14.

10. President Ford's statehood bill remains the best piece of legislation on this regard. See United States, Cong., *Puerto Rico Statehood Act of 1977,* 95th Cong., 1st sess., H. Doc. 95-49.

11. United States, Department of State, Senior Seminar Policy, *The Problem of Puerto Rico's Political Status,* 1974-75; Office of the Assistant Secretary of Defense, "Puerto Rico: Commonwealth, Statehood or Independence," Memorandum to U.S. President Gerald Ford, 12 July 1977; United States, Library of Congress, *Puerto Rico: Independence or Statehood? A Survey of Historical, Political, and Socio-economic Factors, with Pro and Con Arguments* (Washington: Congressional Research Service, 1977); United States, Library of Congress, *Treating Puerto Rico as a State Under Federal Tax and Expenditure Programs* (Washington: Congressional Research Service, 1977); United States, Library of Congress, *Puerto Rico; Commonwealth, Statehood, or Independence?* (Washington: Congressional Research Service, 1978); United States, Department of State, "Puerto Rico's Status: A Problem for the Eighties"

(Internal Report, 1980); General Accounting Office, *Puerto Rico's Political Future: A Divisive Issue with Many Dimensions* (Washington: GAO, 1981).

12. Edgardo Meléndez, *Puerto Rico's Statehood Movement* (Westport, Conn.: Greenwood Press, 1988), Chpt. 2 and 3. Also, Mariano Negrón Portillo, "El liderato anexionista antes y después del cambio de soberanía," *Revista del Colegio de Abogados de Puerto Rico,* October 1972, 369-91.

13. *Ibid.,* ch. 4.

14. *Ibid.,* ch. 5; Aarón G. Ramos, ed., Introduction, *Las ideas anexionistas en Puerto Rico bajo la dominación norteamericana* (Río Piedras: Editorial Huracán, 1987).

15. PNP politics are discussed in Meléndez, Chpt. 6 and 7; Ramos; Ilya Villar Martínez and Haroldo Dilla Alfonso, "Las tendencias anexionistas en el proceso político puertorriqueño," *El Caribe Contemporáneo,* June 1982:70-91; and Luis Martínez Fernández, *El Partido Nuevo Progresista* (Río Piedras: Editorial Edil, 1986).

16. Partido Republicano, *Asamblea Republicana celebrada en San Juan,* (San Juan: Imprenta de "El País," 1-2 July 1899:29, 32; Pilar Barbosa, ed., *Orientando al pueblo, 1900-1921,* (San Juan: Imprenta Venezuela, 1939), 37, 42, 110.

17. Reece B. Bothwell, "Puerto Rico en la Federación Americana," *El Estado,* April-May 1949:9, 11.

18. Luis A. Ferré, *El propósito humano,* ed. Antonio Quiñones Calderón (San Juan: Ediciones Nuevas, 1972).

19. Carlos Romero Barceló, *La estadidad es para los pobres* (San Juan, 1973).

20. Carlos Romero Barceló, *Forjando el Futuro,* ed. Antonio Quiñones Calderón (Hato Rey: Ramallo Bros., 1978); Carlos Romero Barceló, "Puerto Rico, U.S.A.: The Case for Statehood," *Foreign Affairs, Fall 1980:60-81; Grupo de Investigadores Puertorriqueños, Breakthrough From Colonialism,* (Río Piedras: Editorial de la Universidad de Puerto Rico, 1984), 2 vols.

21. United States, Cong., Senate, Committee on Energy and Natural Resources, *Hearings on the Political Status of Puerto Rico,* 101st Cong. 1st sess. S.710, S.711, and S.712 (Washington: GPO, 1989) 122-142.

22. United States, Cong., Senate, Committee on Energy and Natural Resources, *Puerto Rico Status Referendum Act,* 101st Cong., 1st sess., 3-7.

23. PNP President Romero Barceló has acknowledged this in response to one of his critics; he argued that "To demand [status] definitions to the plebiscite bill is not in our favor. On the contrary, it goes against us." *El Nuevo Día,* 31 October 1990:18.

24. *Political Status of Puerto Rico,* 47.

25. United States, Cong., Senate, *Political Status of Puerto Rico, Hearings on July 11, 13, and 14, 1989,* (Washington: GPO, 1989):25-26.

26. *Political Status of Puerto Rico,* 369-70, 404-405.

27. The CBO September 1989 report appears in *Political Status of Puerto Rico,* 53-62.

28. *Puerto Rico Status Referendum Act,* 26.

29. *Puerto Rico Status Rererendum Act,* 63-67.

30. *El Mundo,* April 6, 1990:4-5.

31. Patrick J. Buchanan, "Puerto Rico as Our 51st State?" *Washington Times*, 26 February 1990; and Buchanan, "Let Puerto Rico Be a Nation," *New York Post*, 16 May 1990. Buchanan challenged President Bush in the 1992 Republican presidential primaries. One of Buchanan's main issues against Bush was the president's support for statehood. An example of new attacks on Puerto Rican statehood by the Republican right is Richard A. Viguerie and Steven Allen, "To Bush: The Right Has Other Choices," *The New York Times*, 14 June 1990:A27; George F. Will, "Does Puerto Rico Belong Within the Federal Union?," and Buchanan, "Puerto Rico Asserts Her Nationhood," both published in *The Washington Post*, and reprinted in *The San Juan Star*, 24 March 1991:24.

32. "Puerto Rico Referendum Killed," *The Washington Post*, 28 February 1991.

Chapter 3

1. B. de la Torre, "Navy Builds Up Base," *Caribbean Business*, 23 July 1986:18.

2. For an analysis of U.S. military installations in the entire insular Caribbean see H. García Muñiz, *Decolonization, Demilitarization, and Denuclearization in the Caribbean* (Miami: Latin American and Caribbean Center, Florida International University, 1989). An extensive bibliography on security forces and foreign military presence in the Caribbean, including installations, can be found in H. García Muñiz and B. Vélez Natal, eds. *Bibliografía Militar del Caribe* (Río Piedras: Centro de Investigaciones Históricas, Universidad de Puerto Rico, forthcoming). The most comprehensive works on military installations are Robert Harkavy, *Great Power Competition for Overseas Bases* (New York: Pergamon, 1982) and *Bases Abroad: The Global Foreign Military Presence* (New York: Oxford, 1989).

3. In this work I use H.G. Hagerty's definition of "base" and "facility," whose main distinction relates to both size and tenancy. A base is usually a larger complex, including both operating and supporting assigned personnel; a facility tends to be smaller, with a more limited function, and few operating personnel regularly resident. An "installation" is a generic term, applicable to both. H.G. Hagerty, *Forward Deployment in the 1970's and 1980's*, National Security Affairs Monograph 77-2 (Washington: National Defense University, 1977):32.

4. Most of the information of this section dealing with the pre-First World War period was taken from M.E. Estades Font, *La presencia militar de Estados Unidos en Puerto Rico, 1898-1918: Intereses estratégicos y dominación colonial* (Río Piedras: Editorial Huracán, 1988).

5. No information has been found on the dispossession and removal of any community in Guantánamo. For a moving account of the Culebra experience see C.C. Feliciano, *Apuntes y comentarios de la colonización y liberación de la isla de Culebra* (Culebra, 1981).

6. C.T. Hull, Lieut., U.S.N., and F.W. Hoadley, "U.S.A. Naval Communication Service, Naval Radio Station NAU," in *El libro de Puerto Rico/The Book of Porto Rico*, E. Fernández García, ed. (San Juan: El Libro Azul Pub. Co., 1923), 719.

7. For details see Chapter 2 of H. García Muñiz, *Los Estados Unidos y la militarización del Caribe,* (Río Piedras: Instituto de Estudios del Caribe, Universidad de Puerto Rico, 1988).

8. J. Pastor Ruiz, *Vieques antiguo y moderno,* (Yauco: Tip. Rodríguez Lugo, 1947), 206. My translation.

9. One document says: "My proposal is that the present population of Vieques be transported and resettled in the Island of St. Croix...I discussed this proposal with Governor Pinero [sic]. He received it with enthusiasm." Memorandum from Irwin W. Silverman, Acg. Director, Div. of Territories and Island Possessions, Dept. of the Interior, to Oscar Chapman, Under Secretary of Interior, Dept. of Interior, 8 August 1947, Colección Viequense, Escuela Germán Rieckehoff, Vieques, Puerto Rico.

10. In the 1980 congressional hearings, the mayor of Vieques told the U.S.V.I. delegate: "Congressman Evans...knows very well that there are many people of Vieques residing in the neighboring islands of St. Croix and St. Thomas that have had to abandon this island because of economic conditions...that do not permit the people of Vieques, after they finish high school, to stay on the island because there are no economic opportunities here for those who have graduated or for our people." United States, Cong., House, Committee on Armed Services, *Hearings before the Panel to Review the Status of Navy Training Activities in the Island of Vieques* (Washington: GPO, 1980) 216. See also C. Senior, *The Puerto Rican Migrant in St. Croix,* (Río Piedras: Social Science Research Center, 1947).

11. Planning Board, Office of the Governor, "Need for a Study of Land Holdings of Armed Forces in Puerto Rico," Record Group 136 Office of the Territories, Classified Files, 1907-1951, Box 930, National Archives, Washington, D.C.

12. L.D. Langley, "Roosevelt Roads, Puerto Rico, U.S. Naval Base, 1941-," in *United States Navy and Marine Corps Bases, Overseas,* P. Coletta and J.K. Dauer, eds. (Westport, Conn.: Greenwood, 1985) 149.

13. Frank C. Nash, "United States Military Bases Report to the President by December, 1957," *Declassified Document Quarterly Catalogue,* 4.

14. Adm. L. Baggett Jr., USN, CINC, U.S. Atlantic Command, "U.S. Atlantic Command: Strengthening the Forward Strategy," *Defense* November/December, 1987:30.

15. U.S. Forces, Caribbean, previously known as the Antilles Defense Department, had its headquarters in Key West and was responsible for the conduct of joint and combined exercises in the Caribbean Basin as well as the implementation of the security assistance program for countries in the Caribbean area, including the Dominican Republic, Haiti, Jamaica, Trinidad and Tobago, and the island states of the Regional Security System of the Eastern Caribbean. The phasing out of U.S. Forces, Caribbean was the result of a cost-cutting study which said that "[I]n all the important contingencies imaginable it appears the command will either get in the way or be ignored." D.J. Vander Schaaf, Chairman, *Review of Unified and Specified Command Headquarters,* Secretary of Defense Study Team, February 1988, 42.

16. For an excellent analysis of the new developments see M. Klare, "The U.S. Military Faces South," *The Nation,* 18 June 1990:841, 858-861.

17. See, for example, United States, Cong., Senate, Committee on Armed Services, *National Security Strategy,* 100th Cong., 1st sess., (Washington: GPO, 1987) 912-916. For a discussion on U.S. command structure in the Caribbean see H. García Muñiz, *Estratégia,* 219-231.

18. L. Chavez, "Salvador Leader Says the FBI is Training Investigation Squad," *New York Times,* 30 May 1984:A1, 13.

19. For an extensive document-based analysis see, Estado Libre Asociado, Comisión de Derechos Civiles, *Discriminación y persecución por razones políticas: La práctica de mantener listas, ficheros y expedientes de ciudadanos por razón de su ideología política,* 1 February 1989, Chapter 3.

20. Raymond Carr, *Puerto Rico: A Colonial Experiment* (New York: Vintage, 1984) 311.

21. For details see H. García Muñiz, "Defense Policy and Planning in the Caribbean: An Assessment of the Case of Jamaica on its 25th Independence Anniversary," *Caribbean Studies 21* 1988: 67-123.

22. See J. Enders, *La presencia militar de Estados Unidos en Puerto Rico* (Río Piedras: Proyecto Caribeño de Justicia y Paz, 1980) 1-10, and J. Rodríguez Beruff, *Política militar y dominación: Puerto Rico en el contexto latinoamericano* (Río Piedras: Editorial Huracán, 1988) 172-174.

23. "Case Study and Justification Folder and Environmental Impact for Retaining Fort Buchanan at Minimum Essential," FORSCOM, Ft. McPherson, Georgia, Revised 26 October 1976, Section 1, 6, quoted in Enders, *Presencia* 10.

24. Añejo 1: W.M. Arkin, "The Treaty of Tlatelolco, Nuclear Weapons and Puerto Rico. Findings for the Bar Association of Puerto Rico Special Commission on the Nuclear Weapons Threat," in Colegio de Abogados de Puerto Rico, *Informe de la Comisión Especial sobre Armamentos Nucleares y el Tratado para la Proscripción de las Armas Nucleares en América Latina* (San Juan, 17 August 1984) 3.

25. See L.H. Gelb, "U.S. Has Contingency Plan to Put A-Arms in 4 Countries, Aids Say," *New York Times,* 13 February 1985:1.

26. In return the navy was to relocate all naval activities (except communications) from the San Juan area to Roosevelt Roads. See "Memorandum for the Naval Aide to the President on Puerto Rico Real Estate Negotiations," 14 December 1961, *Declassified Document Quarterly Catalogue 8 (1982).*

27. Document 75: "Letter to President John F. Kennedy from Luis Muñoz Marín, Governor of Puerto Rico, 28 December 1961," Covington and Burling, *Culebra Legislative History Presented to: The Hon. Ramn Feliciano, Mayor of the Municipality of Culebra* (Culebra, 18 October 1975).

28. Carr, 312. For summaries presenting the anti- and pro-Navy positions respectively see L.L. Cripps, *Human Rights in a United States Colony* (Cambridge, Mass.: Schenkman, 1982), 115-38, and E. Langhorne, *Vieques: A History of a Small Island* (Vieques: The Vieques Conservation and Historical Trust), 62-86.

29. In his early days at Covington & Burling in the late 1960s, Copaken was assigned Culebra as a pro bono case, but when Hernández Colón was elected governor in 1972 the firm started to bill the Commonwealth. See M. Cohen, "Making Rain in the Caribbean," *American Lawyer* 17 March 1986:17-21.

30. In accordance with the Culebra agreement, the Commonwealth offered the navy the use of the two smaller uninhabited off-shore islands Desecheo and Monito, but they were rejected because they did not comply with the navy's requisites. See United States, Cong., *Subcommittee on Real Estate, Consideration of and Hearings on the Acquisition Report No. 102 and Disposal Report No. 300* (Washington: GPO, 1970).

31. Camp García was deactivated in 1978. Due to its presence prostitution had been rampant in Vieques for years. A navy sympathizer says that "the town had a flavor of the old West: 154 bars and elaborately caparisoned horses standing outside." Langhorne, 66.

32. L. Luxner, "Pentagon Spending Shrinks Here 4th Year in a Row," *Caribbean Business* 17 November 1988:4.

33. For an excellent analysis see M. Aponte-García, Chapter 6, "Changing Production Patterns and Industrial Policy: United States Military Production in the Caribbean," University of Massachusetts, 1990.

34. "Editorial: Vieques quiere empleos," *El Vocero* 3 February 1989:14, and "Entrelíneas," *El Nuevo Día* 27 February 1989:2, my translation.

35. For a moving account, including photos, see "Conflagration in Monte Carmelo," *The Vieques Times* April 1989:1, 4.

36. D. Hemlock, "Vieques Squatters Dig on Navy Land," *The San Juan Star* 30 May 1989:1.

37. See M. Cap, "Youth of Vieques: Seeking Better Future," *Caribbean Business* 18 May 1989:14. For demographic and economic data on Vieques see J.A. Bonnet Bentez, *Vieques en la historia de Puerto Rico* (San Juan: F. Ortiz Nieves, 1977).

38. C.J. Friedrich, *Puerto Rico: Middle Road to Freedom* (New York: Rinehart & Co., 1959) 72, my emphasis.

39. United States, Cong., Senate, Committee on Energy and National Resources, "Prepared Statement of Brig. Gen. M.J. Byron, Acting Deputy Assistant Secretary of Defense, 11 July 1989," 10.

40. Thomas F. Eagleton, "Base Realignments and Closures," *Report of the Defense Secretary's Commission,* December 1988: 39, 88. U.S. military installations in Puerto Rico and the Virgin Islands were considered as being "inside the United States."

41. See "Discriminate Deterrence," *Report of the Commission on Integrated Long-Term Strategy* January 1988, 10, and James R. Blaker, "US Overseas Basing System Faces a Difficult Transition," *Armed Forces Journal International* February 1989, 65-67.

42. See United States, Cong., House, Committee on the Armed Services, "Naval Training Activities on the Island of Vieques, Puerto Rico," *Report of the Panel to Review the Status of Navy Training Activities on the Island of Vieques,* 96th Cong., 2nd sess., (Washington: GPO, 1981).

43. United States, Department of Defense, Office of the Secretary of Defense, *Base Structure Report for FY1988* 56-57.

Chapter 4

1. See for example, Germán Delgado Passapera, *Puerto Rico: Sus luchas emancipadoras* (San Juan: Editorial Cultural, 1984) and Juan Manuel Carrión, "The Origins of Puerto Rican Nationalism: Precocity and Limitations of the Nineteenth Century Independece Movement" in *Rethinking the Nineteenth Century: Contradictions and Movements*, Francisco Ramírez, ed. (Westport, Conn.: Greenwood Press, 1988).

2. See Gordon K. Lewis, *Puerto Rico: Freedom and Power in the Caribbean*, (New York: Monthly Review Press, 1964) and Raymond Carr, *Puerto Rico: A Colonial Experiment* (New York: Vintage Books, 1984).

3. See A.G. Quintero Rivera, *Conflictos de Clase y Política en Puerto Rico* (San Juan: Ediciones Huracán, 1976) and José Luis González, *El país de cuatro pisos* (San Juan, Ediciones Huracán, 1980).

4. A.D. Smith, *The Ethnic Origin of Nations,* (Cambridge, MA: Basil Blackwell, 1988).

5. Immanuel Wallerstein, *The Politics of the World Economy: The States, the Movements and the Civilizations,* (Cambridge: Cambridge University Press, 1984), 20.

6. See for example A.G. Quintero Rivera, "Notes on the Puerto Rican National Development: Class and Nation in a Colonial Context," *Marxist Perspectives* Spring 1980, and Wilfredo Mattos Cintrón, *La Política y lo Político en Puerto Rico* (Mexico City: ERA, 1980).

7. See Emilio González Díaz, "Las bases del consenso político en la Colonia: El problema de la democracia en Puerto Rico," *El Caribe Contemporáneo,* (México), March-June 1980 and Wilfredo Mattos Cintrón, "La formación de la hegemonía de Estados Unidos en Puerto Rico y el independentismo," *Homines* (Puerto Rico), vol. 2, 1987-88.

8. On the Caribbean Basin Initiative see Hibourne A. Watson, "The Caribbean Basin Initiative," in *Contemporary Marxism,* 1985; and Emilio Pantojas, "Hacia la reestructuración de la hegemonía: La complementariedad entre los Niveles militar, económico, y político del proyecto norteamericano para la Cuenca del Caribe," in *Puerto Rico en el Caribe Hoy,* Carmen Gautier Mayoral, ed.(San Juan: CLASCO/CEREP, 1988).

9. Juan Mari Brás, *El Independentismo en Puerto Rico: Su Pasado, su Presente y su Porvenir* (San Juan: Editorial CEPA, 1984).

10. A history of anti-nationalist repression in the 1950s can be found in Ivonne Acosta, *La Mordaza,* (San Juan: Edil, 1987).

Chapter 5

1. Puerto Rico Planning Board, *Income and Product, 1984,* Table 2 and *Economic Report to the Governor, 1987-88,* Table 2.

2. Puerto Rico Planning Board, *Serie histórica del empleo, desempleo y el grupo trabajador en Puerto Rico, 1984,* Table 4.

3. Gross per capita income, in 1954 constant dollars, increased from $1,183 in 1973 to $1,281 in 1979. This represents an annual rate of growth of 1.4 percent, the lowest rate of growth between two peak years in the post-war period. However, gross per capita income actually declined to $1,249 in 1986. Puerto Rico Planning Board, *Income and Product, 1984,* Table 1.

4. Puerto Rico Planning Board, *Income and Product, 1984,* Table 19.

5. Edwin Meléndez, "Accumulation and Crisis in the Post-war Puerto Rico Economy," Unpublished Ph.D. Dissertation, University of Massachusetts, 1985, Table 4.

6. Puerto Rico Department of Labor, *Annual Report,* several years.

7. United States, Department of Commerce, *Economic Study of Puerto Rico,* Vol. 2:37.

8. For an analysis of the alternative explanations of the economic crisis, see Edwin Meléndez "Post-war Schools of Political Economy in Puerto Rico: Contrasting Views on the Open Economy and Economic Crisis," *Nature, Society, and Thought* Vol. 1, no. 2 (1988).

9. Edwin Meléndez's estimates using data from *Income and Product, 1984, Economic Report of the Governor, 1987-88,* and unpublished data.

10. Edwin Meléndez's estimates using data from *Income and Product, 1984,* and *Economic Report,* Tables 18, 19, 20.

11. For a detailed analysis of the tendencies in these variables see Edwin Meléndez, "Crisis económica y el programa económico anexionista, 1977-1984," in J. M. Carrion, E. Meléndez and A. Ramos, *Nuevos Estudios de la Política Puertorriqueña,* (Río Piedras: Editorial Huracán, forthcoming). I have estimated the Puerto Rican profit rate from 1977 to 1984 as follows:

Year	Profit Rate
1977	0.13
1978	0.15
1979	0.16
1980	0.17
1981	0.16
1982	0.07
1983	0.07
1984	0.08

12. *Income and Product, 1984,* Tables 2 and 6.

13. Puerto Rico Department of Labor and Human Resources. *Census of Manufacturing,* several years.

14. *Economic Report,* several tables; and Council of Economic Advisors, *Economic Report to the President, 1989,* Table B.83.

16. Puerto Rico Department of Labor, *Annual Report,* several years. Trade-dependence ratio refers to exports plus imports as a proportion of gross domestic product.

17. *Income and Product, 1984,* Tables 1, 3, and 29.

18. For a more detailed analysis of the post-industrial society argument, see Edwin Meléndez, "Crisis económica y estrátegias de desarrollo en Puerto Rico," in C. Gautier-Mayoral and Nazario-Trabal, eds., *Puerto Rico en los 1990,* (Río Piedras: Centro de Investigaciones Sociales, 1988).

19. Twin-plant projects are not all financed with 936 funds. The U.S. government requires that beneficiary countries have signed a Tax Exchange Agreement but only four countries had done it by 1988. For a more comprehensive analysis, see Carmen Deere and Edwin Meléndez, "Economic Crisis and U.S. policies Towards the Caribbean," memo, University of Massachusetts, 1989.

20. The ratio of foreign capital inflow (F) to the outflow of profits generated from past investments (FPY) is greater then one when F is greater than FPY. Data for F/FPY is only available for 1985 and 1986. In these years, F/FPY was 0.73 and 0.22 respectively. This pattern of foreign investment of capital is no different from that of the 1977-84 period. However, one can infer broad tendencies in profitability and foreign reinvestment of capital based on the tendencies of the variables which affect them. Interested readers should refer to my estimation of profit and reinvestment equations in "Accumulation and Crisis in a Small and Open Economy: the Postwar Social Structure and Accumulation in Puerto Rico," *Review of Radical Political Economics,* forthcoming.

21. Raymond Carr, *Puerto Rico: A Colonial Experiment,* (New York: Vintage Books, 1984).

Chapter 6

1. V. Oppenheimer, *The Female Labor Force in the United States* (Westport, Conn.: Greenwood, 1977), 65.

2. History Task Force of the Center for Puerto Rican Studies, *Labor migration under capitalism: The Puerto Rican Experience* (New York: Monthly Review Press, 1979); L. Reynolds and P. Gregory, *Wages, productivity and industrialization in Puerto Rico* (Homewood, IL: Irwin, 1965); R. Silva-Bonilla, "Amas de casa en la fuerza de trabajo asalariado en Puerto Rico: Un estudio del lenguaje como mediación ideológica en la reificación de la conciencia femenina (Housewives in the salaried work force in Puerto Rico: A study of language as ideological mediation in the reification of feminist consciousness), Ph.D. dissertation, Union for Experimental Colleges and Universities, 1982; United States, Dept. of Commerce, *Economic Study of Puerto Rico* (2 vols.) (Washington: GPO, 1979).

3. Y. Azize, *Luchas de la mujer en Puerto Rico, 1989-1919* (San Juan: Graficor, 1979); I. Picó-Vidal, "The History of Women's Struggle for Equality in Puerto Rico" in *Sex and Class in Latin America,* J. Nash and I. Safa, eds. (South Hadley, Mass.: J.F. Bergin, 1980); M. Rivera-Quintero, "Incorporación de las mujeres al mercado de trabajo en el desarrollo del capitalismo (Incorporation of women into the labor market in the development of capitalism)" in *La mujer en la sociedad puertorriqueña,* E. Acosta-Belén (Rio Piedras: Ediciones Huracán, 1980).

4. D. Elson and R. Pearson, "Nimble fingers make cheap workers: An analysis of women's employment in Third World export manufacturing" *Feminist Review* 1981:87-107; L. Lim, *Women Workers in Multinational Corporations: The case of the electronics industry in Malaysia and Singapore* Occasional Paper No. 9, University of Michigan-Ann Arbor, Women's Studies Program, 1978; H. Safa, "Runaway shops and female emploment: The search for cheap labor" *Signs* (1981) 7:418-33.

5. M.P. Fernández-Kelly, "Contemporary production and the new international division of labor," in *The Americas in the new international division of labor* Steven E. Sanderson, ed. (New York: Holmes & Meier, 1985); F. Frobel, J. Heinrichs, and O. Kreye, *The new international division of labour.* (Cambridge: Cambridge University Press, 1980); Saskia Sassen, *The mobility of labor and capital* (Cambridge: Cambridge University Press, 1988).

6. Azize, 7.

7. U.S. Dept. of Commerce, 1979[2]:246.

8. H. Barton, "Distinctive characterstics of the Puerto Rican economy," Unpublished document, 1966; Reynolds and Gregory.

9. V. Guzmán and V. R. Esteves, *El problema del desempleo en Puerto Rico* (San Juan: Banco Gubernamental de Fomento Para Puerto Rico, 1963).

10. Economic Development Administration, "Economic development in Puerto Rico during the last twenty years," *Report of the Office of Economic Research,* (San Juan: Imprenta del Gobierno, 1971) 20.

11. Comisión de Derechos Civiles de P.R., "Resumen de conclusiones y recomendaciones del Informe de la Comisión de Derechos Civiles sobre la igualdad de derechos y oportunidades de la mujer puertorriqueña," Department of Political Sciences, University of Puerto Rico, Rio Piedras, 1972:2.

12. Economic Development Administration, "Resumen del desarrollo economico de Puerto Rico," (San Juan: Imprenta del Gobierno, 1982) 10.

13. Reynolds and Gregory, 22-23.

14. H. Barton, *An appraisal of industrial incentives in Puerto Rico,* Report prepared for the Economic Development Administration, San Juan, 1976: 2.

15. Barton, 1966:13.

16. H. Barton, "Puerto Rico's industrial future," Paper presented at the Sixth Annual Meeting of the Puerto Rico Economics Association, San Juan, 1957, 16-7.

17. Barton, 1957:13.

18. Barton, 1966:13-14.

19. EDA, 1982:10.

20. Barton, 1957:17.

21. Sanderson, 1985: 5.

22. Frobel et al., 1980; Nash and Fernández-Kelly 1983; Safa, "Runaway shops"; S. Sanderson, "A critical approach to the Americas in the new international division of labor" in *The Americas in the new international division of labor* Steven E. Sanderson, ed. (New York: Holmes & Meier, 1985); R. Trajtenberg, "Transnacionales y fuerza de trabajo en la periferia: Tendencias recientes en la internacionalización de la producción (Transnationals and labor force in the periphery: Recent tendencies in the internationalization of production) Instituto Latinamericano de Estudios

Transnacionales, Mexico, 1978; P. Vuskovic, "Latin America and the changing world economy" *NACLA* (1980) 14:2-15.

23. Fernández-Kelly, 1985; Sassen.

24. S. Amin, "Self-reliance and the new international economic order," *Monthly Review* No. 29, 1977:5.

25. D. Barkin,"Proletarianization," in *The Americas* Steven E. Sanderson, ed.

26. Sassen.

27. Fernández-Kelly, 1985; J. Nash, "The impact of the changing international division of labor on different sectors of the labor force" and R. T. Snow, "The new international division of labor and the U.S. work force: The case of the electronics industry" in *Women and men and the international division of labor,* J. Nash, and M. P. Fernández-Kelly, eds. (Albany: SUNY Press, 1983).

28. Elson and Pearson; Fernández-Kelly, 1985; Lim; Safa.

29. Fernández-Kelly, 1985:208.

30. J.A. Bustamante, "Maquiladoras: A new face of international capitalism on Mexico's northern frontier," in *Women and men* J. Nash and M.P. Fernandez-Kelly, eds.; Fernández-Kelly, 1983.

31. A. Corten and I. Duarte, "Proceso de proletarizacion de mujeres: Las trabajadores de industrias de ensamblaje en la Republica Dominicana," Paper presented at the XIV Congreso Latinoamericano de Sociologia, San Juan, 1981.

32. M. Garrity, "The assembly industries in Haiti: Causes and effects," *Journal of Caribbean Studies* 2 1981:25-35; A. Lebel and F. Lewis, *Report on Haitian factory women* U.S. Agency for International Development, Washington, DC, 1983.

33. M. Gill, "Women, work and development," in *Women, work and development,* Joycelin Massiah, ed., (Cave Hill: Institute for Social and Economic Research, University of the West Indies, 1984).

34. L. Bolles, "Kitchens hit by priorities: Employed working-class Jamaican women confront the IMF," in *Women and men,* J. Nash and M.P. Fernandez-Kelly, eds.

35. E. Abraham-Van Der Mark, "The impact of industrialization on women: A Caribbean case," in *Women and men,* J. Nash and M.P. Fernández-Kelly, eds.

36. D. Kelly, *Hard work, hard choices: A survey of women in St. Lucia's export-oriented electronic factories,* (Cave Hill: Institute of Social and Economic Research, University of the West Indies, 1987).

37. Elson and Pearson.

38. J. Salaff, *Working Daughters of Hong Kong* (New York: Cambridge University Press, 1981).

39. R. Grossman, "Women's place in the integrated circuit," *Pacific Research 9* 1979:2-17; Lim.

40. F. Deyo and P. Chen, *Female labour force participation and earnings in Singapore,* Bangkok: Clearinghouse for Social Development in Asia, 1976; Lim; A. Wong, "Planned development, social stratification, and the sexual division of labor in Singapore" *Signs* (1981) 7:434-52.

41. Grossman.

Chapter 7

1. Donald Castillo Rivas, *Acumulación de capital y empresas transnacionales,* (Mexico City: Siglo Veintiuno, 1980) 144-45, and United States, Department of Commerce, *Economic Study of Puerto Rico, Vol. II* (Washington: GPO, 1979) 56.

2. United States, Department of Commerce, *Economic Study, Vol. I, 34 and Vol. II, 445-449.*

3. Comité para el Desarrollo Económico de Puerto Rico Inc., "Un estudio del subcomité para el desarrollo económico de Puerto Rico," Vol. I, (San Juan: January 1984) 52-53 and Annex 26-28.

4. James L. Dietz, epilogue, *Historia Económica de Puerto Rico,* (Río Piedras: Ediciones Huracán, 1989).

5. Michael Beaud, *A History of Capitalism,* (New York: Monthly Review Press, 1983), 194-200 and Joyce Kolko, *Restructuring the World Economy,* (New York: Pantheon, 1988) Ch. 1.

6. Edwin Meléndez, "Crisis económica y estratégia de desarrollo en Puerto Rico," in Carmen Gautier Mayoral and Néstor Nazario Trabal, eds., *Puerto Rico en los 1990s,* (Río Piedras: Universidad de Puerto Rico, Centro de Investigaciones Sociales, 1988), 197 and United States Department of Commerce, *Economic Study,* Vol. II, 66-67.

7. United States, Department of the Treasury, *The Operation and Effect of the Possessions Corporation System of Taxation; First Annual Report,* (Washington: Department of the Treasury, 1978), 64-65; United States, Department of Commerce, *Economic Study,* Vol. II, 563.

8. Still about 30 percent of all bank deposits derive from 936 funds; *Puerto Rico Business Review* Dec 1991/Jan 1992:2.

9. The scale began at 90 percent of applicable Commonwealth income and property taxes during the first five years of operations, and declined to 75 percent exemption during an additional five years, for a total of ten years of partial exemption in highly industrialized areas. In areas classified as intermediate and low-industrial development zones, additional exemptions of 65 and 55 percent were possible over two additional five-year blocks; for companies locating in the island municipalities of Vieques and Culebra, a further five-year, 50 percent tax exemption was available. See Economic Development Administration, *Industrial Incentive Act, 1978* (San Juan: Economic Development Administration, 1979) 2, 20-25.

10. Economic Development Administration, *Industrial Incentive Act, 1978* 17-19, 41.

11. In 1987, a Tax Incentives Law was passed by the PPD-dominated government. This law reverted to a flat 90% tax exemption rate for the full period of exemption to all qualifying industries, thus eliminating both the declining exemption scale and the lower rate that had been made applicable to services in the original legislation introduced by the PNP in 1978. Note, too, that the new legislation was designated the "Tax Incentives Law," whereas all prior legislation had been called "Industrial Incentives." This change reflects the shifting emphasis in promotion toward service industries.

12. José R. Madera, "The Economic Development Administration of Puerto Rico: The Present and the Future," *Puerto Rico U.S.A.* (EDA, Dec. 1980) Vol. 20, No. 4, 3.

13. Junta de Planificación, *Informe económico al gobernador, 1989* (San Juan: Junta de Planificación, 1990).

14. Economic Development Administration, *Puerto Rico's Caribbean Development Program.* (Hato Rey: EDA, no date), 3.

15. U.S. International Trade Commission, *Annual Report on the Impact of the Caribbean Basin Economic Recovery Act on U.S. Industries and Consumers, Third Report, 1986,* 122 (Washington: USITC, September 1988) 3-7.

16. Coopers & Lybrand, Inc.,"Twin Plants for Puerto Rico and the Eastern Caribbean: Estimated Manufacturing Costs," March 16, 1983, corporate mimeo; John Stewart, "Puerto Rico Shouldn't be Fearful of Twin Plant Concept," *The San Juan Star* Aug 28, 1983:B-3; John Stewart, "The Twin Plant Concept in the Caribbean Basin," *Puerto Rico Business Review 9,* Jan-Feb 1984:2.

17. Strategic Development Council for Puerto Rico, *Puerto Rico's Caribbean Development Program, Including Use of 936 Funds,* (San Juan: CDP, July 1991).

18. Economic Development Administration, *Puerto Rico's Caribbean Development Program: A Progress Report to the Ways and Means Committee of the U.S. House of Representatives* (San Juan: EDA, Caribbean Development Office, September 15, 1988):1-3.

19. Economic Development Administration, *Puerto Rico's Caribbean Development Program: Second Progress Report to the Ways and Means Committee of the U.S. House of Representatives,* (San Juan: EDA, Caribbean Development Office, March 15, 1990), Chapter 5.

20. Junta de Planificación, *Informe Económico al Gobernador, 1983* (San Juan: Junta de Planificación, 1984), XV/17-XV/18.

21. *Caribbean Business* September 17, 1987:1.

22. Emilio Pantojas-García, *Development Strategies as Ideology: Puerto Rico's Export-led Industrialization Experience* (Boulder, CO: Lynne Reinner, 1990) Table 5.5.

23. Caribbean Development Office, "Projects in Operation," mimeo, July 1990.

24. James L. Dietz, "Maquiladoras in the Caribbean: Puerto Rico, the Dominican Republic and the Twin Plant Program," Paper presented to the XV International Congress of the Latin American Studies Association, Miami, Florida, December 1989.

25. Economic Development Administration, *Caribbean Development Program: Second Progress Report.*

26. Emilio Pantojas-García, "The CBI and Economic Restructuring in the Caribbean and Central America," *Caribbean Studies* Vol. 20, 1988: 46-58; Economic Development Administration, 1990:xv-xvi.

27. Dietz, "Maquiladoras"; James L. Dietz and Emilio Pantojas-García, *Maquiladoras in the Caribbean: The Political Economy of Export-Led Industrialization* (in progress, 1993), Chapter 4.

Chapter 8

1. *Rescatar* means to recover or rescue something that rightfully belongs to you. Therefore, a land invasion, a *rescate*, for the Puerto Rican *rescatadores* was the recovery of territory that belonged to them by moral right and not by the legal right of private property. Although the academic literature uses the concept of "land invasion" to refer to this process, I will use the concept of *rescate*. A *rescate* or an organized land invasion is a form of political pressure on the State and it implies a certain political awareness. Organized land invasions are a socio-political event because, through a popular mobilization to obtain a shelter, a specific relationship to the State is established.

2. Two ideologically divergent newspapers were used to gather the historical data for the accounts: the *San Juan Star* and *Claridad*. I had to rely mostly on these accounts because the governmental documents were scarce and incomplete. Personal interviews of the actors were used to verify some of the events.

3. For a detailed explanation of these reforms and their ideological-political justifications see Leonardo Santana, *Planificación y Política*, (San Juan: Editorial Cultural, 1989).

4. Robert William Stevens, "Los Arrabales de San Juan: Una perspectiva histórica" en *Revista de Ciencias Sociales* Jan-June, 1985: 175.

5. Stevens, 178.

6. See Joaquín Villamil, "El Modelo de Crecimiento Dependiente," *Revista Interamericana de Planificación*, 10, September 1976: 64-86.

7. "Revelan Pobres constituyen 80 percent Población Isla," *El Mundo* 11 May 1970:18-B and "Más de Quinientos Mil Puertorriqueños se Benefician del Programa de Distribución de Alimentos," *El Mundo* 10 June 1971:11-B.

8. D. Colón, A. Fabían, M. González, I. Pacheco, and L. Santiago, "Las Invasiones de Terrenos en Puerto Rico: Una Alternativa a la Política Pública Existente," Master's thesis, (Río Piedras: University of Puerto Rico, 1977).

9. See Liliana Cotto, "Trends in the Puerto Rican Labor Movement: State Employees' Organization and Strike Militance in the First Luster of the Seventies," *Homines*, 6, 1989: 174.

10. An urban struggle is a popular, organized mobilization around an urban demand by a specific social sector. In this case the demand is housing.

11. See Manuel Castells, "Squatters and the State: The Dialectics between Social Integration and Social Change," *The City and the Grassroots*, (Berkeley: University of California Press, 1983) 190.

12. "Villa Justicia Hooks Into Water Line," *San Juan Star* 12 February 1972:13 and "Squatters Take Over Gurabo Public Lands," *San Juan Star* 26 April 1971:16.

13. "Comunidad Villa Eloísa Protesta por Orden Desahucio de Juez," *Claridad* 4 July 1971:6.

14. "Crean Organización Rescate de Tierras," *Claridad* 14 February 1971:5.

15. "Residentes de Toa Baja Demandan les Cedan Tierras," *Claridad* 12 August 1973, 5.

16. "Concentración de Rescatadores Mañana," *Claridad* 14 May 1975:11 and "Reprochan Silencio de Legisladores," *Claridad* 3 June 1975:9.

17. Sonia Marrero, "Insisten en Ver al Gobernador," *Claridad* 12 May 1975:3.

18. Sonia Marrero, "Terrorismo contra Rescatadores," *Claridad* 13 May 1975:9.

19. For the complete story on the dismantling by state officials of the marathon picket see "Via Crucis," *Claridad* 10 May 1975:1; also "Carolina Apoya a los Rescatadores," *Claridad* June 3, 1975:9. Finally, the personal interview with Carlos Gorrín, one of the attorneys of the demonstrators (May 25, 1988) gave me a more humane view of the action.

20. For a detailed discussion on this subject see Tilman Evers, Clarita Muller-Pantenberg, and Stefanie Spessart, "Movimientos Barriales y Estado: Luchas en la Esfera de la Reproducción en America Latina," *Revista Mexicana de Sociología,* 44 April-June 1982:703-756.

21. "32 Squatters are arrested in Gurabo," *San Juan Star* 5 June 1971:3; "The New Hard Line with Squatters" *San Juan Star* August 6, 1971: E-6; "Gobierno Arrasa Comunidades Pobres" *Claridad* 8 August 1971:3

22. "Via Crucis," *Claridad* 10 May 1975:1.

23. "Threatened Squatters Claim Moral Right," *San Juan Star* 9 March 1975:3.

24. "Evicted Squatters Picket La Fortaleza," *San Juan Star* 3 April 1971:15.

25. "Ferré Orders Investigation Into Evictions," *San Juan Star* 4 April 1971:3.

26. "Turbas del PNP Aislan vecinos de Villa Kennedy," *Claridad* 11 April 1971:1, 18.

27. See Evers et al., "Movimientos," 173.

28. "Jefe de la CRUV dirige destruccion de viviendas" *Claridad* February 27, 1972:3; "Familias de Caguas ocupan terrenos" 11 April 1971:19; "100 Invaders' Shacks Demolished in Ponce" *San Juan Star* 21 February 1972:2.

29. For details see "Vecinos de Villa Tiros Dispuestos a Luchar para Conservar sus Hogares," *Claridad* 23 November 1969:8.

30. "Mayaguez, San Germán, Cabo Rojo, Continúan Rescate de Terrenos," 13 February 1972:3. "Aqui Vamos Pa' Encima," *Claridad* 6 February 1972:12.

31. "PIP Militants Guard Gurabo Land Takers," *San Juan Star* 26 May 1971:6.

32. "Unidos Rescatadores Tierras del Oeste se Organizan Contra la Represión," *Claridad,* 20 February 1972:3.

33. "Estados Unidos Descongelará Fondos Viviendas Públicas, Medidas Benefician a la Isla," *El Mundo* 22 March 1973:1.

Chapter 9

1. Julia Kristeva, interviewed by N.Nishikawa.' There is a misogynist, anti-intellectual type of fascism that erupts precisely at the moment a woman attempts to come into being, where she is advancing without a shield, because when you write a novel you can not shield yourself in concepts. You advance on the open and you are a perfect target for anybody's darts, that is a difficult moment.' (Quote translated by C. Suárez-B.) "Entre le Temps Passé et le Temps a Venir," *Iichiko,* May 1990.

2. Women are also very important in the Santería and other popular cults such as the Mita sect. It is a pity that their role in these groups has not been studied more thoroughly. Some interesting insights can be found in Nélida Agosto, *The Mita Congregation: an Anthropological Study of a Revivalist Sect in Puerto Rico* (Ph.D. dissertation, Oxford University, 1984, regrettably still unpublished).

3. Héctor Meléndez, "El estado criollo," *El Nuevo Día,* 2 August 1989.

4. Editorial, *Mujeres en Marcha,* newsletter, Organización Puertorriqueña de la Mujer Trabajadora, December 1989. For statistics on the economic situation of women in Puerto Rico, see *Boletín social* (San Juan: Junta de Planificación de Puerto Rico, Estado Libre Asociado de Puerto Rico, October 1984); *Compendio de estadísticas sociales* (San Juan: Junta de Planificación de Puerto Rico, 1985) and *La participación de la mujer en la fuerza laboral* (San Juan: Departamento del Trabajo y Recursos Humanos, October 1987). The yearly Economic Reports to the Governor from the Junta de Planificación are also very useful.

5. Idsa Alegría Ortega, "Mujeres y elecciones, 1988," *Diálogo* University of Puerto Rico, February 1989. For example, as a result of the last elections there are four women senators, three congresswomen and four mayors, a decline from the 1984 elections.

6. Within the three main political parties in Puerto Rico today, the New Progressive Party (pro-statehood), the Popular Democratic Party (the governing party, which is autonomist), and the Independence Party, the most militant women's group is *Mujeres Progresistas* (Progressive Women) of the New Progressive Party, but it is of a reformist nature and subordinated to statehood politics.

7. Alaine Touraine, *Introducción a la sociología,* (Barcelona: Editorial Ariel, 1978).

8. Juanita Colombani, "Elogian y critican a la Senadora Muñoz Mendoza," *El Mundo* 28 July 1990.

9. Agnes J. Montano, "La mujer en la política," *Imagen* San Juan, Puerto Rico, September 1988, 49.

10. Maritza Díaz Alcaide and Agnes J. Montano, "Escaso liderato de femeninas en el PIP," *El Mundo* 29 July 1990.

11. Wilfredo López Montañez, taped interview by Margarita Mergal, March 1988.

12. "Organizaciones y proyectos sobre la mujer puertorriqueña," *Pensamiento Crítico,* 8:44, May/June 1985, 21.

13. Margarita Mergal, "Por qué el tema femenino-feminista en las Ciencias Humanas?" in *Hacia un currículo no sexista* (Cayey: Proyecto Pro Mujer, Universidad de Puerto Rico, Recinto de Cayey, 1992).

14. In Latin America and there is a growing body of literature on the subject. For example, see Virginia Vargas Valente, "Reflexiones sobre la construcción del movimiento social de mujeres" in various authors, *Movimientos sociales y educación popular en Perú* (Lima: Nuevos Cuadernos CELATS, No. 9, 1986); Various authors, "Mujeres latinoamericanas," *Diez ensayos y una historia colectiva* (Lima: Flora Tristán, Centro de la mujer peruana, 1988); *Tomando fuerzas para volar con fibra,* Memoria del primer y segundo encuentro-taller sobre teoría feminista (Ballenita, Ecuador: Centro de Acción de la Mujer y Centro de Información y Apoyo a la Mujer,

1986-87); Cecilia Millán, "¿Y si la sociología quedará embarazada? análisis del discurso sociológico," *Ciencia y Sociedad*, 8:1, January/March, 1988; Ana Sojo, *Mujer y política, ensayo sobre el feminismo y el sujeto popular* (San José, Costa Rica: Editorial DEI, 1988).

15. Arcilio Alvarado, hijo, "La mujer ante el plebiscito," *El Nuevo Día* 10 March 1990.

16. Ibid.

17. Georg Lukács, *Historia y conciencia de clase*, (México: Editorial Grijalbo, 1969).

18. Jane Flax, "Postmodernism and gender relations in feminist theory," *Signs* (Summer 1987): 621.

19. Antonio Gramsci, *La formación de los intelectuales*, (México: Editorial Grijalbo, 1967).

20. Néstor Braunstein, "¿Cómo se construye una ciencia?" in Braunstein, et al., *Psicología ideología y ciencia*, (México City: Siglo Veintiuno, 1975).

21. Gerda Lerner, Appendix and Definitions, *The Creation of Patriarchy*, (New York: Oxford University Press, 1986).

22. *Feministas en Marcha* holds a yearly ceremony conferring the "Golden Pig Award" to the TV ad they consider the grossest, most sexist, and insulting to women. They have already exerted considerable influence on the advertising industry.

23. Roland Barthes, "Strip-tease," *Mitologías* (México City: Siglo Veintiuno, 1980), 150; "Respuestas," interview by Jean Thibaudeau in *¿Por dónde empezar?* (Barcelona: Tusquets Editor, 1974), 59.

24. Velda González, taped interview by Margarita Mergal, April 1988. "El problema del poder," *Forum: Mujer y poder en Puerto Rico*, Biblioteca General de Puerto Rico, March 8, 1989.

24. See Multi-Search, Inc., "La familia puertorriqueña hoy," *Estudio de familias, Partes I and II* (San Juan, 1986).

25. Virginia Vargas Valente, *El aporte de las rebeldía de las mujeres*, (República Dominicana: CIPAF, 1988).

Chapter 11

1. Isolina Ferré and Pedro Vales, *Métodos y estratégias para el trabajo en comunidad*, (Puerto Rican Community Foundation, 1988); Aida Negrón de Montilla, *Americanization in Puerto Rico and the Public School System, 1900-1930*, (Río Piedras: Editorial Universitaria, 1975).

2. Law Num. 68 of August 28, 1990, 3 L.P.R.A. 391-400.

3. That statement in the first chapter of the law ends a bitter and very contested effort of the U.S. Government to impose English as the official language of instruction. For additional information on U.S. Government's Americanization efforts see Aida Negrón de Montilla, *The Americanization of the Public Schools*. Official reform efforts were made in the last century in reference and in relation to U.S. reform efforts and schemes. The language issue has been a central issue in our debates.

4. "Educators Skeptical About School Reform", *The San Juan Star* 5 August 1990.

5. "Juan Domingo is a barrio in Guaynabo, a city southeast of San Juan. The barrio has more than 700 hundred household units in less than 30 acres; the community is divided into eight main sectors defined by their access to the road: Los Robles, Tintillo, Sevilla, Las Flores, Polvorín and Fondo del Saco. Its extreme poverty stands in direct contrast with the cheerfulness and solidarity among the people, the constant presence of music, the enthusiasm about doing things together and sharing what they have." (Ana Maria García Blanco, "Constructing a Ship While at Sea—A New Approach to Schooling, " PhD Thesis, Harvard University, Graduate School of Education 1990, 43.

6. "Estudiantes dan F al sistema educativo," *El Mundo,* 4 November 1989.

Lately there is also anxiety over the security of students, teachers, and staff due to an increasing level of violence and gang activity. Just recently one school in the metropolitan area closed two days after being attacked by a youth gang who hurt one of the students. A joint decision by parents and officials to close the school two days was taken in order to allow them to implement tighter security measures.

7. This type of decision affects the great majority of Puerto Ricans if we consider the fact that in 1988 only 50,000 families on the island had an income of more than $25,000 a year while approximately 535,000 families received less than $10,000 a year. Of the latter group, around 250,000 received a total income of less than $5,000. Taken from Banco Popular, "Most Families are feeling the squeeze," *The San Juan Star,* September 1990:B-2, 3. According to the same source, around 320,000 "middle class" families earn an income ranging from $7,500 to $25,000. We are very conscious of the difficulties of this type of description of the social structure. These numbers, nevertheless, give some basic benchmarks with which to visualize some important elements of the island's class structure. A more elaborated formulation is beyond the scope of this essay.

For a detailed discussion of the socioeconomic conditions of the Puerto Rican urban poor, see Helen Iken Safa, *The Urban Poor of Puerto Rico, a Study in Development and Inequality,* (New York: Holt, Rinehart and Winston, Inc., 1973).

Under the new law, the Secretary of Education remains directly in charge of 20 essential areas of the school system including the development of educational policies and short-term goals, the establishment of basic curricula offerings and the minimal skills that each student must develop, the design of new schools, contracting with private corporations to construct new schools, organizing parents' trainings, and so on.

8. In many ways it is possible to identify some critical "corporatist" elements in the relation between the *Asociación* and the PPD controlled government. Generally this labor union gets preferential treatment from the government in terms of access to the decision-making process which is, in turn, reciprocated with the union by a great deal of political loyalty. The *Asociación* was a key player in the final draft of the school reform bill and was instrumental in eliminating important sections of the law that would reduce the power of school principals and superintendents which they represent.

9. "Estudiantes dan F al sistema educativo."

10. "Retoman a la Escuela," *El Nuevo Día,* 30 July 1988.

11. Rubén Arrieta, *El Mundo* 3 August 1988.

12. The private school system has been adamantly opposed to declaring Spanish the official language of the island government even though that would have no impact at all on the language of instruction in private schools. It also underscores how important it is for those institutions to "project" themselves as the "representatives" of the English language in the Puerto Rican public opinion. About 15 percent of the students are in private schools and constitute a well-recognized socio-economic "status" symbol.

13. Ana Helvia Quintero Rivera, "A collaborative effort between the University of Puerto Rico and the Public School—an experience of reform", *Harvard Educational Review* November 1989.

14. James P. Comer, "Educating Poor Minority Children", *Scientific American* November 1988:47.

15. Comer, 47.

16. José Javier Colón, et al., "Entitlements of Latino Students in the Massachusetts Public Educational System," working paper presented by Multicultural Education, Training and Advocacy (META) for the Mauricio Gastón Institute for Latino Community Development and Public Policy of the University of Massachusetts, 1990.

17. Juan Pablo Adorno Galán, resident of the barrio and worker of the New School in Ana María García Blanco, "Constructing a Ship."

18. Fernando Picó, *Vivir en Caimito,* (Río Piedras: Ediciones Huracán, 1989).

19. Picó.

20. Carl Boggs, *Social Movements and Political Power,* (Philadelphia: Temple University Press, 1986).

Chapter 13

1. Robert Heilbroner, "The Coming Meltdown of Traditional Capitalism,") *Ethics and International Affairs* (New York: Carnegie Council on Ethics and International Affairs, 1988), 69.

2. Heilbroner, "Meltdown" and "Reflections: The Triumph of Capitalism," *The New Yorker,* 1989 [date?].

3. These exercises set out to capture key dimensions and consequences of increasing interpenetration and interdependence of the U.S. economy, primarily with Mexico and Puerto Rico, as major instances of an ongoing "silent integration" of hemispheric social formations. Refer also to Robert McCleery, Bradford Barham and Clark Reynolds, "The Challenge of United States-Mexico Economic Interdependence,") Stanford, CA: Americas Program, Stanford University; Raul Hinojosa Ojeda, "Interdependence and Class Relations: A Long View Perspective on the U.S. and Latin America," *Conference on the New Interdependence in the America: The Challenges to Economic Restructuring, Political Redemocratization and Foreign Policy,* Stanford University, 1989.

4. Susan George, *A Fate Worse Than Debt: The World Financial Crisis and the Poor* (New York: Grove Press, 1988); Sue Branford and Bernardo Kucinski, *The Debt Squads: The U.S., the Banks and Latin America (New Jersey: JED Books, 1988)*.

5. Lee Smith, ed., *The Cuomo Commission Report* (New York: Simon and Schuster, 1988).

6. Edwin Meléndez Velez, "Accumulation and Crisis in the Post-War Puerto Rican Economy," University of Massachusetts (Amherst) Ph.D. dissertation in Economics, 1985; James L. Dietz, *Economic History of Puerto Rico: Institutional Change and Capitalist Development* (Princeton: Princeton University Press, 1986); Eliezer Curet, "Development Policies for Small Countries," American University, Ph.D. dissertation in Economic, 1984; Perdo A. Caban, "The Colonial State and Capitalist Expansion in Puerto Rico," *Centro de Estudios Puertorriquenos Bulletin* (New York: Hunter College) II, 6, 1989; Frank Bonilla and Ricardo Campos, "A Wealth of Poor: Puerto Ricans in the New Economic Order," *Daedalus* 110, 2, 1981.

7. Reynolds.

8. Curet.

9. Bonilla and Campos, "Wealth."

10. Frank Levy, "Changes in the Distribution of American Family Incomes," *Science* 436, 1987; Junta de Planificación de Puerto Rico, *Serie Historica del Empleo, Desempleo y Grupo Trabajador en Puerto Rico, 1983* (Santurce: Puerto Rico: 1983).

11. Richard B. Freeman, ed., *Immigration, Trade and the Labor Market (Cambridge, MA: National Bureau of Economic Research, 1988)*.

12. Richard Santillan, "The Midwest: 1915:1986," in *Latinos and the Political System,* Chris F. Garcia, ed. (Notre Dame, IN: University of Notre Dame Press, 1988).

13. Frank Bonilla and Ricardo Campos, *Industry and Idleness* (New York: Centro de Estudios Puertorriqueños, Hunter College, CUNY, 1986); Marta Tienda and Ding-Tzann Li, "Minority Concentration and Earnings Inequality: Blacks, Hispanics and Asians Compared," *American Journal of Sociology* 93, 1987:1.

14. Martin Carnoy, Hugh Daley, and Raul Hinojosa Ojeda, forthcoming [TITLE??].

15. Robert Brubaker, "Traditions of Nationhood and Politics of Citizenship," *States and Social Structure Newsletter* (New York: Social Science Research Council, 1987).

16. Carlos Ala Santiago Rivera, "Union Organizing in the Pharmaceutical Industry," Graduate Center for Workers' Education, CUNY, Conference on Technology and the Transformation of Work, 1989.

17. Victor Botbaum and Carol O'Cleareacain, "Labor Market Issues and Policies," *Occasional Papers No. 3* (New York: Center for Labor Management Policy Studies, CUNY, 1989).

18. Edgar de Jesus, "When Workers Move Forward...," *Centro de Estudios Puertorriqueños Bulletin* New York: Hunter College, CUNY, II, 1989:5.

19. Hobart A. Spalding, Jr., "Latin American Unions and International Labor Networks," *Latin American Research Review* XXIV, 1989:2.

20. Midwest Center for Labor Research, "Solidarity Across Borders: U.S. Labor in a Global Economy," *Labor Research Review* Chicago, IL, VIII, 1989:1.

21. Benjamin R. Ringer, *"We the People" and Others* (New York: Tavistock Publications, 1983).

22. Frank Bonilla, "Hispanics and American Studies," *American Character and Culture in the 1980s: Pluralist Perspectives,* Colloquium sponsored by the University of Massachusetts (Boston), 1982.

23. Armando Rendon, "Latinos: Breaking the Cycle of Survival to Tackle Global Affairs," in Chris F. Garcia ed., *Latinos.*

Chapter 14

1. For Kent's personal version of the whole affair see his autobiographical work, *This is My Own,* (New York:, 1955), 501-506.

2. A multi-faceted artist, Kent was best known for his "Greenland" paintings. His works were displayed in prestigious museums not only in the United States, but in South America and Europe as well. Since his youth, Kent had been involved in many progressive causes, fighting railroads and banks, and organizing workers. During the Great Depression, Kent thrust himself into the center of the cultural and political struggle. By the mid-1930s, he was working closely with the Communist Party of the United States (CPUSA). The most complete biographical study on Kent is David Traxel, *An American Saga: The Life and Times of Rockwell Kent,* (New York: , 1980).

3. The island, he wrote years later, "was as luxuriantly beautiful as one might picture the Garden of Eden to have been. A people living in such poverty as I have never seen. Here, I thought, looking down from the densely forested heights down over the waving fronds of palm trees to the sunlit, cultivated plain and blue ocean, one might make the home of his heart's desires; and from here, I realized had fled countless thousands of disinherited children to seek a haven in the filthy tenements of Harlem." Kent, *It's Me O Lord,* 501.

4. Kent, *Own,* 313.

5. Thomas Mathews, *La Política Puertorriqueña y el Nuevo Trato* (Río Piedras:, 1975), 313.

6. Kent, *Own,* 504; "Revolt Plea Seen in Kent's Mural," *New York Times,* 11 September 1937:19.

7. To protect Black, Kent always maintained the secrecy of the degree of her involvement in the whole affair. See Traxel, *Saga,* 182.

8. Kent, *Own,* 307; "Revolt Plea Seen in Kent's Mural,"11 September 1937:19.

9. "Kent Quite Willing to Paint White Men," *New York Times,* 22 September 1937:22. "Edificio correos en Washington ostenta incripcion pro-independencia de Puerto Rico," *El Imparcial,* 22 September 1937:22, 24; "Carta del Senor Kent," *La Democracia,* 26 September 1937:4, 5.

10. "Mural Stirs Ire of Puerto Ricans," *New York Times,* 15 September 1937:26.

11. Ibid.

12. "Iglesias gestiona permiso para cambiar el mural," *El Mundo,* 16 September 1937:3.

13. "Importante mitin de la J. Nacionalista," *La Voz,* 17 September 1937:10; "Mitin Pro Presos de Puerto Rico," *La Voz,* 18 September 1937:4; "Veleda Nacionalista en

el Park Palace," *La Voz,* 22 September 1937:4; "Junta Nacionalista Commemora 'El Grito de Lares' en N.Y.," *La Voz,* 24 September 1937: 10.

14. "De Rockwell Kent a los Nacionalistas," *La Voz,* 28 September 1937:4.

15. "A pesar de Iglesias, el Mural de Rockwell Kent permanecera en su sitio," *La Democracia,* 24 September 1937:4.

16. Kent, *Own,* 309; "Carta de Rockwell Kent," *La Democracia,* 26 September 1937:4-5.

17. Ibid., 310-311.

18. "A Kent no le encomendaron ningun mural sobre Puerto Rico. Así lo informo a Iglesias el Secretarios de Tesoro Morgenthau," *El Mundo,* 13 October 1937:5, 16.

19. "Farley Censorship Hits Kent Mural, New Message to Puerto Rico Asked," *New York Times,* 2 November 1937: 27; Kent, *Own,* 310.

20. "Farley Censorship."

21. Kent, *Own,* 311; "Another Painter to Blot Kent Mural," *New York Times,* 3 November 1937:25.

22. Kent, *Own,* 311-312.

23. "Rockwell Kent, que presencio caso Albizu tiene prueba Jurado fue amanado," *El Imparcial,* 6 November 1937:4.

24. "Another Painter."

25. Kent, *Own,* 312.

26. "Kent Paid in Full by Treasury Check," *New York Times,* 3 November 1937:19.

27. "Se gestiona que el pintor Kent venga a declarar en juicio de Ponce," *El Imparcial,* 8 November 1937:3.

28. "No permiten a Kent declarar en Ponce," *El Imparcial,* 21 November 1937:48, 15; "La corte no permitio declarar a Rockwell Kent," *La Democracia,* 21 November 1937:1, 8.

29. "Puesto que Puerto Rico quiere terminar su 'status' colonial enteramente antiamericano, Estados Unidos debe permitir que sin retraso los puertoriqueños se hagan enteramente iguales al pueblo americano," *La Democracia,* 23 November 1937:1.

30. Kent, *Own,* 356-357.

31. Kent, *It's Me,* 503.

Chapter 15

1. W. Mattos Cintrón, *La política y lo político en Puerto Rico,* (MéxicoCity: ERA, 1980) Chapter 1.

2. See G. Delgado Pasapera, *Puerto Rico: sus luchas emancipadoras,* (CITY?: Editorial Cultural, 1984) for independence movements in the second half of the nineteenth century.

3. W. Mattos Cintrón, "La formación de la hegemonía de Estados Unidos en Puerto Rico y el independentismo. Los derechos civiles y la cuestión nacional," *El Caribe Contemporáneo* Jan-Jun 1988, México. A previous version of this paper is in *Hómines,* March 1987-Feb. 1988.

4. W. Mattos Cintrón, *Puerta sin casa*, (Río Piedras: Ediciones La Sierra, 1984) 91-93. Also, A. G. Quintero Rivera, *La lucha obrera en Puerto Rico*, (CEREP, YEAR?) 7 and G. L. García y A. G. Quintero Rivera, *Desafío y solidaridad*, (CITY: Ediciones Huracán, 1982) 32-34.

5. A. Gramsci, *El materialismo histórico y la filosofía de Benedetto Croce*, (México: Juan Pablos Editor, 1975) 217.

6. For a view of the enormous cultural activity of the working class at the beginning of the century, see R. Dávila Santiago, *El derribo de las murallas*, (Río Piedras: Editorial Cultural, 1988) Chapter 3.

7. A. G. Quintero, *La lucha obrera*, 7.

8. An example of this virtual criminalization: in 1919 a group of university students sent a letter to the House of Representatives petitioning a declaration of independence. The Commissioner of Instruction, Miller, demands from the university's authorities, the names of the petitioners so as to deny them access to the teaching profession. In A. Negrón de Montilla, *La americanización en Puerto Rico y el sistema de instrucción pública*, (Río Piedras: Editorial Universitaria, 1977) 185. Such criminalization has prevailed to this day. See I. Acosta, *La mordaza*, (Editorial Edil, 1987) for the period of the late 1940s and early 1950s. Until recently the government had kept close surveillance of thousands of citizens whose only crime was their advocacy of independence. See *Claridad, 4-10 August 1989 and 25-31 August 1989.*

Such a political climate has had important effects within Puerto Rican society which can be shown in the Cerro Maravilla murders in 1978 when a group of members of the Intelligence Division of the police murdered two persons who had been already detained after being led by an undercover agent supposedly to blow up some communications towers.

Several pro-independence groups, particularly the Nationalist Party, have used repression as the principal explanation of the weak political support of independence among the Puerto Rican people. While political repression has abounded in different periods of time in Puerto Rico, it has not been the principal means to guarantee the presence of the United States in the country. Repression, especially in its figure as criminalization, has served as a useful mean for the definition of the boundaries within which non coercive means act. See Mattos-Cintrón, *La formación*.

9. It must be stressed that throughout this paper hegemony will be used in its gramscian sense, that is, a dominion that stems out of non-coercive means. It should not be confused with ideology or propaganda because it can also be developed through direct material means such as financial aid, food coupons and other sorts of social assistance programs.

10. See García and Quintero, *Desafío*.

11. A prior but short-lived attempt was the *Partido de la Independencia* founded by R. Matienzo Cintrón.

12. W. Mattos Cintrón, "La formación", 42-46. See also L. Ferrao, *Pedro Albizu Campos y el nacionalismo puertorriqueño*, (Editorial Cultural, 1990), 257-291.

13. W. Mattos Cintrón, *La política*, 74.

14. For an economic analysis of this period, see, E. Pantojas-García, *Development strategies as ideology,* (Rio Piedras: Editorial de la Universidad de Puerto Rico, 1990), Chapter 3. Also J.L. Dietz, *Economic History of Puerto Rico,* (New Jersey: Princeton University Press, 1986), Chapter 4.

15. A program is a set of political principles, practices and proposed frameworks for a society. It is not merely an ideological statement since it also summarizes ongoing political practices, so it should not be confused with a platform which usually deals only with the proposed framework.

16. For an analysis of the 1982 struggle inside the PSP, see H. Meléndez Lugo, *El fracaso del proyecto PSP de la pequeña burguesía,* (Río Piedras: Editorial Edil, 1984). Also, W. Mattos Cintrón, *Puerta sin casa.*

17. For an analysis of the crisis and its restructuring, see E. Pantojas-García, 135-138, 144-158. Also, W. Mattos Cintrón, *La política,* 148-168.

18. W. Mattos Cintrón, *La política,* 154.

19. The MSP merged with the *Partido Socialista Revolucionario* in the 1980s to form the *Movimiento Socialista de Trabajadores* (MST). It has an important influence in several unions.

20. A space it shares with the *Partido Comunista Puertorriqueño* and the recently formed *Frente Socialista* (FS).

21. See the U.S. Senate bill S. 712.

22. Under pressure of the PIP, the Puerto Rican Civil Liberties Commission and the PSP newspaper, *Claridad,* the state has returned most—but not all—of these dossiers to the people surveilled. The magnitude of the operation, involving tens of thousands of suspects, indicate the enormous effort and expense that the colonial government went through to keep in check people perceived as potential criminals.

23. It has been estimated that "The federal tax subsidy for operating in Puerto Rico equalled 11 percent of total 1989 earnings at Pfizer, 8.3 percent at Coca Cola, 10 percent at Phillips-Van Heusen, 3 percent at Stride-Rite and 5 percent at Digital equipment." among others. T.G. Donlan, "The 51st State", in *Barron's,* 3 September 1990.

24. The PSP has indeed been critical of some of the "official" socialist bloc's actions. As the MPI it criticized the invasion of Czechoslovakia and, later, already as PSP, it also criticized the intervention in Afghanistan. These positions are totally coherent with a party that defends independence against a nation—the United States—that has tried to legitimize its role on the island through the validation of its 1898 military intervention. On the other hand, the Polish events in 1981 became a vexing matter. While at first, the PSP sided with the workers, the leadership sensed that such a decision would put in jeopardy the support received from the "official" socialist world; and after all, the struggle in Poland could be seen as a Polish internal affair. When Jaruzelki's coup became a fact, the PSP leadership remained silent. Democratic principles were not in the same footing as foreign intervention.

25. The real intellectual driving force of this law has been Professor Pedro Juan Rúa. In 1978 he developed the thesis that language was the main element defining a nation, and that only through conflict with opposing forces is a nation and a nationality developed. Almost alone, at the beginning, he singled out the English

Only movement in the United States as the main opposing force in the language question, and delivered several lectures throughout the island sensibilizing public opinion on the subject. Diverse groups and personalities later on coalesced into this effort. The PPD, for its own political motives deriving from the need to expose the anti-national character of the PNP, decided to adopt the language issue. See, P. J. Rúa, "Nación, lengua y cultura I y II" in *Teoría y crítica,* (Río Piedras: Editorial Edil, 1984) and "Idioma, universidad nacional y acción política" in *Resistencia nacional y Acción universitaria,* (Río Piedras: Editorial Edil, 1988).

The approval of this law caps a long effort by the Hernandez-Colon Administration to attract Spanish and other European capitals as a means of reinforcing the current economic model of the Commonwealth. It is evident that such a model relying on 936 industries for growth is unwise, given the possible effects of Congressional intervention and the North American Free Trade Agreement (NAFTA). The PPD appeal to Spanish capital has had an unexpected result: for the first time in nearly ninety years, an hispanic country, which was also the former colonial power in Puerto Rico, has exercised considerable influence in the island appealing to the common ties that link Puerto Rico to the Iberoamerican nations. This has irked the pro-annexation forces that have seen Spain's presence not only as a booster to the Commonwealth but also as a cultural deterrent to statehood. As a result there has been a very vocal campaign by the PNP-dominated press against the language law, and Spain's influence.

26. See for example the recent case of a runaway plant leaving Indiana to settle in Puerto Rico. The plant belongs to American Home Products Corporation and in September 1990 positioned itself to close its facility in Elkhart. (*Keep Whitehall Open,* 24 September 1990, a publication of the Oil, Chemical and Atomic Workers Union, Local 7-515, Elkhart, Indiana.)

27. That there is an ample social base for a workers' movement could be seen from the massive demonstration of organized labor on March 8, 1990, against the government's plans to sell and privatize the telephone company. Status politics, however, is at the moment a hindrance for that movement to coalesce.

28. Probably the most documented effort is the PSP's. See, W. Mattos Cintrón, *Puerta sin casa.* For an analysis of the MPI see Meléndez, *El fracaso del proyecto PSP* and W. Mattos Cintrón, Breve historia del Partido Socialista Puertorriqueño, PSP, 1979.

About the Contributors

Frank Bonilla, Thomas Hunter Professor, Hunter College, is Director of the Interuniversity Program for Latino Research and Director of the Center for Puerto Rican Studies-CUNY. He is the author or co-author of several books, including *The Failure of Elites, Student Politics in Chile, Labor Migration under Capitalism, Industry and Idleness, and the Politics of Change in Venezuela.*

Pedro Cabán is Associate Professor of Political Science and Chairperson of the Department of Puerto Rican and Hispanic Caribbean Studies at Rutgers University. He served as Chairperson of the Board of Directors of the Institute for Puerto Rican Policy. He has published numerous articles on labor, colonialism and the state in Puerto Rico in *Latin American Perspectives, Journal of Latin American Studies, Revista de Ciencias Sociales* and other journals.

Juan Manuel Carrión has a Ph.D. in Sociology and teaches at the University of Puerto Rico. Previously, he taught at the State University of New York at Binghamton and at Rutgers University in New Brunswick, NJ. He is currently working on a book about nationalism and class struggles in twentieth century Puerto Rico.

José Javier Colón Morera, Ph.D. cand., has been heavily involved with Puerto Rican communities in the U.S. in school reform initiatives. He is currently teaching at the Political Science Department of the University of Puerto Rico.

Liliana Cotto is assistant professor, Department of Social Sciences, General Studies Faculty, University of Puerto Rico, Río Piedras. She is the author of several articles on the *rescate* movement (squatters) of the 70's in Puerto Rico. She is currently doing research on the relation between social struggles and social movements in Puerto Rico and the Dominican Republic during the 80's.

James Dietz is Professor of Economics and Latin American Studies, California State University, Fullerton. He is the author of *Economic History of Puerto Rico.* (Princeton University Press, 1986; in Spanish, Ed. Huracán) and co-editor of and contributor to *Latin America's Economic Development* and *Progress Toward Development in Latin America.* He is currently working on a book, *Maquilas in the Caribbean,* with Emilio Pantojas-García.

Angelo Falcón, a political scientist, is President and Founder of the Institute for Puerto Rican Policy in New York City. He is a contributor to the forthcoming reader, *The 1988 Elections and the Latino Vote,* co-editor of the book *Latinos and politics: A Select Research Bibliography* and of the forthcoming book *Latino Voices: Mexican, Puerto Rican and Cuban Perspectives on American Politics*. He is a Co-Principal Investigator with the Latino National Political Survey (LNPS).

Ana María García Blanco is a recent Graduate from the Harvard Graduate School of Education and is presently directing, with other members of the community, the New School in Juan Domingo.

Humberto García-Muñiz is Associate Researcher, Institute of Caribbean Studies, University of Puerto Rico, Rio Piedras. He is the author of *Boots, Boots, Boots: Intervention, Regional Security and Militarization in the Caribbean* (1986), *La Estrategia de Estados Unidos y la Militarización del Caribe* (1988) and has more recently co-authored (with Betsaida Vélez Natal) the *Bibliografía Militar del Caribe* (1992). He has published articles in academic journals in Puerto Rico, Mexico, Spain and Great Britain.

Edgardo Meléndez is Assistant Professor, Department of Political Science, University of Puerto Rico-Río Piedras. He is the author of a book and several articles on the Puerto Rican statehood movement. He is currently doing research on the independence and annexationist movements in Cuba and Puerto Rico in the late nineteenth century.

Edwin Meléndez is Associate Professor of Urban Studies and Planning at the Massachusetts Institute of Technology and Director of the Mauricio Gaston Institute for Latino Community Development and Public Policy of the University of Massachusetts. He is co-editor of *Hispanics in the U.S. Labor Force* and co-author of *In the Shadows of the Sun: Caribbean Development Alternatives and U.S. Policies,* and *Mink Coats Don't Trickle Down: The Economic Assault on Women and People of Color*. He has published on the economic crisis in Puerto Rico, Latinos' inequality in the U.S. labor markets, and employment strategies for Latino workers.

Wilfredo Mattos-Cintrón is Associate Professor at the Facultad de Ciencias Naturales, Universidad de Puerto Rico, Río Piedras. He has published several books and articles on Puerto Rican politics and history, including *La política y lo político en Puerto Rico* (México: ERA, 1980) and *Puerta sin casa* (Río Piedras: Ediciones La Sierra, 1984). He has also written two novels, *El cerro de los buitres* and *El cuerpo bajo el puente*.

Margarita Mergal is Full Professor at the Social Sciences Department of the General Studies Faculty of the Río Piedras campus of the University of Puerto Rico. She is co-author of *Participación de la mujer en la historia de Puerto Rico, las primeras décadas del siglo XX* and of its video version. Author of many essays, militant feminist, she is currently doing research on the development of feminism in the Hispanic Caribbean.

Emilio Pantojas-García is a political sociologist who works on development issues in the Caribbean and Chair of the Department of Latin American and Caribbean Studies at SUNY/Albany. He recently published *Development Strategies as Ideologies: Puerto Rico's Export-led Industrialization Experience (Lynne Reinner, 1990)*.

Palmira Ríos is Assistant Professor of Urban Policy at the Graduate School of Management and Urban Policy of the New School for Social Research. Formerly, she was Deputy Director of the Center for Immigrant and Population Studies of the College of Staten Island, CUNY and faculty member of the Department of Puerto Rican Studies at Lehman College and Department of Sociology at SUNY-Binghamton. Ríos is the author of several articles on women and work, ethnic and racial relations, and is currently co-editing *Gender, Labor, and Migration: Puerto Rican Women in the 20th Century* (forthcoming, Temple University Press).

Carlos Rodríguez Fraticelli is presently an Assistant Professor in the Departamento de Ciencias Sociales, Facultad de Estudios Generales, Universidad de Puerto Rico, Río Piedras.

Carlos Alá Santiago-Rivera is Associate Professor at the Graduate School of Public Administration, University of Puerto Rico-Río Piedras Campus. He is currently a co-investigator with CLASCO's Latin American Labor Commission. Previously, he was Visiting Professor at the Graduate Center for Workers Education (Brooklyn College, CUNY), and has also held positions at the Labor Education Center (Rutgers University), the Universidad Centroamericana (Nicaragua), and the Universidad National Autónoma de Piura (Perú). He has published extensively on labor in Puerto Rico and Nicaragua, collective bargaining in higher education, and economic restructuring and technological change in the pharmaceutical industry.

Index

Foraker Act, 22, 42
Fort Buchanan, 59-60
FTPR (Labor Federation of Puerto Rico), 148
FUPI (Federation of Pro-Independence Students), 75

G
Gallisa, Carlos, 35, 206
General Workers' Council (Concilio General de Trabajadores, CGT), 148
Gideon, Kenneth W., 33
González, José Luis, 70
González, Velda, 140
Government Development Bank, 85-86
Government Planning Board, 161
Gramsci, Antonio, 202
Grenada, 59, 62
    invasion of, 59, 64
Guantánamo, 53-54, 55-56
Guaynabo, educational reform in, 158, 159, 164-165, 166-169

H
Heilbroner, Robert, 181
Hernández, Zaida, 134
Hernández Colón, Rafael, 4
    as governor after 1984, 3, 79, 85-87, 110, 174-175, 178
    as governor in mid-1970s, 26, 28, 61, 85
Higher Education Board (La Junta Rectora de Educación), 161
hotel industry, 154
House Bill 4765 (HR 4765), 2, 32, 36, 38
House Committee on Interior and Insular Affairs, 32
House Insular Affairs Subcommittee, 2, 35-36, 174
housing, 120-121. See also rescates
HR 4765 (House Bill 4765), 2, 32, 36, 38

Hurricane Hugo, 63, 152, 187

I
Iglesias Pantín, Santiago, 194, 195
illiteracy, 30, 161
income:
    below poverty level, 30, 235
    per capita, 30, 80, 85, 108, 183
independence movement, 15-16
    detachment of, from popular struggles, 15, 126-127, 133, 201-204, 213-214
    in the 1989-1991 plebiscite process, 4, 13, 33-34, 35, 63, 175
    in the 1930s. See Nationalist Party
    see also Puerto Rican pro-Independence Party
    limited support for, 5, 72, 143, 177-178, 201-204
    repression of, 13, 75, 191-192, 203, 206-207, 211. See also Cerro Maravilla murders
    and socialism, 5, 74, 204-209, 210-211, 213-214
Industrial Incentive Act of 1978 (Law 26), 107-108, 183
industrial restructuring, 143-144, 153
Institute for Puerto Rican Policy (IPR), 173-174, 176, 177, 178
intelligentsia, 202
internal migration, 120
international division of labor, 90, 98-101, 115
Interuniversity Program for Latino Research (IUP), 184
investment, 22, 80, 81, 84, 98, 183
    high profits on, in Puerto Rico, 8, 22, 29, 81, 114, 216-217
    in twin plants, 109-112
    see also transnational corporations; tax benefits

J
Johnston, Bennett, 3, 32-33, 34-35
Jones Act of 1917, 43

Robeson, Paul, 189
Rodríguez Cristóbal, Angel, 62
Romero Barceló, Carlos, 27, 48-49,
　50, 62, 83, 84, 209
Roosevelt, Franklin D., 189-190
Roosevelt Roads naval base, 55, 56,
　60
　use of, for U.S. interventions in
　　Central America and the Carib-
　　bean, 58, 59, 64, 65
Rúa, Pedro Juan, 241-242
Ruíz, Angel L., 150

S
S712. See Senate Bill 712
San Ildefonso, 54
schools, 30, 54, 156-164, 165-166, 169
　in Barrio Juan Domingo,
　　Guaynaba, 158, 159, 164-165,
　　166-169
Section 936 of Internal Revenue
　Code, 6, 8, 28-30, 103, 106-107,
　210
　and Caribbean Basin Initiative,
　　110-112
　controversy over, within U.S. gov-
　　ernment, 29-30, 86, 110
　impact of, 8, 29, 86, 106-107, 108,
　　113-114
　as issue in 1989-1991 plebiscite
　　process, 6, 33, 34, 52
Senate Bill 712 (S712), 2, 32, 34, 35,
　38, 49-50
Senate Energy and Natural Resources
　Committee (ENR), 2-3, 32, 51, 174
Senate Finance Committee, 2-3
Serrano, José, 175
services sector, 107-108, 146
Smith, A.D., 70
Snyder, Cecil, 191
socialism, 73, 208-209, 210, 213-214.
　See also Puerto Rican Socialist
　Party
Socialist Party, 69, 203. See also
　Coalición Socialista-Republicana

Spain, 67
Spanish Harlem, 194-195
Spanish language, 33, 48, 50-51, 180,
　213
squatter movement, 9-10, 10-11, 120
statehood movement, 41, 44-52, 82-
　84, 137, 214
　before the 1960s, 44, 194
　limited support for, among U.S.
　　Puerto Ricans, 177-180
　mixed reactions to, in Washing-
　　ton, 2, 14, 41, 44-45, 46-47, 49-
　　52, 211-212
　Popular Democratic Party's efforts
　　to eclipse, 24, 26-27
　support for, among low-income
　　Puerto Ricans, 6, 8-9, 44, 47, 83
　see also New Progressive Party
status debates. See Commonwealth,
　efforts to "enhance"; independ-
　ence movement; plebiscite pro-
　cess of 1989-1991; statehood
　movement
strikes, 80, 149, 185
sugar industry, 46, 119

T
Taft-Hartley Law, 80
Taller Salud (Health Workshop), 136
tax incentives, 7-8, 28-30, 51, 96, 107-
　108, 229. See also Section 936 of
　Internal Revenue Code
Tax Reform Act of 1976, 8
Tax Reform Act of 1986, 86, 111
teachers, 135
Teachers' Association (Asociación de
　Maestros), 160
telephone workers, 154
tollgate tax, 107
transfer programs, 30, 43-44, 46, 82.
　See also food stamps
transnational corporations (TNCs):
　domination of Puerto Rican econ-
　omy by, 81

About South End Press

South End Press is a nonprofit, collectively-run book publisher with over 150 titles in print. Since our founding in 1977, we have tried to meet the needs of readers who are exploring, or are already committed to, the politics of radical social change.

Our goal is to publish books that encourage critical thinking and constructive action on the key political, cultural, social, economic, and ecological issues shaping life in the United States and in the world. In this way, we hope to give expression to a wide diversity of democratic social movements and to provide an alternative to the products of corporate publishing.

If you would like a free catalog of South End Press books or information about our membership program—which offers two free books and a 40% discount on all titles—please write us at South End Press, 116 Saint Botolph Street, Boston, MA 02115.

Other titles of interest from South End Press

Storm Signals:
Structural Adjustment and Development
Alternatives in the Caribbean
Kathy McAfee

Mask of Democracy:
Labor Supression in Mexico Today
Dan LaBotz

Workers of the World Undermined:
American Labor's Role in U.S. Foreign Policy
Beth Sims

The Sun Never Sets:
Confronting the Network of Foreign U.S. Military Bases
Joseph Gerson and Bruce Birchard, eds.